A SCOTS HAIRST

BY LEWIS GRASSIC GIBBON

Novels   *Sunset Song*

Cloud Howe

Grey Granite

These three novels comprise the trilogy entitled *A Scots Quair* (Eighth impression 1969.)

Biography   *Niger: The Life of Mungo Park*

Scottish Scene (in collaboration with Hugh
MacDiarmid)

BY J. LESLIE MITCHELL

Hanno

Stained Radiance

The Thirteenth Disciple

The Calends of Cairo

Three Go Back

The Lost Trumpet

Persian Dawns, Egyptian Nights

Image and Superscription

Spartacus

The Conquest of the Maya

Gay Hunter

BY J. LESLIE MITCHELL AND LEWIS GRASSIC GIBBON

Nine Against the Unknown

BY IAN S. MUNRO

Leslie Mitchell: Lewis Grassic Gibbon
(Oliver & Boyd)

A SCOTS HAIRST

Essays and Short Stories

Lewis Grassic Gibbon

EDITED AND INTRODUCED BY

IAN S. MUNRO

HUTCHINSON OF LONDON

HUTCHINSON & CO *(Publishers)* LTD
3 Fitzroy Square, London W1

London Melbourne Sydney Auckland
Wellington Johannesburg Cape Town
and agencies throughout the world

First published 1967
Second impression February 1969
Third impression January 1972
Fourth impression July 1974

Printed in Great Britain by litho on antique wove paper
by R. J. Acford Ltd., Industrial Estate, Chichester, Sussex.

ISBN 0 09 085200 1

CONTENTS

INTRODUCTION

The name of Lewis Grassic Gibbon is a key one in modern Scottish literature. This writer's unique contribution to letters and influence on the development of the novel are accepted not only in his own country but in places as far apart geographically and culturally as Hungary and U.S.A. Yet his writing career spans only seven years during which he published seventeen books.

James Leslie Mitchell was born in 1901 at Hillhead of Seggat, Auchterless, in Aberdeenshire, but most of his early impressionable years were spent in the little farm-croft of Bloomfield which stands on a hill above the village of Arbuthnott in Kincardineshire.

The source is important—Mitchell was deeply conscious and fiercely proud of his peasant origins, and his awareness of this background is at the heart of the best of his work. *A Scots Quair* is rooted and grounded on this stretch of land between the Grampians and the North Sea, and on that lonely croft on the edge of the moor, high on the Reisk road. Up there relics of the distant past remain in plenty—cairns and forts, standing-stones and burial chambers, flints for a boy to collect. Less remote reminders of a heritage linger in the lands across the moor—the farms of Bogjorgan and Clochnahill, the fatherland of Robert Burns, inspiration for a boy to ponder. But the direct impetus for the Grassic Gibbon books came neither from remote or nearer past but from the scenes and folk of Mitchell's own time—the background of those red-clay fields of the Mearns and the folk who knew and worked them.

Mitchell's fruitful Arbuthnott schooldays were followed by a varied and at times tempestuous career in journalism and the Services, until for the last seven years of a life which ended in

1935 at the early age of thirty-four, he became a full-time writer.

The literary products of those seven years ranged from novels, short stories and essays to biography and archaeology. Many of these works reached a high standard and won considerable critical approval in their own field. But by far the greater part of the achievement was the work written under the pseudonym of Lewis Grassic Gibbon, and in particular the three novels *Sunset Song*, *Cloud Howe*, and *Grey Granite*, which make up the great trilogy of the Mearns *A Scots Quair*, probably the most ambitious single effort in Scottish fiction.

The nature and significance of this achievement is being more clearly understood with the passing years. It is certainly the work of a literary pioneer, but the innovating power of Grassic Gibbon's writing is tempered by a profound sense of tradition which links *A Scots Quair* with the heritage of the past. The technical success is a considerable one. Attempting the difficult task of inserting the Scots idiom into an alien tongue Gibbon managed to preserve the rhythm and vitality of native expression without distorting the English language. He found an original and most effective style which he varied with superb literary orchestration to suit each developing situation. He combined recognisable notes and cadences in his interpretation of the countryside, he blended the vigour of local speech with the poetry of realism to achieve complete character involvement, and in *Sunset Song* especially created a perfect unity and expressed deep artistic truth.

Although *A Scots Quair* is undoubtedly the major achievement other Grassic Gibbon writings have a similar quality; the short stories and essays in particular are not only outstanding examples of difficult arts but are an integral part of the writer's treasury. It would be difficult to find the equivalent of *Clay* as a short story or the equal of *The Land* as an essay.

Certainly the five short stories of the Mearns are among the best of the century. In locale and idiom they are of the same genre as *Sunset Song* and in their own medium match the effect and accomplishment of the famous novel. The success-

ful television adaptation of *Sunset Song* introduced Lewis Grassic
Gibbon to many who had not known his work previously, and
the forthcoming screen versions of these stories should have
similar appeal. The best of the essays are also vital to a full
appreciation and understanding of the writer. For instance a
study of *The Land* in relation to *Sunset Song* suggests a key as well
as a parallel to the major work. In this respect and in many others
it seems essential that these small masterpieces so long out of
print should once again be available to students of literature
and general readers.

Like most great writers Mitchell was uneven in his work.
Hasty composition, over-pressure of work, excesses in style
and matter all have contributed to lapses in taste and
standard. Nevertheless the greater part of this subsidiary
material can stand by itself, while the remainder is important
as background, source, and development material. Comparison between the English and Scottish material is inevitable,
and while the former suffers in comparison to the latter, each
has its relevance in the moulding and development of the
finished writer.

The schoolboy essays, the early poems, the first Leslie
Mitchell stories, all have significance on this count, while the
fascinating snatches of the last 'work in progress' now published for the first time prompt speculation on the nature of
the books that might have followed *A Scots Quair* if the author
had not died so young.

Despite the bitter loss of a writer of this stature at the
height of his creative power, the work remaining is impressive
by any standard. It is common now to measure this writer's
work against the best in any modern literature, and to talk
of the Mearns of Grassic Gibbon in the same sense as one
speaks of the Wessex of Thomas Hardy or the Dublin of
James Joyce. *A Scots Quair* must remain as the peak of the
achievement but the smaller pieces in this volume can be
said to mark significant and at times spectacular stages in
the progress towards the heights.

Catterline   I.S.M.
Kincardineshire

GIBBON: SHORT STORIES

Editor's note

The Scottish short stories have been out of print practically since Mitchell's death in 1935. All five were included in *Scottish Scene*, that remarkable miscellany written jointly by Lewis Grassic Gibbon and Hugh MacDiarmid and dedicated to their friend Helen B. Cruickshank. Three of the stories *Clay*, *Smeddum*, and *Greenden* had been published previously in the *Scots Magazine*, and *Clay* and *Smeddum* have been included in some post-war anthologies.

All five are examples of the writer at his best. The quality of *Clay* has been mentioned in the introduction, and *Smeddum* and *Sim* are not far behind. Meg Menzies of Tocherty who provides a living definition of smeddum, is a character from the same mould as Ma Cleghorn of *Grey Granite*, while the study of Sim with its subtle understanding of the ploughman's mind is reminiscent of other Segget dwellers in *Cloud Howe*. Rob Galt of *Clay* is of course a 'blood relative' of *Sunset Song's* Long Rob of the Mill, both deriving from a living source in the person of Mitchell's father-in-law Rob Middleton.

Greenden holds something of Greek tragedy in its development, and at times recalls the mood of *The House with the Green Shutters*. *Forsaken* with its Communist theme is more of a curiosity than the others, hovering uneasily at times between the Mitchell of *Calends of Cairo* and the Gibbon of *Grey Granite*.

The remaining impression of the stories is the mood invoked by the poetic realism, distinctive local flavour in language and humour, and power of dramatic writing. Always the background of the Mearns is vivid and authentic, while the blending of dialogue with narration to form a satisfying unity is a notable technical achievement.

SMEDDUM

She'd had nine of a family in her time, Mistress Menzies, and brought the nine of them up, forbye—some near by the scruff of the neck, you would say. They were sniftering and weakly, two-three of the bairns, sniftering in their cradles to get into their coffins; but she'd shake them to life, and dose them with salts and feed them up till they couldn't but live. And she'd plonk one down—finishing the wiping of the creature's neb or the unco dosing of an ill bit stomach or the binding of a broken head—with a look on her face as much as to say *Die on me now and see what you'll get!*

Big-boned she was by her fortieth year, like a big roan mare, and *If ever she was bonny 'twas in Noah's time,* Jock Menzies, her eldest son would say. She'd reddish hair and a high, skeugh nose, and a hand that skelped her way through life; and if ever a soul had seen her at rest when the dark was done and the day was come he'd died of the shock and never let on.

For from morn till night she was at it, work, work, on that ill bit croft that sloped to the sea. When there wasn't a mist on the cold, stone parks there was more than likely the wheep of the rain, wheeling and dripping in from the sea that soughed and plashed by the land's stiff edge. Kinneff lay north, and at night in the south, if the sky was clear on the gloaming's edge, you'd see in that sky the Bervie lights come suddenly lit, far and away, with the quiet about you as you stood and looked, nothing to hear but a sea-bird's cry.

But feint the much time to look or to listen had Margaret Menzies of Tocherty toun. Day blinked and Meg did the same, and was out, up out of her bed, and about the house, making the porridge and rousting the bairns, and out to the byre to milk the three kye, the morning growing out in the east and a wind like a hail of knives from the hills. Syne back to the kitchen again she would be, and catch Jock, her eldest, a clour in the lug that he hadn't roused up his sisters and brothers; and rouse them herself, and feed them and scold, pull up their breeks and straighten their frocks, and polish their shoes and set their caps straight. *Off you get and see you're not late*, she would cry, *and see you behave yourselves at the school. And tell the Dominie I'll be down the night to ask him what the mischief he meant by leathering Jeannie and her not well.*

They'd cry *Ay, Mother*, and go trotting away, a fair flock of the creatures, their faces red-scoured. Her own as red, like a meikle roan mare's, Meg'd turn at the door and go prancing in; and then at last, by the closet-bed, lean over and shake her man half-awake. *Come on, then, Willie, it's time you were up.*

And he'd groan and say *Is't?* and crawl out at last, a little bit thing like a weasel, Will Menzies, though some said that weasels were decent beside him. He was drinking himself into the grave, folk said, as coarse a little brute as you'd meet, bone-lazy forbye, and as sly as sin. Rampageous and ill with her tongue though she was, you couldn't but pity a woman like Meg tied up for life to a thing like *that*. But she'd more than a soft side still to the creature, she'd half-skelp the backside from any of the bairns she found in the telling of a small bit lie; but when Menzies would come paiching in of a noon and groan that he fair was tashed with his work, he'd mended all the ley fence that day and he doubted he'd need to be off to his bed—when he'd told her that and had ta'en to the blankets, and maybe in less than the space of an hour she'd hold out for the kye and see that he'd lied, the fence neither mended nor letten a-be, she'd just purse up her meikle wide mouth and say nothing, her eyes with a glint as though she half-laughed. And when he came drunken home from a mart she'd shoo the children out of the room, and take off his clothes and put him to bed, with an extra nip to keep off a chill.

She did half his work in the Tocherty parks, she'd yoke up the horse and the sholtie together, and kilt up her skirts till you'd see her great legs, and cry *Wissh!* like a man and turn a fair drill, the sea-gulls cawing in a cloud behind, the wind in her hair and the sea beyond. And Menzies with his sly-like eyes would be off on some drunken ploy to Kineff or Stone-hive. Man, you couldn't but think as you saw that steer it was well that there was a thing like marriage, folk held together and couldn't get apart; else a black look-out it well would be for the fusionless creature of Tocherty toun.

Well, he drank himself to his grave at last, less smell on the earth if maybe more in it. But she broke down and wept, it was awful to see, Meg Menzies weeping like a stricken horse, her eyes on the dead, quiet face of her man. And she ran from the house, she was gone all that night, though the bairns cried and cried her name up and down the parks in the sound of the sea. But next morning they found her back in their midst, brisk as ever, like a great-boned mare, ordering here and directing there, and a fine feed set the next day for the folk that came to the funeral of her orra man.

She'd four of the bairns at home when he died, the rest were in kitchen-service or fee'd, she'd seen to the settling of the queans herself; and twice when two of them had come home, complaining-like of their mistresses' ways, she'd thrashen the queans and taken them back—near scared the life from the doctor's wife, her that was mistress to young Jean Menzies. *I've skelped the lassie and brought you her back. But don't you ill-use her, or I'll skelp you as well.*

There was a fair speak about that at the time, Meg Men-zies and the vulgar words she had used, folk told that she'd even said what was the place where she'd skelp the bit doctor's wife. And faith! that fair must have been a sore shock to the doctor's wife that was that genteel she'd never believed she'd a place like that.

Be that as it might, her man new dead, Meg wouldn't hear of leaving the toun. It was harvest then and she drove the reaper up and down the long, clanging clay rigs by the sea, she'd jump down smart at the head of a bout and go gathering and binding swift as the wind, syne wheel in the horse to the cutting again. She led the stooks with her bairns to help, you'd see them at night a drowsing cluster under the moon on the harvesting cart.

And through that year and into the next and so till the speak died down in the Howe Meg Menzies worked the Tocherty toun; and faith, her crops came none so ill. She rode to the mart at Stonehive when she must, on the old box-cart, the old horse in the shafts, the cart behind with a sheep for sale or a birn of old hens that had finished with laying. And a butcher once tried to make a bit joke. *That's a sheep like yourself, fell long in the tooth.* And Meg answered up, neighing like a horse, and all heard: *Faith, then, if you've got a spite against teeth I've a clucking hen in the cart outbye. It's as toothless and senseless as you are, near.*

Then word got about of her eldest son, Jock Menzies that was fee'd up Allardyce way. The creature of a loon had had fair a conceit since he'd won a prize at a ploughing match— not for his ploughing, but for good looks; and the queans about were as daft as himself, he'd only to nod and they came to his heel; and the stories told they came further than that. Well, Meg'd heard the stories and paid no heed, till the last one came, she was fell quick then.

Soon's she heard it she hove out the old bit bike that her daughter Kathie had bought for herself, and got on the thing and went cycling away down through the Bervie braes in that Spring, the sun was out and the land lay green with a blink of mist that was blue on the hills, as she came to the toun where Jock was fee'd she saw him out in a park by the road, plough-ing, the black loam smooth like a ribbon turning and wheel-

B

ing at the tail of the plough. Another billy came ploughing behind, Meg Menzies watched till they reached the rig-end, her great chest heaving like a meikle roan's, her eyes on the shape of the furrows they made. And they drew to the end and drew the horse out, and Jock cried *Ay*, and she answered back *Ay*, and looked at the drill, and gave a bit snort, *If your looks win prizes, your ploughing never will.*

Jock laughed, *Fegs, then, I'll not greet for that*, and chirked to his horses and turned them about. But she cried him. *Just bide a minute, my lad. What's this I hear about you and Ag Grant?*

He drew up short then, and turned right red, the other childe as well, and they both gave a laugh, as plough-childes do when you mention a quean they've known over-well in more ways than one. And Meg snapped *It's an answer I want, not a cockerel's cackle: I can hear that at home on my own dunghill. What are you to do about Ag and her pleiter?*

And Jock said *Nothing*, impudent as you like, and next minute Meg was in over the dyke and had hold of his lug and shook him and it till the other childe ran and caught at her nieve. *Faith, mistress, you'll have his lug off!* he cried. But Meg Menzies turned like a mare on new grass, *Keep off or I'll have yours off as well!*

So he kept off and watched, fair a story he'd to tell when he rode out that night to go courting his quean. For Meg held to the lug till it near came off and Jock swore that he'd put things right with Ag Grant. She let go the lug then and looked at him grim: *See that you do and get married right quick, you're the like that needs loaded with a birn of bairns—to keep you out of the jail, I jaloose. It needs smeddum to be either right coarse or right kind.*

They were wed before the month was well out, Meg found them a cottar house to settle and gave them a bed and a press she had, and two-three more sticks from Tocherty toun. And she herself led the wedding dance, the minister in her arms, a small bit childe; and 'twas then as she whirled him about the room, he looked like a rat in the teeth of a tyke, that he thanked her for seeing Ag out of her soss, *There's nothing like a marriage for redding things up.* And Meg Menzies said *EH?* and then she said *Ay*, but queer-like, he supposed she'd no thought of the thing. Syne she slipped off to sprinkle thorns in the bed and to hang below it the great hand-bell that the bothy-billies took them to every bit marriage.

Well, that was Jock married and at last off her hands. But she'd plenty left still, Dod, Kathleen and Jim that were still at school, Kathie a limner that alone tongued her mother, Jeannie that next led trouble to her door. She'd been found at her place, the doctor's it was, stealing some money and they sent her home. Syne news of the thing got into Stone-hive, the police came out and tormented her sore, she swore she never had stolen a meck, and Meg swore with her, she was black with rage. And folk laughed right hearty, fegs! that was a clour for meikle Meg Menzies, her daughter a thief!

But it didn't last long, it was only three days when folk saw the doctor drive up in his car. And out he jumped and went striding through the close and met face to face with Meg at the door. And he cried *Well, mistress, I've come over for Jeannie.* And she glared at him over her high, skeugh nose, *Ay, have you so then? And why, may I speir?*

So he told her why, the money they'd missed had been found at last in a press by the door; somebody or other had left it there, when paying a grocer or such at the door. And Jeannie—he'd come over to take Jean back.

But Meg glared *Ay, well, you've made another mistake. Out of this, you and your thieving suspicions together!* The doctor turned red, *You're making a miserable error*—and Meg said *I'll make you mince-meat in a minute.*

So he didn't wait that, she didn't watch him go, but went ben to the kitchen where Jeannie was sitting, her face chalk-white as she'd heard them speak. And what happened then a story went round, Jim carried it to school, and it soon spread out, Meg sank in a chair, they thought she was greeting; syne she raised up her head and they saw she was laughing, near as fearsome the one as the other, they thought. *Have you any cigarettes?* she snapped sudden at Jean, and Jean quavered *No*, and Meg glowered at her cold. *Don't sit there and lie. Gang bring them to me.* And Jean brought them, her mother took the pack in her hand. *Give's hold of a match till I light up the thing. Maybe smoke'll do good for the crow that I got in the throat last night by the doctor's house.*

Well, in less than a month she'd got rid of Jean—packed off to Brechin the quean was, and soon got married to a creature there—some clerk that would have left her sore in the lurch but that Meg went down to the place on her bike, and there, so the story went, kicked the childe so that he couldn't sit down for a fortnight, near. No doubt that was just a bit lie that they told, but faith! Meg Menzies had herself to blame, the reputation she'd gotten in the Howe, folk said, *She'll meet with a sore heart yet.* But devil a sore was there to be seen, Jeannie was married and was fair genteel.

Kathleen was next to leave home at the term. She was tall, like Meg, and with red hair as well, but a thin fine face, long eyes blue-grey like the hills on a hot day, and a mouth with lips you thought over thick. And she cried *Ah well, I'm off then, mother.* And Meg cried *See you behave yourself.* And Kathleen cried *Maybe; I'm not at school now.*

Meg stood and stared after the slip of a quean, you'd have thought her half-angry, half near to laughing, as she watched that figure, so slender and trig, with its shoulders square-set, slide down the hill on the wheeling bike, swallows were dipping and flying by Kinneff, she looked light and free as a swallow herself, the quean, as she biked away from her home, she turned at the bend and waved and whistled, she whistled like a loon and as loud, did Kath.

Jim was the next to leave from the school, he bided at home and he took no fee, a quiet-like loon, and he worked the toun, and, wonder of wonders, Meg took a rest. Folk said that age was telling a bit on even Meg Menzies at last. The grocer made hints at that one night, and Meg answered up smart as ever of old: *Damn the age! But I've finished the trauchle*

*of the bairns at last, the most of them married or still over young. I'm
as swack as ever I was, my lad. But I've just got the notion to be a bit
sweir.*

Well, she'd hardly begun on that notion when faith! ill the
news that came up to the place from Segget. Kathleen her
quean that was fee'd down there, she'd ta'en up with some
coarse old childe in a bank, he'd left his wife, they were off
together, and she but a bare sixteen years old.

And that proved the truth of what folk were saying, Meg
Menzies she hardly paid heed to the news, just gave a bit
laugh like a neighing horse and went on with the work of
park and byre, cool as you please—ay, getting fell old.

No more was heard of the quean or the man till a two
years or more had passed and then word came up to the
Tocherty someone had seen her—and where do you think?
Out on a boat that was coming from Australia. She was
working as stewardess on that bit boat, and the childe that
saw her was young John Robb, an emigrant back from his
uncle's farm, near starved to death he had been down there.
She hadn't met in with him near till the end, the boat close
to Southampton the evening they met. And she'd known him
at once, thought he not her, she'd cried *John Robb?* and he'd
answered back *Ay?* and looked at her canny in case it might be
the creature was looking for a tip from him. Syne she'd
laughed *Don't you know me, then, you gowk? I'm Kathie Menzies
you knew long syne—it was me ran off with the banker from Segget!*

He was clean dumbfounded, young Robb, and he gaped,
and then they shook hands and she spoke some more, though
she hadn't much time, they were serving up dinner for the
first-class folk, aye dirt that are ready to eat and to drink. *If
ever you get near to Tocherty toun tell Meg I'll get home and see her
sometime. Ta-ta!* And then she was off with a smile, young
Robb he stood and he stared where she'd been, he thought
her the bonniest thing that he'd seen all the weary weeks that
he'd been from home.

And this was the tale that he brought to Tocherty, Meg

sat and listened and smoked like a tink, forbye herself there was young Jim there, and Jock and his wife and their three bit bairns, he'd fair changed with marriage, had young Jock Menzies. For no sooner had he taken Ag Grant to his bed than he'd started to save, grown mean as dirt, in a three-four years he'd finished with feeing, now he rented a fell big farm himself, well stocked it was, and he fee'd two men. Jock himself had grown thin in a way, like his father but worse his bothy childes said, old Menzies at least could take a bit dram and get lost to the world but the son was that mean he might drink rat-poison and take no harm, 'twould feel at home in a stomach like his.

Well, that was Jock, and he sat and heard the story of Kath and her stay on the boat. *Ay, still a coarse bitch, I have not a doubt. Well if she never comes back to the Mearns, in Segget you cannot but redden with shame when a body will ask 'Was Kath Menzies your sister?'*

And Ag, she'd grown a great sumph of a woman, she nodded to that, it was only too true, a sore thing it was on decent bit folks that they should have any relations like Kath.

But Meg just sat there and smoked and said never a word, as though she thought nothing worth a yea or a nay. Young Robb had fair ta'en a fancy to Kath and he near boiled up when he heard Jock speak, him and the wife that he'd married from her shame. So he left them short and went raging home, and wished for one that Kath would come back, a Summer noon as he cycled home, snipe were calling in the Auchindreich moor where the cattle stood with their tails a-switch, the Grampians rising far and behind, Kinraddie spread like a map for show, its ledges veiled in a mist from the sun. You felt on that day a wild, daft unease, man, beast and bird: as though something were missing and lost from the world, and Kath was the thing that John Robb missed, she'd something in her that minded a man of a house that was builded upon a hill.

Folk thought that maybe the last they would hear of

young Kath Menzies and her ill-gettèd ways. So fair stammy-gastered they were with the news she'd come back to the Mearns, she was down in Stonehive, in a grocer's shop, as calm as could be, selling out tea and cheese and such-like with no blush of shame on her face at all, to decent women that were properly wed and had never looked on men but their own, and only on them with their braces buttoned.

It just showed you the way that the world was going to allow an ill quean like that in a shop, some folk protested to the creature that owned it, but he just shook his head, *Ah well, she works fine; and what else she does is no business of mine.* So you well might guess there was more than business between the man and Kath Menzies, like.

And Meg heard the news and went into Stonehive, driving her sholtie, and stopped at the shop. And some in the shop knew who she was and minded the things she had done long syne to other bit bairns of hers that went wrong; and they waited with their breaths held up with delight. But all that Meg did was to nod to Kath *Ay, well, then, it's you—Ay, mother, just that—Two pounds of syrup and see that it's good.*

And not another word passed between them, Meg Menzies that once would have ta'en such a quean and skelped her to rights before you could wink. Going home from Stonehive she stopped by the farm where young Robb was fee'd, he was out in the hayfield coling the hay, and she nodded to him grim, with her high horse face. *What's this that I hear about you and Kath Menzies?*

He turned right red, but he wasn't ashamed. *I've no idea— though I hope it's the worse——. It fell near is——. Then I wish it was true, she might marry me, then, as I've prigged her to do.*

Oh, have you so, then? said Meg, and drove home, as though the whole matter was a nothing to her.

But next Tuesday the postman brought a bit note, from Kathie it was to her mother at Tocherty. *Dear mother, John Robb's going out to Canada and wants me to marry him and go with him. I've told him instead I'll go with him and see what he's like as a man—and then marry him at leisure, if I feel in the mood. But he's hardly any money, and we want to borrow some, so he and I are coming over on Sunday. I hope that you'll have dumpling for tea. Your own daughter, Kath.*

Well, Meg passed that letter over to Jim, he glowered at it dour, *I know—near all the Howe's heard. What are you going to do, now, mother?*

But Meg just lighted a cigarette and said nothing, she'd smoked like a tink since that steer with Jean. There was promise of strange on-goings at Tocherty by the time that the Sabbath day was come. For Jock came there on a visit as well, him and his wife, and besides him was Jeannie, her that had married the clerk down in Brechin, and she brought the bit creature, he fair was a toff; and he stepped like a cat through the sharn in the close; and when he had heard the story of Kath, her and her plan and John Robb and all, he was shocked near to death, and so was his wife. And Jock Menzies gaped and gave a mean laugh. *Ay, coarse to the bone, ill-gettèd I'd say if it wasn't that we came of the same bit stock. Ah well, she'll fair have to tramp to Canada, eh mother?—if she's looking for money from you.*

And Meg answered quiet *No, I wouldn't say that. I've the money all ready for them when they come.*

You could hear the sea plashing down soft on the rocks, there was such a dead silence in Tocherty house. And then Jock habbered like a cock with fits *What, give silver to one who does as she likes, and won't marry as you made the rest of us marry? Give silver to one who's no more than a——.*

And he called his sister an ill name enough, and Meg sat and smoked looking over the parks. *Ay, just that. You see, she takes after myself.*

And Jeannie squeaked *How?* and Meg answered her quiet: *She's fit to be free and to make her own choice the same as myself and the same kind of choice. There was none of the rest of you fit to do that, you'd to marry or burn, so I married you quick. But Kath and me could afford to find out. It all depends if you've smeddum or not.*

She stood up then and put her cigarette out, and looked at the gaping gowks she had mothered. *I never married your father, you see. I could never make up my mind about Will. But maybe our Kath will find something surer. . . . Here's her and her man coming up the road.*

CLAY

The Galts were so thick on the land around Segget folk said if you went for a walk at night and you trod on some thing and it gave a squiggle, it was ten to one you would find it a Galt. And if you were a newcomer up in the Howe and you stopped a man and asked him the way the chances were he'd be one of the brood. Like as not, before he had finished with you, he'd have sold you a horse or else stolen your watch, found out everything that you ever had done, recognized your mother and had doubts of your father. Syne off home he'd go and spread the news round from Galt of Catcraig that lay high in the hills to Galt of Drumbogs that lay low by Mondynes, all your doings were known and what you had said, what you wore next your skin, what you had to your breakfast, what you whispered to your wife in the dead of night. And the Galts would snigger *Ay, gentry, no doubt,* and spit in the vulgar way that they had: the average Galt knew less of politeness than a broody hen knows of Bible exegesis.

They farmed here and they farmed there, brothers and cousins and half-brothers and uncles, your head would reel as you tried to make out if Sarah were daughter to Ake of Catcraig or only a relation through marrying a nephew of Sim of High Rigs that was cousin to Will. But the Galts knew all their relationships fine, more especially if anything had gone a bit wrong, they'd tell you how twenty-five years or so back when the daughter of Redleaf had married her cousin, old Alec that now was the farmer of Kirn, the first bit bairn

16

that came of that marriage—ay, faith, that bairn had come unco soon! And they'd lick at their chops as they minded of that and sneer at each other and fair have a time. But if you were strange and would chance to agree, they'd close up quick, with a look on their faces as much as to say *And who are you would say ill of the Galts?*

They made silver like dirt wherever they sat, there was hardly a toun that they sat in for long. So soon's they moved in to some fresh bit farm they'd rive up the earth, manure it with fish, work the land to death in the space of their lease, syne flit to the other side of the Howe with the land left dry as a rat-sucked swede. And often enough as he neared his lease-end a Galt would break and be rouped from his place, he'd say that farming was just infernal and his wife would weep as she watched her bit things sold here and there to cover their debts. And if you didn't know much of the Galts you would be right sorry and would bid fell high. Syne you'd hear in less than a six months' time that the childe that went broke had bought a new farm and had stocked it up to the hilt with the silver he'd laid cannily by before he went broke.

Well, the best of the bunch was Rob Galt of Drumbogs, lightsome and hearty, not mean like the rest, he'd worked for nearly a twenty-five years as his father's foreman up at Drumbogs. Old Galt, the father, seemed nearly immortal, the older he grew the coarser he was, Rob stuck the brute as a good son should though aye he had wanted land of his own. When they fell out at last Rob Galt gave a laugh *You can keep Drumbogs and all things that are on it, I'll soon get a place of my own, old man.* His father sneered *You?* and Rob Galt said *Ay, a place of my own and parks that are MINE.*

He was lanky and long like all of the Galts, his mouser twisted up at the ends, with a chinny Galt face and a long, thin nose, and eyes pale-blue in a red-weathered face, a fine, frank childe that was kindness itself, though his notion of taking a rest from the plough was to loosen his horses and start in to harrow. He didn't look long for a toun of his own, Pittaulds by Segget he leased in a wink, it stood high up on the edge of the Mounth, you could see the clutter of Segget below, wet, with the glint of its roofs at dawn. The rent was low, for the land was coarse, red clay that sucked with a hungry mouth at your feet as you passed through the evening fields.

Well, he moved to Pittaulds in the autumn term, folk watched his flitting come down by Mondynes and turn at the corner and trudge up the brae to the big house poised on the edge of the hill. He brought his wife, she was long as himself, with a dark-like face, quiet, as though gentry—faith, that was funny, a Galt wedded decent! But he fair was fond of the creature, folk said, queer in a man with a wife that had managed to bring but one bairn into the world. That bairn was now near a twelve years old, dark, like her mother, solemn and slim, Rob spoiled them both, the wife and the quean, you'd have thought them sugar he was feared would melt.

But they'd hardly sat down a week in Pittaulds when Rachel that would trot at the rear of Rob, like a collie dog, saw a queer-like change. Now and then her father would give her a pat and she'd think that he was to play as of old. But instead he would cry *Losh, run to the house, and see if your mother will let you come out, we've two loads of turnips to pull afore dinner.* Rachel, the quean, would chirp *Ay, father,* and go blithe to the shed for her tailer and his, and out they would wade through the cling of the clay and pull side by side down the long, swede rows, the rain in a drifting seep from the hills, below them the Howe in its garment of mist. And the little, dark quean would work by his side, say never a word though she fair was soaked; and at last go home; and her mother would stare, whatever in the world had happened to Rob? She would ask him that as he came into dinner—*the quean'll fair have her death of cold.* He would blink with his pale-blue eyes, impatient, *Hoots, lassie, she'll take no harm from the rain. And we fair must clear the swedes from the land, I'm a good three weeks behind with the work.*

The best of the Galts? Then God keep off the rest! For, as that year wore on to its winter, while he'd rise at five, as most other folk did, he wouldn't be into his bed till near morning, it was chave, chave, chave till at last you would think he'd turn himself into an earthworm, near. In the blink of the light from the lanterns of dawn he would snap short-tempered at his dark-faced wife, she would stare and wonder and give a bit laugh, and eat up his porridge as though he was feared he would lose his appetite halfway through, and muck out the byre and the stable as fast as though he were paid for the job by the hour, with a scowl of ill-nature behind his long nose. And then, while the dark still lay on the land, and through the low mist that slept on the fields not a bird was cheeping and not a thing showing but the waving lanterns in the Segget wynds, he'd harness his horses and lead out the first, its hooves striking fire from the stones of the close, and cry to the second, and it would come after, and the two of them drink at the trough while Rob would button up his collar against the sharp drive of the frozen dew as the north wind woke. Then he'd jump on the back of the meikle roan, Jim, and go swaying and jangling down by the hedge, in the dark, the world on the morning's edge, wet, the smell of the parks in his face, the squelch of the horses soft in the clay.

Syne, as the light came grey in a tide, wan and slow from the Bervie Braes, and a hare would scuttle away through the grass and the peesies waken and cry and wheep, Rob Galt would jump from the back of Jim and back the pair up against the plough and unloose the chains from the horses' britchens and hook them up to the swivel-trees. Then he'd spit on his hands and cry *Wissh, Jim!* no longer ill-natured, but high-out and pleased, and swink the plough into the red, soaked land; and the horses would strain and snort and move canny and the clay wheel back in the coulter's trace, Rob swaying slow in the rear of the plough, one foot in the drill and one on the rig. The bothy billies on Arbuthnott's bents riding their pairs to start on some park would cry one to the other *Ay, Rob's on the go*, seeing him then as the light grew strong, wheeling, him and the horses and plough, a ranging of dots on the park that sloped its long clay rigs to the edge of the moor.

By eight, as Rachel set out for school, a slim dark thing with her well-tackèd boots, she would hear the whistle of her father, Rob, deep, a wheeber, upon the hill; and she'd see him come swinging to the end of a rig and mind how he once would stop and would joke and tease her for lads that she had at the school. And she'd cry *Hello father!* but Rob would say nothing till he'd drawn his horse out and looked back at the rig and given his mouser a twist and a wipe. Syne he'd peek at his daughter as though he'd new woke *Ay, then, so you're off*, and cry *Wissh!* to his horses and turn them about and set to again, while Rachel went on, quiet, with the wonder clouding her face that had altered so since she came to Pittaulds.

He'd the place all ploughed ere December was out, folk said that he'd follow the usual Galt course, he'd showed up mean as the rest of them did, he'd be off to the marts and a dealing in horses, or a buying of this or a stealing of that, if there were silver in the selling of frogs the Galts would puddock-hunt in their parks. But instead he began on the daftest-like ploy, between the hill of Pittaulds and the house a stretch of the moor thrust in a thin tongue, three or four acre, deep-pitted with holes and as rank with whins as a haddock with scales, not a tenant yet who had farmed Pittaulds but had had the sense to leave it a-be. But Rob Galt set in to break up the land, he said it fair cried to have a man at it, he carted great stones to fill up the holes and would lever out the roots when he could with a pick, when he couldn't he'd bring out his horses and yoke them and tear them out from the ground that way. Working that Spring to break in the moor by April's end he was all behind, folk took a laugh, it served the fool fine.

Once in a blue moon or so he'd come round, he fair was

a deave as he sat by your fire, he and your man would start in on the crops and the lie of the land and how you should drain it, the best kind of turnips to plant in the clay, the manure that would bring the best yield a dry year. Your man would be keen enough on all that, but not like Rob Galt, he would kittle up daft and start in to tell you tales of the land that were just plain stite, of this park and that as though they were women you'd to prig and to pat afore they'd come on. And your man would go ganting wide as a gate and the clock would be hirpling the hours on to morn and still Rob Galt would sit there and habber. *Man, she's fairly a bitch, is that park, sly and sleeked, you can feel it as soon as you start in on her, she'll take corn with the meikle husk, not with the little. But I'll kittle her up with some phosphate, I think.* Your man would say *Ay, well, well, is that so? What do you think of this business of Tariffs?* and Rob would say *Well, man, I just couldn't say. What worries me's that park where I've put in the tares. It's fair on the sulk about something or other.*

And what could you think of a fool like that? Though he'd fallen behind with his chave on the moor he soon made it up with his working at night, he fair had a fine bit crop the next year, the wife and the quean both out at the cutting, binding and stooking as he reapered the fields. Rachel had shot up all of a sudden, you looked at her in a kind of surprise as you saw the creature go by to the school. It was said that she fair was a scholar, the quean—no better than your own bit Johnnie, you knew, the teachers were coarse to your Johnnie, the tinks. Well, Rachel brought home to Pittaulds some news the night that Rob came back from the mart, he'd sold his corn at a fair bit price. For once he had finished pleitering outside, he sat in the kitchen, his feet to the fire, puffing at his pipe, his eye on the window watching the ley rise up outside and peer in the house as though looking for him. It was Rachel thought that as she sat at her supper, dark, quiet, a bit queer, over thin to be bonny, you like a lass with a good bit of beef. Well, she finished her meat and syne started to tell the message the

Dominie had sent her home with; and maybe if she was sent to the college she'd win a bursary or something to help.

Her mother said *Well, Rob, what say you to that?* and Rob asked *What?* and they told him again and Rob skeughed his face round *What, money for school? And where do you think that I'll manage to get that?*

Mrs. Galt said *Out of the corn you've just sold*, and Rob gave a laugh as though speaking to a daftie—*I've my seed to get and my drains to dig and what about the ley for the next year's corn? Damn't, it's just crying aloud for manure, it'll hardly leave me a penny-piece over.*

Rachel sat still and looked out at the ley, sitting so still, with her face in the dark. Then they heard her sniff and Rob swung round fair astonished at the sound she made. *What ails you?* he asked, and her mother said *Ails her? You would greet yourself if you saw your life ruined.* Rob got to his feet and gave Rachel a pat. *Well, well, I'm right sorry that you're taking't like that. But losh, it's a small bit thing to greet over. Come out and we'll go for a walk round the parks.*

So Rachel went with him half-hoping he thought to change his mind on this business of college. But all that he did on the walk was to stand now and then and stare at the flow of the stubble or laugh queer-like as they came to a patch where the grass was bare and the crop had failed. *Ay, see that, Rachel, the wretch wouldn't take. She'll want a deep drill, this park, the next season.* And he bent down and picked up a handful of earth and trickled the stuff through his fingers, slow, then dusted it back on the park, not the path, careful, as though it were gold-dust not dirt. So they came at last to the moor he had broken, he smoked his pipe and he stood and looked at it *Ay, quean, I've got you in fettle at last.* He was speaking to the park not his daughter but Rachel hated Pittaulds from that moment, she thought, quiet, watching her father and thinking how much he'd changed since he first set foot on its clay.

He worked from dawn until dark, and still later, he hove great harvests out of the land, he was mean as dirt with the

silver he made; but in five years' time of his farming there
he'd but hardly a penny he could call his own. Every meck
that he got from the crops of one year seemed to cry to go
back to the crops of the next. The coarse bit moor that lay
north of the biggings he coddled as though 'twas his own
blood and bone, he fed it manure and cross-ploughed it
twice-thrice, and would harrow it, tend it, and roll the damn
thing till the Segget joke seemed more than a joke, that he'd
take it to bed with him if he could. For all that his wife saw
of him in hers he might well have done that, Mrs. Galt that
was tall and dark and so quiet came to look at him queer as
he came in by, you could hardly believe it still was the Rob
that once wouldn't blush to call you his jewel, that had many
a time said all he wanted on earth was a wife like he had and
land of his own. But that was afore he had gotten the land.

One night she said as they sat at their meat *Rob, I've still
that queer pain in my breast. I've had it for long and I doubt that
it's worse. We'll need to send for the doctor, I think.* Rob said *Eh?*
and gleyed at her dull *Well, well, that's fine. I'll need to be step-
ping, I must put in a two-three hours the night on the weeds that are
coming so thick in the swedes, it's fair pestered with the dirt, that poor
bit of park.* Mrs. Galt said *Rob, will you leave your parks, just for a
minute, and consider me? I'm ill and I want a doctor at last.*

Late the next afternoon he set off for Stonehive and the
light came low and the hours went by, Mrs. Galt saw nothing
of her man or the doctor and near went daft with the worry
and pain. But at last as it grew fell black on the fields she
heard the step of Rob on the close and she ran out and
cried *What's kept you so long?* and he said *What's that? Why,
what but my work?* He'd come back and he'd seen his swedes
waiting the hoe, so he'd got off his bike and held into the
hoeing, what sense would there have been in wasting his time
going up to the house to tell the news that the doctor wouldn't
be till the morn?

Well, the doctor came in his long brown car, he cried to
Rob as he hoed the swedes *I'll need you up at the house with me.*

c

And Rob cried *Why? I've no time to waste.* But he got at last into the doctor's car and drove to the house and waited impatient; and the doctor came ben, and was stroking his lips; and he said *Well, Galt, I'm feared I've bad news. Your wife has a cancer in the breast, I think.*

She'd to take to her bed and was there a good month while Rob Galt worked the Pittaulds on his own. Syne she wrote a letter to her daughter Rachel that was fee'd in Segget, and Rachel came home. And she said, quiet, *Mother, has he never looked near you? I'll get the police on the beast for this,* she meant her father that was out with the hay, through the windows she could see him scything a bout, hear the skirl of the stone as he'd whet the wet blade, the sun a still lowe on the drowsing Howe, the dying woman in the littered bed. But Mrs. Galt whispered *He just doesn't think, it's not that he's cruel, he's just mad on Pittaulds.*

But Rachel was nearly a woman by then, dark, with a temper that all the lads knew, and she hardly waited for her father to come home to tell him how much he might well be ashamed, he had nearly killed her mother with neglect, was he just a beast with no heart at all? But Rob hardly looked at the quean in his hurry *Hoots, lassie, your stomach's gone sour with the heat. Could I leave my parks to get covered with weeds?* And he gave her a pat, as to quieten a bairn, and ate up his dinner, all in a fash to be coling the hay. Rachel cried *Aren't you going to look in on mother?* and he said *Oh, ay,* and went ben in a hurry. *Well, lass, you'll be pleased that the hay's done fine—. Damn't, there's a cloud coming up from the sea!* And the next that they saw, he was out of the house staring at the cloud as at Judgment Day.

Mrs. Galt was dead ere September's end, on the day of the funeral as folk came up they met Rob Galt in his old cord breeks, with a hoe in his hand, and he said he'd been out loosening up the potato drills a wee bit. He changed to his black and he helped with his brothers to carry the coffin out to the hearse. There were three bit carriages, he got in the first, and the horses went jangling slow to the road. The folk in the carriage kept solemn and long-faced, they thought Rob the same because of his wife. But he suddenly woke *Damn't, man, but I've got it! It's LIME that I should have given the yavil. It's been greeting for the stuff, that park on the brae!*

Rachel took on the housekeeping at Pittaulds, sombre and slim, aye reading in books, she would stand of a winter night and listen to the suck and slob of the rain on the clay and hate the sound as she tried to hate Rob. And sometimes he'd say as they sat at their meat *What's wrong with you, lass, that you're glowering like that?* and the quean would look down, and remember her mother, while Rob rose cheery and went to his work.

And yet, as she told to one of the lads that came cycling up from Segget to see her, she just couldn't hate him, hard though she tried. There was something in him that tugged at herself, daft-like, a feeling with him that the fields mattered and mattered, nothing else at all. And the lad said *What, not even me, Rachel?* and she laughed and gave him that which he sought, but half-absent like, she thought little of lads.

Well, that winter Rob Galt made up his mind that he'd break in another bit stretch of the moor beyond the bit he already had broke, there the land rose steep in a birn of wee braes, folk told him he fair would be daft to break that, it was land had lain wild and unfed since the Flood. Rob Galt said *Maybe, but they're queer-like, those braes, as though some childe had once shored them tight up.* And he set to the trauchle as he'd done before, he'd come sweating in like a bull at night and Rachel would ask him *Why don't you rest?* and he'd stare at her dumbfounded a moment: *What, rest, and me with my new bit park? What would I do but get on with my work?*

And then, as the next day wore to its close, she heard him crying her name outbye, and went through the close, and he waved from the moor. So she closed the door and went up by the track through the schlorich of the wet November moor, a windy day in the winter's nieve, the hills a-cower from the bite of the wind, the whins in that wind had a moan as they moved, not a day for a dog to be out you would say. But she found her father near tirred to the skin, he'd been heaving a great root up from its hold, *Come in by and look on this fairely, lass, I knew that some childe had once farmed up here.*

And Rachel looked at the hole in the clay and the chamber behind it, dim in the light, where there gleamed a rickle of stone-grey sticks, the bones of a man of antique time. Amid the bones was a litter of flints and a crumbling stick in the shape of a heuch.

She knew it as an eirde of olden time, an earth-house built by the early folk, Rob nodded, *Ay, he was more than that. Look at that heuch, it once scythed Pittaulds. Losh, lass, I'd have liked to have kenned that childe, what a crack together we'd have had on the crops!*

Well, that night Rob started to splutter and hoast, next morning was over stiff to move, fair clean amazed at his own condition. Rachel got a neighbour to go for the doctor, Rob had taken a cold while he stood and looked at the hole and the bones in the old-time grave. There was nothing in that and it fair was a shock when folk heard the news in a two-three days Rob Galt was dead of the cold he had ta'en. He'd worked all his go in the ground nought left to fight the black hoast that took hold of his lungs.

He'd said hardly a word, once whispered *The Ley!* the last hour as he lay and looked out at that park, red-white, with a tremor of its earthen face as the evening glow came over the Howe. Then he said to Rachel *You'll take on the land, you and some childe, I've a notion for that?* But she couldn't lie even to please him just then, she'd no fancy for either the land or a lad, she shook her head and Rob's gley grew dim.

When the doctor came in he found Rob dead, with his face to the wall and the blinds down-drawn. He asked the quean if she'd stay there alone, all the night with her father's corpse? She nodded *Oh, yes,* and watched him go, standing at the door as he drove off to Segget. Then she turned her about and went up through the parks, quiet, in the wet, quiet gloaming's coming, up through the hill to the old earth-house.

There the wind came sudden in a gust in her hair as she looked at the place and the way she had come and thought of the things the minister would say when she told him she planned her father be buried up here by the bones of the man of old time. And she shivered sudden as she looked round about at the bare clay slopes that slept in the dusk, the whistle of the whins seemed to rise in a voice, the parks below to whisper and listen as the wind came up them out of the east.

All life—just clay that awoke and strove to return again to its mother's breast. And she thought of the men who had made these rigs and the windy days of their toil and years, the daftness of toil that had been Rob Galt's, that had been that of many men long on the land, though seldom seen now, was it good, was it bad? What power had that been that woke once on this brae and was gone at last from the parks of Pittaulds?

For she knew in that moment that no other would come to tend the ill rigs in the north wind's blow. This was finished and ended, a thing put by, and the whins and the broom creep down once again, and only the peesies wheep and be still when she'd gone to the life that was hers, that was different, and the earth turn sleeping, unquieted no longer, her hungry bairns in her hungry breast where sleep and death and the earth were one.

GREENDEN

Folk laughed when they heard of the creatures coming to sit them down in the farm of Greenden that lay west of the Tulloch by Bervie Water. It was a forty-fifty acre place, the Den, wet in the bottom as well it might be so low it lay there in its woods. In the midst stood the biggings; they were old and right dark: from the kitchen door you looked round and up at a jungle, near, lost from the world, so close around and between the trees the broom plants grew, and the whins. But when night came sometimes over the trees and the rank, wild waste of the moor you'd see through a narrow pass in the woods the last of the sun as it kindled a light on the Grampian Hills and went off to its bed. And that light in the mirk was near as much as a man would see of the world outby from the kitchen door of Greenden.

Well, old Grant had farmed there till he died, a steady old stock—fair strong in the hands if weak in the head, was the speak of Murdoch of Mains. For a body hardly ever made out what he said; he would whisper and whisper, whispering even as he girned at his horse in the lithe of the woods that watched Greenden. Soon's he'd been ta'en, the old mistress moved her into Drumlithie and took a bit cottage, and lived on his silver; and sometimes she'd say to a crony at night *It's fine to be here and with sonsy folk*. They thought at first she would miss her man; the minister came, the Free Kirk loon, he snuffled right godly and said through his nose *You'll meet him Above, Mistress Grant*. But at that she gave a kind of a start, near dropped the teapot, she did, when he spoke. *Will I, then? Ay, fegs, I'll confess I hadn't reckoned that.*

Well, that was the Grants gone out of Greenden, there the ill place lay as the winter wore on, not an offer the factor had for it either; a man could sweat out his guts on a better ploy than manuring the dour red clay of the Den. Syne the news went round it was let at last: the factor had let it to no farming body, but a creature from a town, from Glasgow it was; he'd never handled a plough or a graip and Murdoch at the Mains had a story about him. For he'd driven the creature and his wife round the district, and as they went by the parks at Pittendreich they'd seen a roller of old Pittendreich's there, out in the ley the thing was lying. And the body of a woman had gleyed at the thing: *What a shame to let it get rusty, isn't it?* and looked at Murdoch like a fool of a bairn.

Folk took that through hand with a laugh here and there; some said it was surely a lie, though gey witty, for everybody knew that the Murdoch brute could lie like a tink when the mood was on him. True or not, you began to think of the creatures—Simpson the name was—that had taken Greenden and were moving in there at the February end. Ay, they'd find it a change from their Glasgow streets; they didn't know what it was to work, the dirt that came from the towns.

Well, come at last the Simpsons did to Greenden; their gear and furniture came by Bervie, and the Simpson man went there to hire two carts for the carting down of the stuff. Webster the grocer had no rounds that day and he hired out his carts and drove one himself, George Simpson the other, it was late at night when they came to the Den, down through the thick woods, larch it was there, so close the trunks that the night was dark though the light shone still out on the high road that walked by the sea. But they saw in the Den as they wound down there a lantern kindled at last in the mirk, kindled and shining from the kitchen door. And when the carts came rumbling into the close there the wife of Simpson was standing and waiting, the lantern held in her hand.

And Webster took a bit keek at the creature and half thought she must be but Simpson's daughter, no wife she looked, she was thin and slim, bonny in a way, and her eyes were kind. She laughed up at Simpson coming behind, syne smiled at the grocer, and cried up in an English-like voice: *You've been long. I thought I'd have to spend the night down here— all alone by myself in Greenden.*

Alec Webster said *Well, mistress, you'd have ta'en no ill,* And she nodded to that *I know that fine. . . . And, of course, the country's lovely to live in.* And she smiled at him like a daft-like quean. He glowered back at her, canny, slow and quiet Alec, he couldn't make head nor tail of her yet, her laugh and that quiver she hid in her laugh.

Syne he loosed and helped them in with their gear, a great clutter of stuff they'd brought up from Glasgow, George Simpson he puffed and paiched right sore, big though he was, with a sappy big face, and a look on that face as though some childe had ta'en him a right hard kick in the dowp. But his lungs were gey bad, he told to the grocer; he'd come out to the country for his lungs, he said. And when Murdoch at Mains heard of that he said: *Faith, the creature's more like to mislay his anatomy than pick up a bit on the rigs of the Den.*

So there were the two of them settled in there, Simpson and the little bit snippet of a wife: she looked light enough for a puff of wind to blow her from the kitchen door at night when she opened that door to come out to the grocer as he drove his van down for her orders on Friday. Alec Webster was a kindly stock, and he cried *Losh, Mistress, you're not in your Glasgow now, you'll fair need to keep yourself wrapped up.* But she only laughed *I'm fine—oh listen to the trees!* And the grocer listened, and heard them sough, and turned him his head and glowered at the woods: they were just as aye they had been, he thought, why should a man stand still and listen? He asked her, Ellen Simpson, that, and keeked at her white, still stare. And she started again and smiled at him queer. *Oh, nothing. Sorry. But I can't but listen.*

Well, maybe she knew what she meant, he didn't. He sold
her her orders—she fair had a lot—and drove away up the
February dark; and as he was driving he heard in the dark a
hoasting and hacking out there by the barn, and he thought
of the Simpson childe and his lungs. Faith, he'd come to the
wrong place here for his lungs; it wasn't long likely he would
store the kiln.

Mistress Murdoch went down to tea at Greenden. But she
couldn't abide George Simpson's mistress, the creature fair
got on to her nerves with her flitting here and her tripping
there, and her laugh, and the meikle eyes of her in the small
doll face that she had. She said it was Simpson she pitied,
poor man, with lungs like his and a wife like that, little comfort by day and less in his bed; she herself would rather sleep
with a fluff of a feather than depend on *that* on a coldrife
night.

And then, as daft-like a blether as ever you heard, the
story got about how it was they'd come to move up from
Glasgow to Greenden toun. George Simpson himself it was
that told it one night he dropped in at the Murdoch house—
he would go a bit walk there now and again and gley at the
daughter, Jeannie. And the way of their moving from Glasgow had been when his lungs took bad it was plain that he
wouldn't last out a long while at his clerking; he was fair
for the knackers' yard, you would say. The doctors said he
should leave the town, but he'd little fancy for that himself,
and his wife had less: she was town-bred, and feared at the
country, Ellen: or so he'd aye thought. For next Sunday he'd
gone with her to their kirk, and then it was that a hymn was
sung, and it fair seemed to change Ellen Simpson's mind. And
the hymn was the one that begins with the words:

> *There is a green hill far away,*
> *Beyond a city wall,*
> *Where the dear Lord was crucified,*
> *Who died to save us all.*

So when the Simpsons got back to their house, Ellen Simpson had kept whispering and remembering that tune, and sudden-like she said they must leave the town; they must find a farm where George could work out in the open and mend his ill lungs.

Well, he'd hardly hear of the thing at first, as he told to the Murdochs that night at their house, he thought that work on a farm would kill him. But Ellen had set her mind on the plan, so he set about looking for a place to please her. He'd but little silver to stock up a steading, and land in the south was far overdear, but up in the Mearns he came on Greenden, its rent inside the reach of his pouch. So he'd ta'en his wife up to see it; she'd stared, down in the hollow, and seemed half ta'en back. And then she'd said they must take it, and take it they did, and here now they were; and *she* liked it fine.

And fine well she might, the coarse creature, folk said. It wasn't her had to face up the rains of that year or the coarse ploughing of the ill red clay of Greenden. Ay, Simpson was a fine bit childe, a bit dour, but faith! he was surely a fool as well to let himself be ta'en from a fine town job out to the pleiter and soss of a farm to pleasure that creature his wife and the fancies she'd gotten from hearing a hymn in a kirk. Folk with sense knew that hymns were just things that you sang, douce, and then you forgot the damn things.

Wet it was that spring: March came flooding in rains down the length and breadth of the guttering Howe; every night you'd hear the swash of the water if your place in the bed was next to the wall; the gulls were up from the Bervie beaches and cawing at all hours over the parks. Down in Greenden it was worse than most, and Simpson with his hoast, poor childe might well have kept in his bed and blankets, but his creature of a wife wouldn't hear of that, laughing at him, affronting him into a rage. *Come on, now, George, the day's half dead! And it's fine, a good day for the plough.*

So out he'd to get, and out with his pair, and go slow step-stepping up and down the ley haughs that lined the deep Den.

His ploughing was fair a sight for sore eyes; of a Sunday the bothy billies would come over, they'd take a bit dander down to the Den and stand and laugh as they looked at the drills, they went this way and that: *Damn't man, they've but little sense in towns!* Syne they'd hear Mistress Simpson crying to her hens, and see her, small, like a snippet of a doll, flit over the close on some errand or another, the poor Simpson childe kept to his bed on the Sundays.

Well, the spring wore on, fine planting weather came, by May the sun was blaze of heat, up and down the long Howe folk shook their heads. With a spring like this you might well depend that you'd have a summer with sleet, most-like. But it was well enough while it went, and Murdoch of Mains took a dander down to the Den now and then to see how the Simpson man fared. And faith! he'd been kept with his nose at the grind; he'd his parks as well forward as any other place. Murdoch hadn't set eyes on him near for a month, and fair got a shock as he stopped his roller and stood by to speak. He'd grown thicker and bigger, his face filled out, you could hardly see the town in him at all. Murdoch said *Ay man, you're fair a bit farmer*.

And Simpson smiled wan, right patient-like though, with his sappy red face like an ill-used nout's, and said *Maybe*, and paiched to listen at his lungs. And then he told that each night he went to his bed with a back like to break, but Ellen just laughed, she didn't know what an illness was, he wasn't the man to fear her and tell her. So Murdoch saw fine how the thing was going, the Simpson childe working himself to his grave, with his coarse lungs, too, to please his coarse wife. There was nothing he could do in the matter, he thought, but he said they'd aye be pleased to see Simpson at Mains. He said nothing of Ellen, the bit wife, in that; there was damn the pleasure to be had in the creature: with her laugh and her listening and the flutter of her eyes she fairly got on a body's nerves.

What with rain and with heat the Den was green-lush

right early that year—the grocer thought it came thicker than ever he minded—the broom stopped up the aisles of the larch that stretched up the braes from the old brown biggings of the Den. Ellen Simpson would come running out to the door as she heard the sound of his wheels on the close, and cry him good-day, and bring him the eggs, and stand still while he counted, a slow, canny childe; but once he raised his head and said: *Losh, but it's still!*

And the two of them stood there and listened in that quiet, not a sound to be heard or a thing to be seen beyond the green cup that stood listening around. And Ellen Simpson smiled white and said *Yes, it is still—and I'll take two loaves and some tea now, please.*

And Webster took a look at her: thinner she'd grown, more a wisp than ever, but still with her smile, and he liked her fine, near the only soul in the district that did. Most said she'd grown thinner with temper, faith! girning at her man to get out and start work, and him no more than an invalid, like.

Just luck she hadn't his death on her hands, and you couldn't blame him that he fell in the way, nearly every bit evening he would do it now, of taiking away over the brae from the Den to the Mains and his Murdoch friends. Jeannie Murdoch and he would flirt and would fleer—no harm in their fun, folk 'greed about that: the poor stock was no doubt in need of a laugh, him and that wife with her flutterings that fair set your hackles on edge. He was better than he'd been, he'd confess, would Simpson; all the more reason why he wanted some cheer when he came in about to his own fire at night, not aye to be listening to somebody cry: *Oh, George, do you think your lungs are near better?*

And Jeannie Murdoch would say *No, I'm sure. Sit you down. I'll make you a fine cup of tea.* And George Simpson would laugh out his big, sappy laugh *Faith! you're fine as you're bonny, Jean, lass.*

And Murdoch and his mistress would hear them and gley,

Mistress Murdoch pull down her meikle bit face; maybe she thought Jeannie went over far with a man that was married— no more than fun though their speak might be. If it wasn't for that snippet of a creature, Ellen, you'd think Simpson as fine a goodson as you'd meet, a bit slow at the uptake, maybe a bit dour, but a pretty, upstanding childe he was now.

Folk wondered a bit what she thought of those jaunts, Ellen Simpson down by her lone in Greenden. But she never said a word to a soul about them, not that she saw a many to speak to; she'd just smile, and go running and bring you some tea, kind enough you supposed that the creature was, but you'd never get yourself to like her, somehow; she'd set you at unease till you'd sit and wonder what ailed yourself— till going up home through the dark you'd be filled with fancies daft as a carrying woman, as though the trees moved and the broom was whispering, and some beast with quiet breath came padding in your tracks; and you'd look, and 'twas only a whin that you'd passed. And you'd heave a great breath, outside of the Den, up in the light of the evening sun, though the Den below was already in shadow.

But of nights as that summer wore on to its close she took to standing at her kitchen door while the light drew in and the dark came close: now and then some soul would come on her there, near startle her out of her skin as he cried *Ay, mistress, it's a fine bit night.* And she'd laugh, with her hand at her breast, daft-like, and then turn her head as though half she'd forgotten you, and look up and away out over the trees, and you'd look the same way and see feint the thing. And then maybe you'd look harder and see what it was; it was from the kitchen door alone of Greenden that the swathe of the trees and the broom was broken and through the hollow that was left in the gloaming the sun struck light on the Grampian slopes, long miles away and across the Mearns, shining immediate, yet distant and blue, their green earth-hazed in the heatherbells. And that was the thing that she stood and watched as a daftie would, and you'd scrape your feet, and you'd give a bit hoast, and she'd start and switch round, her face gone white, and say *Oh, I'm sorry, I'd forgotten you were here. Was it George that you wanted to see?*

Well, that was in June, and the June-end came, as bonny as ever it came in the Howe; folk meeting the Simpson man on the road would cry to him for a joke *Ay, man, you're fair smothered away from the world in Greenden.* And, faith! they spoke but the truth, so high was the broom with a mantling of bloom, and the trees a wall green-blinding the place. George Simpson made out of it every bit night over to the Mains' new barn they were building; he'd pretend it was the barn he went over to see, but he'd edge away from it as soon as he might, taik round to the kitchen, and Jeannie would blush: *Step away in, Mr. Simpson. How are you? I'm sure you are tired.*

Well, that barn it was, Webster was to swear, brought to an end that steer at Greenden. He never told the story in a neighbour-like way, he never did that, and he wasn't much liked, for he'd never much news to give a body when you spoke to him at the tail of his van and would drop a bit hint that you'd like to know why the Gordon quean was getting gey stout, and if Wallace was as coarse as they said to his wife, and such newsy-like bits of an interest to folk. He'd just grunt when you spoke and start counting the eggs, and say he was damned if he knew or he cared. So he told the Greenden tale to none but his wife; he thought her the same as himself, did Alec. But faith! she could claik a tink from a door, and soon it was known up and down the Howe, every bit of the happening that night at Greenden.

For he'd driven down late, as aye he had done, the grocer, and was coming in by the yard when he met Ellen Simpson come running up the road; her face was white in the fading light, and twice as she ran he saw her fall; and she picked herself up with blood on her face where a stone had cut as she fell. And Webster stopped his horse and jumped off the van and went running to meet her; and he cried *God, mistress, what's ta'en you—what's wrong?*

And she gabbled as he held her, he saw her eyes wild, syne she quieted a minute and covered her eyes and shivered, hot though the June night was. Then she whispered sudden, he shivered himself *They've done something to my hill, they have taken it away! Oh, I can't stand it now, I can't, I can't!*

And Webster said *What?* He was clean dumb-foundered; and he thought in a flash of old Grant of Greenden—he also had whispered and whispered like that. But she pointed up across the larch-hill and the broom, and he gowked, did the grocer, and saw nothing for a while. Syne he saw that there rose through that howe in the woods, through which you'd once see the light gleam on the hills, the roof and the girders of Murdoch's new barn. He stared at the thing, and then stared at the woman, and at that she broke down and cried like a bairn; she'd no shame before him, she was surely daft.

Oh, I can't stand it longer in this hateful place! It's smothering and killing me, down and lost here, I've been frightened, so frightened since the first hour here. I've tried not to show it, and I know that it's nothing, but the trees—they hate me, the fields, and at night. . . . Oh, I can't stand it longer, not even for George, now they've blocked up that sight of the hill that was mine!

And she cried out more of that stite, and the grocer—he'd aye liked her—was fair in a way: *Whisht, mistress, go in and lie down,* he said, but she whispered: *Don't leave me, don't leave me, I'm frightened!* And the dark came then down over the broom, and the horse stood champing and scraping its hooves, and a howlet began to hoot in the larch while Webster sat by her in the kitchen to quiet her. And she whispered once: *George— he's safe now, he's safe, God died, but I needn't, He saved him, not I.* And syne she was whispering again in her terror: *The trees and the broom, keep off the trees; it's growing so dark I can't see it, the hill. . .*

But at last she grew quiet; he told her to lie down. She went ben from the kitchen and he stood and thought. And he minded her man might be at the Mains; he went out and drew round his grocer's van, and got into it and drove up out of the Den, and whipped his bit beast to a trot for the Mains.

And folk told when he got there he went stamping in the kitchen: George Simpson was sitting with Jeannie and her father; the mistress was off to the pictures at Bervie. And Alec Webster cried *Leave your courting until you're a widower; have you no shame at all to abandon your wife night after night in that hell of a Den?* And George Simpson stood up and blustered *You Bulgar——*, and the grocer said *Away, raise your hand up to me, you big, well-fed bullock, and I'll crack your jaw where you stand.* Old Murdoch came in between them then, and he cried *What is't? What's wrong?*

So Webster told Simpson his wife was gey queer; was he or was he not going home? And Simpson scowled and said *Yes*, and went out with the grocer, and that childe swung round his weary bit horse and lashed it to a trot, and out into the road, and so, in their time, by the track to the Den. And there it was dark as a fireless lum, but far off as they neared to the biggings they heard a voice singing—singing so strange that it raised their hair:

> *There is a green hill far away,*
> *Beyond a city wall,*
> *Where the dear Lord was crucified,*
> *Who died to save us all.*

And it suddenly ceased, and Webster swore, and he lashed the horse, and they came to the close, and Webster jumped down and ran into the house. Behind him went Simpson, more slow—he was feared. In the kitchen it was dark and still as they came. Then the grocer slipped, there was something slippery and wet on the floor. So he kindled a match, and they both looked up, and they saw what it was, and it turned them sick. And a waft of wind came in from the door and the Shape from the beam swung to and fro.

And Webster turned round and went blundering out, as though he couldn't see, and he called to Simpson: *Take her down and I'll go for the doctor, man.*

But he knew right well that that would help nothing, and the thought went with him as he drove through the woods, up out of the Den, to the road that walked by the sea and the green hills that stood to peer with quiet faces in the blow of the wind from the sunset's place.

SIM

What profit hath a man of all his labour which he taketh under the sun?
                                                    Ecclesiastes i., 4.

Sim Wilson came of a fell queer stock, his mother a spinner at the Segget Mills, his father a soldier killed by the Boers. When news of that killing came up to Segget the wife just laughed —*Worse folk than the Boers!*—and went on with the tink-like life that she led. In time that fair grew a scandal in Segget, a body wasn't safe to let her man out of her sight for a minute in case he met in with that Wilson creature and was led all agley with her coarse green glower.

Sim was no more than five years old when at last things came to a head in Segget, his mother went off on a moonlight flit with the widow Grant's son and half of her silver, folk wondered which of the two would last longest. Young Sim was left in an emptied house till his auntie that bade in a house by Drumlithie took pity on the loon and had him down there. She came all a-fuss and a-pant with pity, the aunty, a meikle big creash of a woman, and she said to Sim *You're my dawtie now.* And Sim said *Maybe—if you'll leave me a-be.*

Faith, that was his only care from the first, as sweir a nickum as you'd meet, folk said, sweir at the school as he was at his home, it was fair a disease with the ill-gettèd loon. And an impudent creature he was, forbye, with his glinting black hair and his glinting green eyes, he'd truant from school more often than not and be off in the summer to sleep in the sun under the lithe of a whin or a stook. And once, he was then about ten years old, his auntie came on him high on the brae, in the heat, his chin in his hands as he keeked down through the veils of broom at the teams steaming at work in the parks below. She cried, *You coarse brute, why aren't you at school? Aren't you fair black affronted to lie there and stink?*

Well, Sim just sneered, not feared a wee bit. *No, I'm not. I was watching those fools in that park. You won't find me sossing and chaving like that when I'm a man with a fee of my own. The dafties—not to take a bit rest! . . . Lessons? Away, do you think I am soft?*

And he stuck out his tongue and slipped under her arm, his auntie near greeting with rage as he ran. But she couldn't catch up, loaded down with her creash. Sim was soon out of sight on his way up the hill. He spent the whole day lying flat on his back, the only sweir soul in the hash of the Howe.

Folk said that he'd come to an ill-like end, his sweirty would eat to his bones and they'd rot. But then, near the middle of his thirteenth year, he heard the news in his class at the school that the prize for dux that year was a pound; and all of a jiffy he started to work, like mad, near blinded himself of a night with reading and writing and learning his lessons, the hills hardly saw him except back of a book. And he'd cleverness in him, sweir though he'd been, he was dux for that year, and the dominie delighted.

He said to the loon *You'll do even better*, but Sim just sneered in his impudent way. *I'm finished with chaving at lessons and dirt. I've tried, and I know that they're not worth the sweat.* The dominie was fair took aback to hear that, *You'll gang a hard gait through the world, I fear.* And Sim said *Maybe; but I'll gang it myself. And I'll know what I'm getting ere I gang it at all.*

He fee'd his first fee at Upperhill in Kinraddie. Big-boned he had grown and supple and swack, but as sweir as ever and an ill-liked brute. He'd sneer at his elders and betters in the bothy. *What, work my guts out for that red-headed rat? Whatever for, can you tell me that? Show me a thing that is worth my trauchle, and I'll work you all off the face of the earth!*

The foreman there was a canny-like childe, and the only one that could bear with Sim. They both stayed on for a four-five years, Sim sweir as ever, with his glinting, green eyes, he'd a bigger power for lazing around than a pig in a ree was the speak of the bothy. And young and buirdly, well-happed like a hog, he'd doze through the work of the Upperhill parks, good-natured enough were he letten alone. But sometimes he'd stop from making his brose, of a night, when the bothy was lit by the fire. *And to think that the morn we'll be doing the same!* The billies in the bothy would maybe say *What?* and he'd say *Why, making more brose to eat! And the night after that and the night after that. And we'll get up the morn and slave and chave for that red-headed rat—and go to our beds and get up again. Whatever for, can you tell me that?*

And the brute in one of those unco-like moods would go off on a jaunting down to Segget; and take a dram or so in the Arms; and look round about for a spinner to spite. And if there were such Sim would swagger up to him *Ay, man, you've a look on your face I don't like. And I don't much like your face the look's on.* The spinner would maybe look Sim up and down, with a sneer, and call him a clod-hopping clown, and Sim would take him a bash in the face, and next minute the spinners would pile in on Sim; and when he got back to Upperhill bothy he'd look as though he'd been fed through the teeth of a mill. But he'd say he got in his bed *That was fine. Man, I fairly stirred up that dirt down in Segget!* And next day he'd be sleepy and sweir as before.

Syne he met with Kate Duthie at a dance down in Segget, she was narrow and red-haired, with a pointed chin and hard grey eyes you could strike a spunk on, a quean that worked as maid at the Manse. Well, Sim took a look at her, she one at him; and he fair went daft that minute about her. He waited till that dance was over and said *Can I have the next?* and Kate Duthie said, *Maybe. Who might you be?* And Sim Wilson told her, and Kate gave a laugh, *Oh, only a ploughman.*

As the Upperhill lads walked back that night in a bunch

from the dance they had been to in Segget Sim told them the speak of the grey-eyed quean. The foreman said, *And who might she think that she is? A joskin's as good as any damned maid.* Sim shook his head, *Most maybe; not her. Faith, man, but she's bonny, and I wish that I had her.*

Well, that was only the beginning of the stir, his sweirty went like a mist in June, he was out nearly every bit night after that, down at the Manse or hanging round Segget. Kate sometimes saw him and sometimes she didn't, she kept as cool as a clayed-up coulter. At last it came to a night Sim said *I'm thinking of marrying;* Kate Duthie said, *Oh; well I, wish you joy.* And Sim said *Ay, I'll get that fine—if you'll come and provide it.*

Kate laughed in his face and told him plain she wasn't cut out for a ploughman's wife to drag through her days in a cottar house. Sim said there would maybe be no need to cottar, though he'd never thought of the thing before, he spent every meck he ever had made on drink and coarse queans, any coarseness at all that didn't trouble his sweirty too much. But now with the grey-eyed quean in his arms he felt as he'd done that time when a loon and he made up his mind he would win the school prize. *I'll get a bit place of my own. You'll wait?*

Kate shrugged and said *Maybe, you'll have to risk that.* Sim held her and looked at her, suddenly cuddled her, daft and tight till she nearly screamed, just for a minute, and syne finished with that. *You needn't be feared, I'll wait for my turn. That's just a taste of what I'll yet take. What about a kiss?* And she gave him one, cold, like a peck, but he thought it fine, and lapped it in and put her away and went swinging away home the Kinraddie road; you could hear him nearly a mile from the bothy singing as he climbed up the road in the dark.

Well, God! there fair was a change in him then. It was brose and then brose and syne brose to his meat. The other billies in the bothy would laugh and mock at Sim and cry *What's it all for?* But Sim didn't heed, he saved every penny, he worked extra work, and afore two years, what with saving and scraping, he'd enough silver saved for the rent of Haughgreen.

It lies low down by the Segget burn. The clay of the Mearns has thickened down there till in a dry season a man might well think he stood in the yard of a milk-jar potter, the drills just hillocks and slivers of clay. Its rent was low in spite of its size, the most of the biggings just held together, disheartened-like, as though waiting the time to fall in a rickle on somebody's head. But Sim gave a swagger *I'll manage them fine*, the daft-like gaze on his queer green eyes; and was off every night from the Upperhill bothy, not down as afore to Kate Duthie in Segget, but down to Haughgreen with a saw and an axe, pliers and planes, and the Lord knows what. In the last week afore he was due to move in the Upperhill foreman went down for a look, and he found Haughgreen all shored-up and trig, the house all new papered, with furniture in it, the stable fit to take horses again, the stalls in the byre set well for nout—he'd worked like a nigger had that sweir brute, Sim.

The foreman said 'twas a miracle, just; he was glad that Sim had wakened at last. Sim gave him a clap that near couped him at that *Ay, man, and for why? Because I'll soon have the best quean in the Howe. What think you of that? In my house and my bed!*

That night he tramped to his quean down in Segget, and knocked at the kitchen door of the Manse, and Kate came to it and said *Oh, it's you?* And Sim said *Ay*, with his eyes fit to eat her, *You mind what I asked you near two years back?*

Kate said *What was that?* She thought little of him and knew nothing of his slaving to save for Haughgreen. But he started to tell her, as he stood in the door, that he was a farmer, with a farm of his own, and ready to take her there when she liked.

She gaped and said *Sim, it's not true, is it now?* And he said *Ay, it is*. And she fair seemed to thaw, and speired him up hill and down dale all about it, Sim standing and staring at the white of her neck, white, like cream, and he felt like a cat and licked his lips with a hungry tongue.

Well, she soon said *Ay*, she needed no prigging, foreseeing herself a braw farmer's wife. At the end of the term the two of them married, Sim looked that day as though wedding an angel, not just a quean with a warm, white skin and close grey eyes and a mouth like a mule. Not but that the creature had smiles for the hour, and was awful kind to the ploughmen that came. She danced with the foreman and said *You're a joskin? Maybe my husband will give you a fee?* And the foreman spat, *Well, would he now, then? But you see I'm particular-like about the mistress.*

She would try to put Sim against him for that, the foreman knew, and keeked over at Sim; and he saw his eyes as they fixed on Kate, hungry and daft, more a glare than a glower. And he suddenly minded Sim back in the bothy in the days before he had met with this quean, and that speak of his, *Trauchle the day just to trauchle the morn! But show me a thing that is worth my chave and I'll work you all off the face of the earth!*

Well, he'd gotten the thing, good luck go with him, the foreman thought as he tramped away home up through the grey of the morning mists with the bothy lightless and grey in the dawn, leaving Sim with his hard-eyed quean; you hoped he'd not eat her, that's what he'd looked like.

But faith! she survived, fair the kind to do that. Folk gave a bit laugh at the news from Haughgreen, and shook their heads when they heard that Sim no sooner married was as sweir as before, taking life cool as ever he had done in spite of the nagging and prigging of Kate. The ploughing was on; but Sim Wilson's was not, the parks were lucky did they see him by nine, instead of six, when other childes yoked. Even then he'd do little but stand up and gant or wheeber out loud as he sat on a gate.

Now and then a body would cry to him *Ay, you're ploughing's far back for the season, is't not?* and he'd say, *Damn the doubt.*

What o't though it is? And he'd whistle and stare at the clouds in the Howe, his cat-like eyes a-blink in the sun.

The foreman at last took a taik in about and Sim was as pleased to see him as though he wasn't new-married, new-buried instead. Kate snapped from the room like an ill-ta'en rat; she didn't like the foreman, he didn't like her. And he thought as he sat and waited his dram it was more than likely that she wore the breeks.

But right soon he was changing his mind about that. As they sat at their dram, him and Sim, she came back: *It's dark, and it's time you went for the kye—Gang for them yourself*, Sim said, and never turned. *You enjoy trauchle; well, enjoy some more.*

Kate's face blazed up like a fire with rage, she choked and went out and banged the door. The foreman felt a bit shamed for the quean; Damn't, you could see it wasn't so easy to be married to a sweir, queer brute like Sim; it wouldn't be long that these two together would store the kiln in Haughgreen, you knew.

There were more stammy-gastered than him at the change. For all of a sudden as the May came in Sim seemed to wake up and his sweirty went, he was out at all hours at the work of the parks, chaving like daft at his weed-choked drills. The land had lain fallow, he wasn't too late, and afore folk had well gotten over their gape they saw Sim Wilson was having fine crops manured with the sweat of his own meikle hams. He snored no more in the lithe of a whin and he stopped from ganting by every bit gate.

The reason for that was soon plain to be seen, Kate with a bairn and the creature soon due. The Upperhill foreman met in with Sim one night as he drove from the mart at Stonehive, and the foreman cried up *Ay, man, and how are you?* Sim stopped and cried back *Oh, it's you is it, then? Fine, man, I'm aye fine; I get what I want. Have you heard of the news of what's coming to Haughgreen?*

And he told the foreman of the bairn that was coming, as if

half the Howe didn't know about that, his green glazed eyes all glinting and shining. You'd have thought by the way that Sim Wilson spoke 'twas the first bit bairn that had waited for birth in all the windy Howe of the Mearns. He was daft on it, as daft as he had been a wee while afore to marry its mother. And the foreman thought as he wished him luck there were some that had aye to be looking ahead, and others looked back, and it made little odds, looked you east, looked you west, you'd to work or to die.

Kate had a sore time and let every soul know, but the midwife said that the queer-like thing was the way that that meikle Sim Wilson behaved, not like most of the fathers she ever had known, and she'd known a fell few; they went into three classes—fools, poor fools, and just plain damn fools. Well, the last were mostly the fathers of first-born, they'd wabble at the knees and whiten at the gills and pay no need to aught but the wife. Sim Wilson was different, with his unco green eyes, 'twas the bairn that took him his first minute in the room. He had it in his arms as ready as you please, and cuddled it, chuckled to it—the great silly sumph—till Kate whined out from the bed where she lay *And have you got nothing to say to me now?* And Sim Wilson said *Eh? Damn't, Kate, I'd forgotten you!*

An ill-like thing, that, to say to a wife, but that was the way the brute now behaved; there was nothing he thought on earth worth the price of daddling his bairn up and down in his arms, and swearing she'd winked, and wasn't she a topper? The Upperhill foreman came down for a look, and keeked at the creature, an ordinary bairn, like an ill-boiled swede; but Sim sat and glowered at her, the look in his eyes he'd once turned on Kate ere she lay in his bed—*Man, but I'll make a braw life for this lass—I'll give her education and make her a lady.*

The foreman said he thought education was dirt; if ever he had bairns he'd set them to work. Sim laughed in a way that he didn't much like. *You? Maybe. I was kittled on a different day.*

So the foreman left him, fair angered at that. 'Twas nearly five years ere he saw Sim again, for he moved down the Howe and took a fresh fee and got married himself and had bairns of his own. And sometimes he'd mind of that sweir brute Sim and the speaks of his in the bothy long syne: *Well, what's it all for, all your chaving and care?* And when he'd mind that the foreman would laugh and know that most likely his stomach was wrong.

Though he didn't see Sim he heard now and then of him and his capers down at Haughgreen. Folk told that he'd turned to a slaver, just, he'd fee'd two men and near worked them to death, and himself as well, and long Kate forbye—faith, if she'd thought she did herself well marrying a farmer and setting up braw she'd got many a sore heart since her marriage-morn. Sim gave her no help, he wouldn't fee a maid, he was up and out at the blink of dawn crying his men from their beds to work. He spared neither man nor beast, did Sim; in his four-five years he'd made a fair pile. But he was as ready as ever he had been to blab what he thought, a sneer or a boast. And he'd tell any soul that would care to listen the why and the wherefore he moiled like a mole. *It's that lass of mine, Jean—faith, man, she's a topper! I'm to send her to college, away from this soss, and she'll lack for nothing that money can bring.*

And neither she did. It fair was a scandal, folk said, that plain though they ate at Haughgreen the bairn was fed on this dainty and that. Sim had bought the wee wretch the finest of beds and he'd have her aye dressed like the bairns of gentry. You'd heard afore this of folk daft on a bairn but he was surely the worst in the Howe. Folk shook their heads, he had better look out, 'twas fell unchancy to show over-plain that you thought over-much of any bit bairn.

And faith! folk weren't far wrong in their speak—the bairn didn't die, she was healthy enough, but just when it came for the time of her schooling they seemed to wake up to the fact at Haughgreen. She was unco backward and couldn't speak well, and had funny-like ways; she would croon a bit song all the hours of the day, staring up at the hills of the Howe, not caring a fig what she ate or what wore, only caring to lie in the sun and to sleep.

Sim sent for a specialist out from Dundon and had the bit bairn taken away south and treated and tested and God knows what. That went on a six months and the cost was a ruin, a time of sore hearts and black looks at Haughgreen. And he well might have spared his time and his silver, she came back just the same—the bairn was a daftie, and the doctors said that so she'd remain a bairn of three all the years of her life.

Folk thought it awful, but they gave a bit snicker: *Ay, what will that fool at the Haugh say now?* Well, he went in a kind of daze for weeks, but his work didn't slacken as the foreman had thought—when he heard of the thing he had minded long back how Sim had behaved when he married his Kate and found that angel of common enough clay. But slaving was deep in his bones by now and he couldn't well stop though he wished, you supposed. The foreman met him one day at a roup, sneering and boasting as loudly as ever. But there was a look in the queer green eyes as though he were watching for something he'd tint.

He made no mention of the daftie, Jean, that had answered his question *What's it all for?* Sun, wind, and the batter of rain in his face—well, he'd settle now as others had done, and take it all for the riddle it was, not a race to be run with a prize at the end.

Then the news got about and you knew in a blink why he'd acted so calm with his firstborn, Jean. His wife had brought another bit bairn in the world, a lassie as well, and fine and strong. And soon's it was born Sim Wilson was crying *Is it right in the head, is it right in the head?* The doctor knew neither one way nor the other, but he said *Ay, it's fine,* to quieten the fool.

Sim doted on Jess from the day of her birth, promising her

all as he'd done with Jean—Jean that now he could hardly thole to look on, any more than on Kate, his wife, thin and old. She'd fair withered up had the thin-flanked Kate, except her bit tongue, it could scoriate your skin. But it didn't vex Sim with his daughter Jess, he would stride in the kitchen when he loosened at night: *Where's ma wee quean?* and Jess would cry *Here!* Bonny and trig, like a princess dressed, nothing soft about her like that thing in the corner, hunched up and crooning, aye half-way in sleep. She was clever and bright and a favourite at college, Jess, and Sim swore she should have what she liked, she never need soss with the land and its pleiter, she would marry no joskin, a lady she'd be.

He bled the red clay of Haughgreen near to white to wring silver from it for Jess and her life, to send her to college and give her brave clothes. Fegs, he was fair a long gait from the days when he'd mock at the land—*Ay, come and get ME—get me if you can—I'm not such a fool!*

The foreman had clean forgot him for years, Sim Wilson the sweir and the fairlies he chased; and when next he did hear he could hardly believe one thing in the tale that came swift up the Howe. That thing was the age of the daughter, Jess. *Why, the lassie is only a bairn* he said. But the childe that stopped to pass him the tale said *Faith, no, man, eighteen if a day. Ay, a real coarse quean, and you cannot but laugh at the nasty whack it is in the mouth for that meikle fool that farms Haughgreen!*

There was nothing unco in the tale when told, the kind of thing had been known to the world since the coming of men— and afore that, no doubt, else all the ill pleiter would have never begun. But for that to happen to the dawtie of Sim!— Jess, the student, so haughty and neat, the maid that had led his question so on, up out of the years: *What's it all for?*

It seems that she carried her shame a long time, and the creature that found her out was the daftie. One night when old Sim came home from the fields the daftie pointed at her sister, Jess, and giggled, and mouthed and made slabbering sounds. Sim had paid her no heed a good twenty years, but something in the wrigglings of the creature took him. He cried *What's that?* and glowered at his wife, old Kate, with her thinning face and greyed hair.

But Kate knew nothing, like himself she stared at Jess that sat red-faced by the fire. And then while they stared Jess jumped to her feet, weeping, and ran from the room, and they saw—plain enough the way she was in, they'd been blind.

Old Sim gave a groan as an old horse groans when you drive him his last bit bout up a hill, and stood and stared at the daftie, Jean, that was giggling and fleering there like a bairn, like something tint his life long syne, in the kitchen quiet as the daylight waned.

FORSAKEN

'Eloi! Eloi! lama sabachthani?'

For a while you could not think at all what strange toun this was you had come intil, the blash of the lights dazzled your eyes so long they'd been used to the dark, in your ears were the shammle and grind and drummle of dream-minded slopes of earth or of years, your hands moved with a weight as of lead, draggingly, anciently, so that you glowered down at them in a kind of grey startlement. And then as you saw the holes where the nails had been, the dried blood thick on the long brown palms, and minded back in a flash to that hour, keen and awful, and the slavering grins on the faces of the Roman soldiers as they drove the nails into the stinking Yid. That you minded—but now—now where had you come from that lang hame?

Right above your head some thing towered up with branching arms in the flow of the lights; and you saw that it was a cross of stone, overlaid with curlecues, strange, dreich signs, like the banners of the Roman robbers of men whom you'd preached against in Zion last night. Some Gentile city they had carried you to, you supposed, and your lips relaxed to that, thinking of the Samaritans, of the woman by the well that day whom you'd blessed—as often you'd blessed, pitifully and angrily, seeing the filth and the foolishness in folk, but the kindly glimmer of the spirit as well. Here even in the stour and stench and glare there would surely be such folk—

It was wee Johnny Tamson saw the Yid first—feuch! there

the nasty creature stood, shoggling backward and forward alow Mercat Cross, Johnny kenned at once the coarse brute was drunk same as father was Friday nights when he got his money from the Broo. So he handed a hack on the shins to Pete Gordon that was keeking in at a stall near by to see if he could nick a bit orange. *There's a fortune-teller, let's gang and make faces at him!*

You were standing under the shadow of the Cross and the Friday market was gurling below, but only the two loons had seen you as yet. You saw them come scrambling up the laired steps, one cried *Well, Yid!* and the other had a pluffer in his hand, and he winked and let up with the thing, and ping! on your cheek. But it didn't hurt, though you put up your hand to give it a dight, your hand you hardly felt on your cheek so strange it had grown, your eyen on the loon. Queer that lads had aye been like that, so in Bethlehem long syne you could mind they had been, though you yourself never been so, staring at books, at the sky, at the wan long trail of some northing star that led the tired herdsmen home. . . .

Johnny Tamson was shoggling backward and forward two steps below where the sheeny stood, he'd fallen to a coarse-like singing now, trying to vex the foreign fortune-teller:

> *Yiddy-piddy,*
> *He canna keep steady,*
> *He stan's in an auld nichtgoon!*

But Pete hadn't used his pluffer again, he felt all watery inside him, like. He cried up *Don't vex the man!* for something hurt when he looked in those eyen, terrible queer eyen, like mother's sometimes, like father's once. . . . *Stop it!* he cried to young Johnny Tamson.

Johnny Tamson pranced down the steps at that and circled round Pete like a fell raised cat. *Who're you telling to stop?* he asked, and Pete felt feared to his shackle-bone, Johnny Tamson was a bigger chap than him. So, because he was awful feared he said *You!* and bashed Johnny Tamson one in the neb, it burst into blood like a cracked ink-bottle and Johnny went stitering back and couped, backerty-gets into the stall they'd been sneaking about five minutes before, waiting a chance to nick an orange. Old Ma Cleghorn turned round at that minute, just as Johnny hit the leg of the stall and down it went with a showd and a bang.

You saw the thing that happened and heard the quarrel of the loons, understood in a flash, had moved down from the steps of the Mercat Cross, but had not moved quick enough crash went the stall, and there was the boy Pete staring appalled. As you put your hand on his shoulder he gasped, and looked round: *Oh, it's you!* and was suddenly urgent— *Come on!*

The Yid man wouldn't or he couldn't run, but came loping down the Gallowgate fine, Pete breathing and snorting through his nose and looking back at the stouring market din. Syne he looked at the mannie, and stopt, the street dark: *You'll be all right here*, he said to the mannie, *but they'd have blamed you—they aye blame Yids. Well, so long, I'm away home!*

You looked after the loon and stared round you again at the clorted house-walls of the antrin toun. And then because you went all light-headed you leaned up against the wall of the street, your hand at your eyen as the very street skellacht; till someone plucked at your sleeve. . . .

God damn and blast it, just like young Pete, coming belting against you out in the streets as you were tearing home for your tea: *Father, there's a Yid chap up in the close—with a nightgown on, he looks awful queer.—Well, I'm queer myself, I'm away for my tea.—Father, I want you to take him home with us— you're aye taking queer folk home. . . .* So here was Pa, hauled up to speak to the Yid—and a damned queer-looking felly at that, fair starving the creature was by his look.

Ay, then, Comrade!

You saw something in his face you seemed to know from far-off times, in a lowe of sea-water caught by the sun, in a garden at night when the whit owl grew quiet, that awful night in Gethsemane when you couldn't see the way clear at all, when you were only blank, dead afeared. Comrade! You knew him at once, with your hand to your head, to your heart, in greeting.

PETER!

Ay, that's my name. This young nickum here thinks you're no very well. Will you come in by for a dish of tea?

So next you were walking atween the loon and Peter down one dark street and along another and up dark twisting stairs. And at one of those twists the light from the street shone on the staircase and through on you, and Peter gave a kind of a gasp.

God, man, where was't I kenned you afore?

II

Sick of father and the tosh he piled in the room, books and papers, an undighted hand-press, wasn't room for a quean to do a hand's-turn to get into her outgoing clothes. Mr. Redding had called that evening to Jess: *Miss Gordon, come into the office*, in she'd gone, he was fat, the creash oozed over his collar, and she'd kenned at once when he closed the door the thing he was going to do. And he'd done it, she'd laughed, it hurt, the bloody beast. But she didn't say so, he sweated and loosed her, paiching: *We'll make a night o' it, eh, my Pootsy? I'll pick you up in the car at Mercat Cross.*

Oh, damn! She found herself greeting a bit, not loud, Mother would hear her greeting like a bairn as she minded that. But what else was there for a lassie to do, if she liked bonny things and fine things to eat, and—oh, to be hapt in a fine rug in a car and get a good bed to lie on—even if it was beside that oozing creash in the dark, as it had been afore now. Mind the last time? . . . But she couldn't do anything else, she'd her job to hold on to, a lot of use to find herself sacked, on the Broo, and father with work only now and then

E

and the rest of his time ta'en up with Bolsheviks—he'd be in the jail with it ere all was done, and where would his family be then?

She found the dress and scraped her way intilt, angrily, and heard the whisp-whisp of folk coming in at the kitchen door, wiping their feet on the bass and Mother speaking to them low. She tore the comb through her hair and opened the door and went into the parlour, not heeding them a damn. *Ma*—

You knew that face at once, the long golden throat and the wide, strange eyen and the looping up of the brightsome hair, your heart was twisted with a sudden memory, remembering her sorrow, her repentance, once, that night when she laved your feet with tears, how she followed through the stour of the suns and days of those moons when you trekked your men to El Kuds, Magdalene, the Magdalene.

She thought, Oh gosh, isn't father just awful? another tink brought into the house, a fright of a fool in an old night-gown. If Mr. Redding saw him I'd never hear the end. . . . And she looked at the Yid with a flyting eye, but feared a bit, something queer about him, as though she'd once seen him, once long back—that was daft, where could she have seen him? *Mother, where's my crocodile shoon?*

Ma was seating the Yid by the fire, poor creature, he'd been out in ill weather enough in that silly sark-like thing that he wore. He looked sore troubled in his mind about something, the Lord kenned what, men were like that, Ma never bothered about their daft minds, and their ploys and palavers and blether of right, wrong and hate and all the rest of the dirt,'they were only loons that never grew up and came back still wanting their bruises bandaged. But she thought the Yid was a fine-like stock, for all that, not like some of the creatures—feuch, how they smelt! that Peter would bring from his Bolshevist meetings.

Fegs, lassie, can you no see to the crocodiles yourself—or the alligators either, if it comes to that? Peter was in fair a good humour the night, warming his nieves, steeking and unsteeking them in front of the fire. *Your Ma's to see to the tea for me and this comrade here that young Pete met up by Mercat Cross.*

Jess banged over under the big box bed and found the crocodiles there, oh, no, not cleaned, young Pete was a lazy Bulgar, Ma spoiled him, he never did a thing for his meat, there he sat glowering at that Yid, like a gowk, as though the queer creature were some kind of sweetie. . . . Oh Christ, and they've tint the blasted brushes.

She got down on her knees and raxed out the polish, and started to clean, no body speaking, Ma seeing to the smokies above the fire, Pa warming his hands and Pete just staring, the Yid—Jess looked up then and saw him look at her, she stopped and looked back with a glower of her brows and next minute felt suddenly sick and faint. . . . Oh Gosh, that couldn't have happened to her, not *that*, after that night with Redding? She'd go daft, she'd go out and drown herself if there were a kid——.

You could see in this room with the wide, strange lum and those folk who only half-minded you suddenly a flash in the Magdalene's eyes. She was minding—minding you and the days when she joined the band, the New Men you led, while you preached again chastity, patience and love. The Magdalene minding, her eyes all alowe, in a minute she'd speak as Peter had spoken——

Peter said *Those smokies have fairly a right fine guff. Up with them, Ma, I've the meeting to gang to. Sit in about, Comrade, and help yourself. Queer I thought I'd once met you afore—Dottlet, folk sometimes get, eh, ay? Do you like two lumps or three in your tea?*

You heard yourself say *None, if you please*, though this was a queer and antrin stuff put into a queer and antrin drink. Yet it warmed you up as you drank it then and ate the smoked fish the woman Martha served, with a still, grave face (you minded her face in other time, before that birling of dust went past).

Pete thought as he ate up his bit of a smoky, *My Yid chap was famisht as Pa would say. Look how he's tearing into the fish. May-*

be he'll help me to plane my bookcase after he's finisht. And he called out loud, they all gave a loup, *Will you help me to plane my bookcase, chap? You were once a joiner and should do it just fine.*

The loon, you saw, knew you—or kenned only that? *How did you ken that I carpentered?*

—*Och, I just kent. Will you help me? Ma, there's Will coming up the stair.*

Jess got to her feet and slipped into the room, and banged the door and stood biting her lips, feared, but not now so feared as she'd been. If that was the thing that had happened to her she kenned a place where they'd see to it. Ugh, it made her shiver, that couldn't be helped, she'd see to the thing in spite of the Yid. . . . Och, she was going clean daft, she supposed, what had the Yid to do with it all? Something queer as he stared at her? If she vexed over every gowk that stared she'd be in a damn fine soss ere long. In a damn fine soss already, oh Gosh! . . .

Will thought as he stepped in and snibbed the door, Hello, another recruit for the Cause. A perfect devil for recruits, old Pa—wish to God he'd get some with some sense and go. And he sighed, fell tired, and nodded to the man that sat in the queer get-up by the table. Looked clean done in, poor devil in that fancy gown of his, some unemployed Lascar up from the Docks trying on the old fortune-telling stunt. . . .

Of him you were hardly sure at all—the thin, cool face and the burning eyes and the body that had a faint twist as it moved. And then you minded—a breathing space, an hour at night on the twilight's edge when the trees stood thin as pencil smoke, wan, against the saffron sky, in a village you rested in as a train went through, gurling camels with loping tails, and a childe bent down from a camel back, in the light, and stared at you with hard, fierce, cool eyes. And they'd told you he was a Sanhedrin man, Saul of Tarsus, a hater and contemner of the New Men you led.

Will, this is a comrade that young Pete found. My son's the secretary of the Communist cell. Would you be one of the Party yourself?

Will thought, Just like Pa, simple as ever. Poor devil of a Yid, of course he'll say *Ay*. . . . But instead the man looked up and stared, and seemed to think, and syne nodded, half doubtful. *All things in common for the glory of God.*

Pa said *Ay, just, that's what I tell Will. But he will not have it you can be religious at all if you're communist, I think that's daft, the two are the same. But he kens his job well enough, I'll say that. Eat up, Comrade, you're taking nothing.*

You thought back on that wild march up on El Kuds and the ancient phrases came soft on your lips as you looked at the bitter, cool face of Saul, and you heard yourself say them, aloud in the room. *All things in common in the Kingdom of God, when the hearts of men are changed by light, when sin has ceased to be.*

Will thought, Queer how that delusion still lasts, queer enough in this poor, ragged devil from the Docks. Funny, too, how he said the old, empty words as though they were new and bit and pringled, not the grim, toothless tykes they are. Looked in a funny-like way when he said them, one half-believed one had seen him before. Oh, well, oh hell, couldn't let that pass. Agitprop, even while eating a smoky!

That's been tried and found useless over long, Comrade. Waiting the change of heart, I mean. It's not the heart we want to change, but the system. Skunks with quite normal hearts can work miraculous change for the good of men. People who have themselves changed hearts are generally crucified—like Christ.

—Christ? Who is Christ?

They all glowered at him, Pete fair ashamed, it wasn't fair the poor Yid should be shown up like that. Ma turned to the fire again, Eh me, the Jew felly was unco unlearned, poor brute, with they staring eyen—and whatever had he been doing to those hands of his? Pa reddened and pushed the oat cakes over.

Help yourself, Comrade, you're eating nothing. Never mind about Jesus, he's long been dead.

Jesus? What Jesus was this of theirs, who brought that look of shame to them? Some prophet of antique time, no doubt, this man named as someone you knew had been named. . . . Saul's eyen staring with that question in them—neither the eyen of an enemy nor yet of a frere.

Who was Jesus?

Ma thought, Well, well, and now they'll be at it. Will'll never get his smoky down at all with all this blether he's having on hand telling the poor Jew man about Jesus—Eh me, and the way he speaks, too, right bonny, though no very decent my mother'd have thought. But that was long syne, afore you met in with Peter Gordon and his queer-like notions—scandalized mother off the earth, near, they had! . . . *Will, would you have another smoky?*

—*No, Ma, thank you kindly. . . . So that was the way of it, you see, this Prophet childe started with the notion that men's hearts would first need changing, to make them love one another, care for the State— he called it the Kingdom of God in his lingo. And what happened was that he himself was crucified after leading an army against Jerusalem; syne, hardly was he dead than his followers started making a god of him, quite the old kind of God, started toning down all he'd taught to make it fit in with the structure of the Roman state. They became priests and princes in the service of the temples dedicated to the dead Jesus, whom they'd made a God. . . . And, mind you, that change of heart must have happened often enough to folk when they heard of the sayings of this Jesus. Thousands and thousands changed—but there was no cohesion—no holding together, they put off the Kingdom of God till Eternity: and were tortured and murdered in Jesus' name.*

You stared in the bright sharp eyes of Saul and saw now that he had no knowledge of you. Jesus?—many years ago, he had said. . . . And after that last black night, that hour when you cried to God forsaking you, mad darkness had descended again on the earth, on the faces and souls of Magdalene and Martha, Peter and Saul—Peter there with the old, kind smile on his face, his mind far lost in dreams. And those banners you had led up the passes against El Kuds were put away for the flaunting flag of a God—a God worshipped afar in the strange touns.

Ma cried, *Eh, mighty, the poor childe's no well. Lean back a minute; Pete, open that window; Fegs you fair gave me a turn, man!*

III

Jess Gordon came out from the room all dressed, with her crocodiles on, as they tended the Yid. He opened his eyen as she stepped in the room, Gosh, what need had he to look at her like that, as though he both *kenned* and nearly grat? Well, she didn't care, not a damn, she was going out with Redding, she would tell them all that, that greasy Lascar into the bargain. *What's wrong with him, Ma?*

And now you saw she was not the Magdalene—or the Magdalene after two thousand years with the steel of a Roman sword in her heart, sharper, clearer, colder than of yore, not to be moved by glance or touch or the aura of God that you carried from those Bethlehem days as a loon. This was Magdalene from the thousands of years that drummlet and rumblet into the night since the pain tore deep in your wounded feet. . . .

Ma said, *The childe was feeling the heat, just don't vex him and don't stare at him like that, as though he had done you some ill or other. And where are you off to with your crocodiles on?*

—*To meet a chap if you want to know.* Jess dragged her eyen from those staring eyen. (Damn him, he could stare.) *Ta-ta, folk.*

Ta, ta, they called. She turned at the door. *And ta-ta, YOU.* Her look was a knife.

Pa louped up as she banged the door. *What's ta'en the ill-gettèd bitch the night? Glowering that way at the Comrade here?* . . . *Eh, what did you say?*

You had said only *Peter!* and at that he had turned, for a moment you saw loup into his eyen that love and amazement that had once been his, love and amazement for the leader, not the creed, it died away as he sat down again. And even he you saw now was not the Peter of that other time,

weak and leal and kind he had been, but more of the kindness now, little of the love, forsaken of the trust and utter-
most belief. No thing in him now you could ever touch
except with a cry of despair.

Ma said, *There was nothing to fuss about. Finish your tea,
you've your meeting, Pa. Pete, it's time you were off to your bed. Say
ta-ta now to the gentlemen.*

—*Och, isn't there no time for my bookcase, Ma? All right, all
right, ta-ta, chap.*

The mannie looked and said *Ta-ta.* And again something
came twisting in young Pete's wame. He looked back, white-
faced, from the bedroom door. *Ta-ta. I—liked you awful, you ken.*

—*Hear that?* said Pa. *He's fair ta'en to you, Comrade. Well, I'll
need t'away to the meeting, I doubt. You'll be down there, Will?*

—*Ay will I, worse luck. Is the comrade coming?*

You looked from the face of one to the other, the faces of
Martha and Saul and Peter, and you saw, no mist now hap-
ping your eyen (that mist from past times), they'd no kinship
with you. Saul with the bitter face and creed, a leader once
for that army you led up the heights to El Kuds, never for
that love you had led it with. Looking into his heart with that
ancient power you saw the white, stainless soul that was there,
but love had gone from it, faith and trust, hope even, only
resolve remained. Nothing there but resolve, nothing else
that survived the awful torment your name had become. . . .
And you saw in the face of Martha even something that was
newer or older than you—a cold and a strange and a terrible
thing, a mother of men with the eyen of men, facing fear and
pain without hope as did Saul, wary and cool, unbannered,
unafraid. . . . You shook your head:

No. I maun gang to my hame.

They could never make up their minds what he said next
that minute when he covered his face with his hands, afore he
went out of the house and their lives. Pa said it was something
about some Eliot, Will said the poor Lascar devil had mum-
bled something or other about the Sabbath.

GIBBON: ESSAYS

Editor's note

The Grassic Gibbon essays add a new dimension to this form
—holding more dramatic intensity than is usual in the
medium. Like the Scottish stories they are all reprinted from
The Intelligent Man's Guide to Albyn to give that MacDiarmid-
Gibbon tour-de-force its alternative title. Incidentally Mac-
Diarmid was among the first to recognise the vitality and
important innovating power of Gibbon's writing. In return
L.G.G. put on record his view that Hugh MacDiarmid was
'a great poet—writing the only poetry Scotland has produced in the last hundred years—stuff unexpected and
beautiful, mellow and keen.' And whatever views are held on
the presence or absence of a Scottish Renaissance it must be
admitted that these two were key figures in the renewed
creative vigour of the early thirties.

The link between the magnificent essay on *The Land* and
Sunset Song has been noted and the parallels between the
words of Chris in character and Mitchell in person are open
to most interesting comparison and speculation. This essay
was written in a mood of heightened perception after the
author's return visit to Arbuthnott and the lands of the
Mearns in the late summer of 1933.

The Ramsay MacDonald essay aroused much controversy.
In one sense it is an amazing indictment, a devastatingly
destructive attack on 'the wrecker of the Socialist Party'
which displays Mitchell's power of invective at its strongest.
Yet Mitchell himself claimed that his portrait of Ramsay

wasn't unfair—merely dark, and although not everyone would agree with this estimate there is a measure of latent sympathy and a perceptive understanding in the closing sentences of the essay.

Some inhabitants of Glasgow and Aberdeen were slow to forgive Mitchell for his description of their native cities. There is a biting and bitter note in the essay on Glasgow and although Aberdeen received somewhat lighter punishment not everyone was grateful. Both sketches were strongly coloured by personal experiences—there is a distinct auto-biographical note in the Aberdeen essay.

The treatment of the theme in *Religion* is not unexpected, *The Antique Scene* contains some doubtful history and some interesting speculation, and *Literary Lights* is a mixture of balanced and prejudiced criticism with an interesting novelty in a fragment of self-assessment.

Although on any estimate *The Land* stands out among the essays, the others hold much of interest, and are certainly never dull. And they help towards understanding of the man without explaining the enigma of the writer.

THE LAND

1 *Winter*

I like the story of the helpful Englishman who, when shown a modern Scots Nationalist map with 'Scotland Proper' stretching from John o' Groats to the Tweed, and 'Scotia Irredenta' stretching from the Tweed to the Mersey, suggested 'Scotland Improper' in place of the latter term. The propriety of Northern England to rank as a section of Scotland may have political justice; it certainly has no aesthetic claim. If I look out on the land of Scotland and see it fouled by the smoking slag-heaps of industrialism rightwards and leftwards, a long trailing rift down the eastern coast and a vomiting geyser in Lanarkshire, I feel no stirrings of passion at all to add those tortured wastes of countryside, Northumbria and Lancashire, to the Scottish land. I like the grey glister of sleet in the dark this night, seen through the unblinded window; and I like this idle task of voyaging with a pen through the storm-happed wastes of Scotland in winter; but I balk at reaching beyond the Border, into that chill land of alien geology and deplorable methods of ploughing. This paraffin lamp set beside me on the table was lit for the benefit of myself and Scotland Proper: I shrink from geographical impropriety to-night as my Kailyard literary forerunners shrank from description of the bridal bed.

And now that I bend to the task and the logs are crackling so cheerfully and the wind has veered a point, and there's a fine whoom in the lum, it comes on me with a qualm that

perhaps I have no qualifications for the task at all. For if
the land is the enumeration of figures and statistics of the
yield of wheat in the Merse or the Carse of Gowrie, fruit-
harvesting in Coupar-Angus, or how they couple and breed
their cattle in Ayrshire, I am quite lost. And if the land is the
lilting of tourist names, Strathmore, Ben Lomond, Ben
Macdhui, Rannoch, Loch Tay and the Sidlaw Hills, I confess
to bored glimpses of this and that stretch of unique countryside, I confess that once (just such a night as this) I journeyed
up to Oban; and the train was bogged in a snow-storm; and I
spent shivering hours in view of Ben Cruachan; and once an
Anglo-Gaelic novelist took me round Loch Lomond in his
car and we drank good whisky and talked about Lenin; and
an uncle once dragged me, protesting, up Lochnagar, in
search of a sunrise that failed to appear—the sun hid that
morning in a diffusion of peasoup fog; and I've viewed the
Caledonian Canal with suitable commercial enthusiasm and
recited (as a small boy at concerts) verse about the Dee and
Don, they still run on (a phenomenon which elicited complacent clappings of commendation from my audiences);
and I've eaten trout by Loch Levenside. But I refuse the
beetling crags and the spume of Spey; still I think they are
not The Land.

That is The Land out there, under the sleet, churned and
pelted there in the dark, the long rigs upturning their clayey
faces to the spear-onset of the sleet. That is The Land, a dim
vision this night of laggard fences and long stretching rigs.
And the voice of it—the true and unforgettable voice—you
can hear even such a night as this as the dark comes down,
the immemorial plaint of the peewit, flying lost. *That* is The
Land—though not quite all. Those folk in the byre whose
lantern light is a glimmer through the sleet as they muck and
bed and tend the kye, and milk the milk into tin pails, in
curling froth—they are The Land in as great a measure.
Those two, a dual power, are the protagonists in this little
sketch. They are the essentials for the title. And besides,

quite unfairly, they are all so intimately mine that I would give them that position though they had not a shadow of a claim to it.

I like to remember I am of peasant rearing and peasant stock. Good manners prevail on me not to insist on the fact over-much, not to boast in the company of those who come from manses and slums and castles and villas, the folk of the proletariat, the bigger and lesser bourgeoisies. But I am again and again, as I hear them talk of their origins and beginnings and begetters, conscious of an over-weening pride that mine was thus and so, that the land was so closely and intimately mine (my mother used to hap me in a plaid in harvest-time and leave me in the lee of a stook while she harvested) that I feel of a strange and antique age in the company and converse of my adult peers—like an adult himself listening to the bright sayings and laughters of callow boys, parvenus on the human scene, while I, a good Venriconian Pict, harken from the shade of my sun circle and look away, bored, in pride of possession at my terraced crops, at the on-ding of rain and snow across my leavened fields. . . .

How much this is merely reaction from the hatreds of my youth I do not know. For once I had a very bitter detestation for all this life of the land and the folk upon it. My view was that of my distant cousin, Mr. Leslie Mitchell, writing in his novel *The Thirteenth Disciple:*

'A grey, grey life. Dull and grey in its routine, Spring, Summer, Autumn, Winter, that life the Neolithic men brought from the south, supplanting Azilian hunger and hunting and light-hearted shiftlessness with servitude to seasons and soil and the tending of cattle. A beastly life. With memory of it and reading those Catholic writers, who, for some obscure reason, champion the peasant and his state as the ideal state, I am moved to unkindly mirth . . . unprintably sceptical as to Mr. Chesterton or his chelas ever having grubbed a livelihood from hungry acres of red clay, or re-

garding the land and its inhabitants with other vision than
an obese Victorian astigmatism.'

Not, I think, that I have gone the full circle and have
returned among the romantics. As I listen to that sleet-drive
I can see the wilting hay-ricks under the fall of the sleet and
think of the wind ablow on ungarmented floors, ploughmen
in sodden bothies on the farms outbye, old, bent and wrinkled
people who have mislaid so much of fun and hope and high
endeavour in grey servitude to those rigs curling away, only
half-inanimate, into the night. I can still think and see these
things with great clarity though I sit in this warm room and
write this pleasant essay and find pleasure in the manipulation of words on a blank page. But when I read or hear our
new leaders and their plans for making of Scotland a great
peasant nation, a land of little farms and little farming communities, I am moved to a bored disgust with those pseudo-
literary romantics playing with politics, those refugees from
the warm parlours and lights and policemen and theatre-
stalls of the Scots cities. They are promising the New Scotland a purgatory that would decimate it. They are promising
it narrowness and bitterness and heart-breaking toil in one of
the most unkindly agricultural lands in the world. They are
promising to make of a young, ricketic man, with the phthisis
of Glasgow in his throat, a bewildered labourer in pelting
rains and the flares of head-aching suns, they are promising
him years of a murderous monotony, poverty and struggle
and loss of happy human relationships. They promise that of
which they know nothing, except through sipping of the
scum of Kailyard romance.

For this life is for no modern man or woman—even the
finest of these. It belongs to a different, an alien generation.
That winter that is sweeping up the Howe, bending the
whins on Auchindreich hill, seeping with pelting blasts
through the old walls of Edzell Castle, malagarousing the
ploughed lands and swashing about and above the heavy

cattle-courts where in darkness the great herds lie cud-chewing and breath-blowing in frosty steam, is a thing for most to be stared at, tourist-wise, endured for a day or a week. This night, the winter on the countryside, the crofter may doze contentedly in the arm-chair in the ingleneuk and the mistress yawn with an equal content at the clock. For you or I or young Simon who is taking his girl to the pictures it is as alien and unendurable in permanence as the life of the Kamtchatkan.

11 *Spring*

Going down the rigs this morning, my head full of that un-accustomed smell of the earth, fresh and salty and anciently mouldy, I remembered the psalmist's voice of the turtle and instinctively listened for its Scots equivalent—that far cooing of pigeons that used to greet the coming of Spring mornings when I was a boy. But the woods have gone, their green en-circlement replaced by swathes of bog and muck and rank-growing heath, all the land about here is left bare in the North wind's blow. The pigeons have gone and the rabbits and like vermin multiplied—unhappily and to no profit, for the farmers tell me the rabbits are tuberculous, dangerous meat. Unshielded by the woods, the farm-lands are assailed by enemies my youth never knew.

But they are fewer and fewer, the cultivated lands. Half of them are in grass—permanently in grass—and browsed upon by great flocks of sheep, leaving that spider-trail of grey that sheep bring to pastures. We are repeating here what the Border men did in Badenoch and the Highlands—eating away the land and the crofter, killing off the peasant as surely as in Russia—and with no Russian compensation. If the little dykes and the sodden ditches that rivuleted in the Springs of bygone times with the waters hastening to the Forthie—the ditches that separated this little farm from that —were filled and obliterated by a sovkholz with tractors and high enthusiasm and a great and tremendous agricultural hope, I at least could turn to the hills and the heath—that other and older Land—with no more regret than the sensitive felt in the passing of the windjammers and the coming of the steamboats. But instead there has come here only a brainless greed, a grabbing stupidity, the mean avariciousness and planlessness of our community in epitome. I do not wonder that the rabbits are tuberculous: the wonder is that they are not jaundiced as well.

It was then that I thought what a fine and heartsome smell has rank cow-dung as the childe with the graip hurls it steady heap on heap from the rear of his gurling cart. They sell stuff in Paris in little bottles with just that smell, and charge for it handsomely, as they may well do, for it is the smell that backgrounds existence. And then (having come to the end of the rig and looked at the rabbit-snare and found it empty and found also a stone whereon to sit) I fell into another meditation: this dung that backgrounded existence, this Autumn's crops, meal for the folk of the cities, good heartsome barley alcohol—would never be spread, never be seeded, never ground to bree, but for the aristocracy of the earth, the ploughmen and the peasants. These are the real rulers of Scotland: they are the rulers of the earth!

And how patient and genial and ingenuously foulmouthed and dourly wary and kindly they are, those self-less aristos of Scotland. They endure a life of mean and bitter poverty, an order sneered upon by the little folk of the towns, their gait is a mockery in city streets, you see little waitresses stare haughtily at their great red, suncreased hands, plump professors in spectacles and pimples enunciate theses on their mortality and morality, their habits of breeding and their shiftlessness—and they endure it all! They endure the chatter of the city salons, the plannings of this and that war and blockade, they endure the pretensions of every social class but their own to be the mainspring and base of human society—they, the masters, who feed the world! . . . And it

F

came on me that all over Great Britain, all over Europe this morning, the mean fields of France and fat pastures of Saxony and the rolling lands of Roumania those rulers of the earth were out and about, bent-backed at plodding toil, the world's great Green International awaiting the coming of its Spartacus.

There are gulls in from the sea this morning, wheeling in comet tails at the heels of this and that ploughman, a dotting of signatures against the dark green of the Bervie braes. Here the land is red clay, sour and dour, but south, by Brechin, you come to that rich loam land that-patterns Scotland like a ragged veil, the lovely land that even here erupts in sudden patches and brings tall corn while the surrounding fields wilt in the baking clay. The clay is good for potatoes in the dry years, however—those dry years that come every decade or so for no reason that we know of here in the Howe, for we are beyond the 'mountain-shadow' that makes of Donside and Braemar the tourist's camping-ground. . . .

In the sunlight, down by Kinneff, the fog-horn has begun its wail, the sun has drawn great banks of mist out of the North Sea and now they are billowing over Auchendreich like the soft, coloured spume from a washing-tub. But left-wards the sun is a bright, steely glare on the ridged humps of the Grampians, hastening south into the coming of Summer, crowned with snow in their upper haughs—much the same mountains, I suppose, as the Maglemosians looked on that Spring day in the youth of the world and the youth of Scotland when they crossed the low lands of the Dogger Bank and clambered up the rocks of Kinneff into a still and untenanted Scotland. The great bear watched them come, and the eagle from his Grampian eyrie and scattering packs of wolves on the forest fringes saw that migration of the hunters seven thousand years ago. They came over Auchendreich there, through the whins and heath, and halted and stared at the billowing Howe, and laughed and muttered and squatted and stared—dark men, and tall, without gods or kings, classes or culture, writers or artists, free and happy, and all the world theirs. Scotland woke and looked at them from a hundred peaks and stared a shy virgin's amaze.

All winter the cattle were kept to the byres. This morning saw their first deliverance—cows and stirks and stots and calves they grumphed and galumphed from the byre to the park and squattered an astounded delight in the mud, and boxed at each other, and stared a bovine surprise at the world, and went mad with delight and raced round the park, and stood still and mooed: they mooed on a long, devilish note, the whole lot of them, for nearly two minutes on end and for no reason at all but delight in hearing their own moo. They are all of mixed breed, except one, a small Jersey cow of a southron coldness, who drops her aitches, haughtily, and also her calves. The strains are mostly shorthorn, with a dash of Highland, I suspect: a hundred years of mixed pasturing and crop-rotation weeded out the experimental breeds and left these satisfying mongrels. Presently (after racing a grocer' grocer's cart for the length of the field and all but hamstringing themselves on the boundary fence) they abandoned playfulness and took to grazing, remembering their mission was to provide fat carcases for the slaughter-shed——.

We balk from such notions, in Spring especially, in especial as the evening comes with that fresh smell all about it, impregnating it, the kind of evening that has growth and youngness and kindliness in its essence—balk from the thought of our strange, unthinking cruelties, the underpit of blood and suffering and intolerable horror on which the most innocent of us build our lives. I feel this evening that never again will I eat a dead animal (or, I find myself guarding the resolve with the inevitable flippancy, a live one). But that resolve will be gone to-morrow: the Horror is beyond personalism, very old and strange and terrible. Even those hunters all those millenia ago were eaters of flesh.

It is strange to think that, if events never die (as some of the wise have supposed,) but live existence all time in Eternity, back through the time-spirals, still alive and aware in that world seven thousand years ago, the hunters are *now* lying down their first night in Scotland, with their tall, deep-bosomed sinewy mates and their children, tired from trek. . . . Over in the west a long line of lights twinkles against the dark. Whin-burning—or the camps of Maglemose?

III *Summer*

I cycled up the Glen of Drumtochty to-day. It was very hot, the heat was caught in the cup of the Howe and spun and stirred there, milkily, by little currents of wind that had come filtering down through the Grampian passes. In the long, dusty stretches of roadway my shadow winked and fluttered perspiringly while I followed in a sympathetic sweat. This till we pass down into the Glen itself, when the over-shadowing hills flung us a cool shade. There the water sparkled and spun coolly, so coldly, a little burn with deep brown detritus winding amidst the broom and the whins. To the left the reafforested Drumtochty Hill towered up dazzlingly impossible in purple. This Tyrian splendour on Drumtochty Hill is probably unmatched in all Scotland, very breath-taking and strange, alien to Scotland: it is a wonder, a flamboyant flaunting of nature that comes for a month on our dour hill-lands and we stare at it, sober, Presbyterian, from our blacks and browns—much as Mac-Diarmid visioned the Scots on Judgement Day staring at

> 'God and a' his gang
> O' angels in the lift,
> Thae trashy, bleezin' French-like folk
> Wha garred them shift. . . .'

Beyond the contours of Drumtochty, through the piping of that stillness, snipe were sounding. I got off my bicycle to listen to that and look round. So doing I was aware of a

sober fact: that indeed all this was a little disappointing. I
would never apprehend its full darkly colourful beauty until
I had gone back to England, far from it, down in the smooth
pastures of Hertfordshire some night I would remember it
and itch to write of it, I would see it without the unessentials
—sweat and flies and that hideous gimcrack castle, nestling
—(Good God, it even *nestled!*) among the trees. I would see it
in simplicity then, even as I would see the people of the land.

This perhaps is the real land; not those furrows that haunt
me as animate. This is the land, unstirred and greatly un-
touched by men, unknowing ploughing or crops or the coming
of the scythe. Yet even those hills were not always thus. The
Archaic Civilization came here and terraced great sections of
those hills and reared Devil Stones, Sun Circles, to the great
agricultural gods of ancient times—long ago, before Pytheas
sailed these coasts, while Alexander rode his horse across the
Jaxartes there were peasants on those hills, on such a day as
this, who paused to wipe the sweat from their faces and look
with shrewd eyes at the green upspringing of the barley
crops. . . . By night they slept in houses dug in the earth,
roofed with thatch, and looked out on a wilder and wetter
Howe, but still with that passion of purple mantling it in this
month. They are so tenuous and yet so real, those folk—and
how they haunted me years ago! I had no great interest in
the things around me, I remember, the summer dawns that
came flecked with saffron over the ricks of my father's farm,
the whisper and pelt of the corn-heads, green turning to
yellow in the long fields that lay down in front of our front-
door, the rattle and creak of the shelvins of a passing box-
cart, the chirp and sardonic *Ay!* of the farming childe who
squatted unshaven, with twinkling eyes, on the forefront of
the shelvin . . . but the ancient men haunted those woods and
hills for me, and do so still.

I climbed up the top of Cairn o' Mount with my bicycle
and sat and lunched and looked about me: and found it very
still, the land of Scotland taking a brief siesta in that midday

hour. Down in the north the green parks, miles away, were like plaques of malachite set on the table of some craftsman of ancient Chichen-Itza or Mexico, translucent and gleaming and polished. One understood then, if never before, how that colour—green—obsessed the ancient civilization with its magic virtues. It was one of the colours that marked a Giver of Life—reasonably, for those crops are surely such Givers? It is better land here than in my homeland—darker, streaked with clay, but with a richer sub-soil. Between the green of the corn and barley shone the darker stretches of the tattie-shaws, the turnip tops, and the honey brown of the clover. Bees were humming about me: one came and ate jam from my sandwiches, some discontented apian soul unfulfilled with the natural honey of the heather-bells and longing for the tart, sharp tastes of the artificial.

He is not alone in that. In the days of my youth (I have that odd pleasure that men in the early thirties derive from thinking of themselves as beyond youth: this pleasure fades in the forties) men and women still lived largely on the food-stuffs grown in the districts—kale and cabbage and good oat-meal, they made brose and porridge and crisp oatcakes, and jams from the blackberry bushes in the dour little, sour little gardens. But that is mostly a matter of the past. There are few who bake oatcakes nowadays, fewer still who ever taste kale. Stuff from the grocer's, stuff in bottles and tins, the canned nutriments of Chicago and the ubiquitous Fray Bentos, have supplanted the old-time diets. This dull, feculent stuff is more easy to deal with, not enslaving your whole life as once the cooking and serving did in the little farms and cottars' houses—cooking in the heat of such a day as this on great open fireplaces, without even a range. And though I sit here on this hill and deplore the fusionless foods of the canneries, I have no sympathy at all with those odd souls of the cities who would see the return of that 'rich agricultural life' as the return of something praiseworthy, blessed and rich and generous. Better Fray Bentos and a seat in the pictures with your man of a Saturday night than a grilling baking of piled oatcakes and a headache withal.

They change reluctantly, the men and women of the little crofts and cottar houses; but slowly a quite new orientation of outlook is taking place. There are fewer children now plodding through the black glaur of the wet summer storms to school, fewer in both farm and cottar house. The ancient, strange whirlimagig of the generations that enslaved the Scots peasantry for centuries is broken. In times gone by a ploughman might save and scrape and live meanly and hardly and marry a quean of like mettle. And in time they would have gathered enough to rent a croft, then a little farm; and all the while they saved, and lived austere, sardonic lives; and their savings took them at last to the wide cattle-courts and the great stone-floored kitchen of a large farm. And all the while the woman bred, very efficiently and plentifully and with out fuss—twelve or thirteen were the common numberings of a farmer's progeny. And those children grew up, and their father died. And in the division of property at his death each son or daughter gathered as inheritance only a few poor pounds. And perforce they started as ploughmen in the bothies, maids in the kitchens, and set about climbing the rungs again—that their children might do the same.

It kept a kind of democracy on the land that is gone or is going; your halflin or your maid was the son or the daughter of your old friends of High Rigs: your own sons and daughters were in bothies or little crofts: it was a perfect Spenglerian cycle. Yet it was waste effort, it was as foolish as the plod of an ass in a treadmill, innumerable generations of asses. If the clumsy fumblements of contraception have done no more than break the wheel and play of that ancient cycle they have done much. Under these hills—so summer-hazed, so immobile and essentially unchanging—of a hundred years hence I do not know what strange master of the cultivated lands will pass in what strange mechanical contrivance: but

he will be out with that ancient yoke, and I send him my love
and the hope that he'll sometime climb up Cairn o' Mount
and sit where I'm sitting now, and stray in summery thought
—into the sun-hazed mists of the future, into the lives and
wistful desirings of forgotten men who begat him.

IV *Autumn*

I have a daughter four years old who was born in England
and goes to school there, and already has notions on ethnology. Occasionally she and I debate and fall out, and her final
triumphant thrust is 'You're only Scotch!'

Autumn of all seasons is when I realize how very Scotch I
am, how interwoven with the fibre of my body and personality is this land and its queer, scarce harvests, its hours of reeking sunshine and stifling rain, how much a stranger I am, south,
in those seasons of mist and mellow fruitfulness as alien to my
Howe as the olive groves of Persia. It is a harder and slower
harvest, and lovelier in its austerity, that is gathered here, in
September's early coming, in doubtful glances on the sky at
dawn, in listening to the sigh of the sea down there by Bervie.
Mellow it certainly is not: but it has the most unique of tangs,
this season haunted by the laplaplap of the peesie's wings, by
great moons that come nowhere as in Scotland, unending
moons when the harvesting carts plod through great thickets
of fir-shadow to the cornyards deep in glaur.

These are the most magical nights of the land: they endure
but a little while, but their smells—sharp and clear, com-
mingled of fresh horse-dung and dusty cornheads—pervade
the winter months. The champ and showd of a horse in that
moonsprayed dark and the guttural 'Tchkh, min!' of the
forker, the great shapes of cattle in the parks as you ride by,
the glimmer far away of the lights of some couthy toun on the
verge of sleep, the queer shapes of post and gate and stook—
Nature unfolds the puppets and theatre pieces year after
year, unvaryingly, and they lose their dust, each year

uniquely fresh. You can stand and listen as though for the
lost trumpet of God in that autumn night silence: but indeed
all that you are listening for is a passing peewit.

It is strange how Scotland has no Gilbert White or H. J.
Massingham to sing its fields, its birds, such night as this, to
chronicle the comings and goings of the swallows in simple,
careful prose, ecstasy controlled. But perhaps not so strange.
We Scots have little interest in the wild and its world; I
realize how compassed and controlled is my own interest, I
am vague about sparrows and tits, martins and swallows, I
know little of their seasons, and my ignorance lies heavily
upon me not at all. I am concerned so much more deeply
with men and women, with their nights and days, the things
they believe, the things that move them to pain and anger and
the callous, idle cruelties that are yet undead. When I hear or
read of a dog tortured to death, very vilely and foully, of some
old horse driven to a broken back down a hill with an over-
loaded cart of corn, of rats captured and tormented with red-
hot pokers in bothies, I have a shudder of disgust. But these
things do not move me too deeply, not as the fate of the old-
time Cameronian prisoners over there, three miles away in
Dunnottar; not as the face of that ragged tramp who went by
this afternoon; not as the crucifixion of the Spartacist slaves
along the Appian Way. To me it is inconceivable that sincere
and honest men should go outside the range of their own
species with gifts of pity and angry compassion and rage when
there is horror and dread among humankind. I am unreasonably and mulishly prejudiced in favour of my own biological
species. I am a jingo patriot of planet earth: 'Humanity right
or wrong!'

Particularly in Autumn. At noon I crossed a field off which
the last of the stooks had been lifted and led captive away,
the gaping stubble heads pushed through the cricks of clay,
the long bouts of the binder wound and wheeled around the
park, where the foreman had driven his team three weeks
before. And each of those minute stubble stalks grew from

seed that men had handled and winnowed and selected and ploughed and harrowed the earth to receive, and sown and tended and watched come up in the rains of Springs and the hot Summer suns—each and all of these—and out and beyond their kindred trillions in the other parks, up to the biggings of Upperhill there, and south through all the chave of the Howe to the black lands that start by Brechin and roll down the coast till they come to the richness of Lothian and the orchards of Blairgowrie. . . . This is our power, this the wonder of humankind, our one great victory over nature and time. Three million years hence our descendants out on some tremendous furrowing of the Galaxy, with the Great Bear yoked to The Plough and the wastes of space their fields, will remember this little planet, if at all, for the men who conquered the land and wrung sustenance from it by stealth and shrewdness and a savage and surly endurance. Nothing else at all may endure in those overhuman memories: I do not think there is anything else I want to endure.

The ricks loom tall and white in the moonlight about their yellow bosses: folk are loosening the heavy horses from the carts and leading them tramp, tramp across the cobbles of the close: with a scrape and clatter by the water-trough and a silence and then the sound of a slavering long, enjoyable long suction: I feel thirsty in sympathy with that equine delight of cool, good water in a parched mouth and throat. Then a light blinks through the cobwebs of the stable, an impatient voice says *Wissh!* and harvest is over.

Quiet enough here, because the very young and irresponsible are not here. But elsewhere, nights like this, up and down the great agricultural belts of Scotland, in and about the yards and the ricks, there is still some relic of the ancient fun at the last ingathering of the sheaves—still a genial clowning and drinking and a staring at the moon, and slow, steady childes swinging away to the bothies, their hands deep down in their pouches, their boots striking fire from the cobbles; still maids to wait their lads in the lee of the new-built stacks, and be cuddled and warm and happy against brown, dank chests, and be kissed into wonder on the world, and taste the goodness of the night and the Autumn's end. . . . Before the Winter comes.

To-morrow the potato harvests, of course. But somehow they are not real harvests, they are not truly of Autumn as is the taking in of the corn. It is still an alien plant, the potato, an intruder from that world of wild belief and wilder practice that we call the New, a plant that hides and lairs deep down in the midst of back-breaking drills. The corn is so ancient that its fresh harvesting is no more than the killing of an ancient enemy-friend, ritualistic, that you may eat of the flesh of the God, drink of his blood, and be given salvation and life.

GLASGOW

Glasgow is one of the few places in Scotland which defy personification. To image Edinburgh as a disappointed spinster, with a hare-lip and inhibitions, is at least to approximate as closely to the truth as to image the Prime Mover as a Levantine Semite. So with Dundee, a frowsy fisher-wife addicted to gin and infanticide, Aberdeen a thin-lipped peasant-woman who has borne eleven and buried nine. But no Scottish image of personification may display, even distortedly, the essential Glasgow. One might go further afield, to the tortured imaginings of the Asiatic mind, to find her likeness—many-armed Siva with the waistlet of skulls, or Xipe of Ancient America, whose priest skinned the victim alive, and then clad himself in the victim's skin. . . . But one doubts anthropomorphic representation at all. The monster of Loch Ness is probably the lost soul of Glasgow, in scales and horns, disporting itself in the Highlands after evacuating finally and completely its mother-corpse.

One cannot blame it. My distant cousin, Mr. Leslie Mitchell, once described Glasgow in one of his novels as 'the vomit of a cataleptic commercialism'. But it is more than that. It may be a corpse, but the maggot-swarm upon it is very fiercely alive. One cannot watch and hear the long beat of traffic down Sauchiehall, or see its eddy and spume where St. Vincent Street and Renfield Street cross, without realizing what excellent grounds the old-fashioned anthropologist appeared to have for believing that man was by nature a

brutish savage, a herd-beast delighting in vocal discordance
and orgiastic aural abandon.

Loch Lomond lies quite near to Glasgow. Nice Glas-
wegians motor out there and admire the scenery and calcu-
late its horse-power and drink whisky and chaff one another
in genteelly Anglicized Glaswegianisms. After a hasty look
at Glasgow the investigator would do well to disguise himself
as one of like kind, drive down to Loch Lomondside and
stare across its waters at the sailing clouds that crown the
Ben, at the flooding of colours changing and darkling and
miraculously lighting up and down those misty slopes, where
night comes over long mountain leagues that know only the
paddings of the shy, stray hare, the whirr and cry of the
startled pheasant, silences so deep you can hear the moon
come up, mornings so greyly coloured they seem stolen from
Norse myth. This is the proper land and stance from which to
look at Glasgow, to divest oneself of horror or shame or
admiration or—very real—fear, and ask: Why? Why did men
ever allow themselves to become enslaved to a thing so
obscene and so foul when there was *this* awaiting them here—
hills and the splendours of freedom and silence, the clean
splendours of hunger and woe and dread in the winds and
rains and famine-times of the earth, hunting and love and the
call of the moon? Nothing endured by the primitives who
once roamed those hills—nothing of woe or terror—ap-
proximated in degree or kind to that life that festers in the
courts and wynds and alleys of Camlachie, Govan, the
Gorbals.

In Glasgow there are over a hundred and fifty thousand
human beings living in such conditions as the most bitterly
pressed primitive in Tierra del Fuego never visioned. They
live five or six to the single room . . . . And at this point,
sitting and staring at Ben Lomond, it requires a vivid mental
jerk to realize the quality of that room. It is not a room in a
large and airy building, it is not a single-roomed hut on the
verge of a hill; it is not a cave driven into free rock, in the

sound of the sea-birds as that old Azilian cave in Argyll: it is
a room that is part of some great sloven of tenement—the
tenement itself in a line or a grouping with hundreds of its
fellows, its windows grimed with the unceasing wash and
drift of coal-dust, its stairs narrow and befouled and steep, its
evening breath like that which might issue from the mouth of
a lung-diseased beast. The hundred and fifty thousand eat
and sleep and copulate and conceive and crawl into childhood in those waste jungles of stench and disease and hope-
lessness, sub-humans as definitely as the Morlocks of Wells—
and without even the consolation of feeding on their oppres-
sors' flesh.

A hundred and fifty thousand . . . and all very like you or
me or my investigator sitting appalled on the banks of Loch
Lomond (where he and his true love will never meet again).
And they live on food of the quality of offal, ill-cooked, ill-
eaten with speedily-diseased teeth for the tending of which
they can afford no fees; they work—if they have work—in
factories or foundries or the roaring reek of the Docks toil-
some and dreary and unimaginative hours—hour on hour,
day on day, frittering away the tissues of their bodies and the
spirit-stuff of their souls; they are workless—great numbers
of them—doomed to long days of staring vacuity, of shoeless-
ness, of shivering hidings in this and that mean runway when
the landlords' agents come, of mean and desperate beggings
at Labour Exchanges and Public Assistance Committees;
their voices are the voices of men and women robbed of man-
hood and womanhood. . . .

The investigator on Loch Lomondside shudders and turns
to culture for comfort. He is, of course, a subscriber to *The
Modern Scot*, where culture at three removes—castrated, disembowelled, and genteelly vulgarized—is served afresh each
season; and has brought his copy with him. Mr. Adam
Kennedy is serializing a novel, *The Mourners*, his technique a
genteel objectivity. And one of his characters has stopped in
Glasgow's Kelvingrove, and is savouring its essence:

John's eyes savoured the spaciousness of the crescent, the formal curve of the unbroken line of house façades, the regimentation of the rows of chimney-pots, the full-length windows, the unnecessarily broad front steps, the feudal basements—savoured all these in the shimmering heat of the day just as his nose had savoured the morning freshness. It was as good for him to walk round these old terraces as to visit a cathedral. He could imagine now and then that he had evoked for himself something of the atmosphere of the grand days of these streets. The world was surer of itself then, sure of the ultimate perfectability of man, sure of the ultimate mastery over the forces that surrounded him. And if Atlas then no longer had the world firm on his shoulder, the world for all that rested on the same basis of the thus-and-thusness of things. With such a basis you could have that sureness of yourself to do things largely as had been done before. But the modern mind was no longer sure of itself even in a four-roomed bungalow. Its pride was the splitting of its personality into broods of impish devils that spent their time spying one on the other, It could never get properly outside itself, could never achieve the objectivity that was capable of such grandly deliberate planning as in these streets.'

Glasgow speaks. The hundred and fifty thousand are answered. Glasgow has spoken.

This, indeed, is its attitude, not merely the pale whey of intellectualism peculiar to *The Modern Scot*. The bourgeois Glaswegian cultivates aesthetic objectivity as happier men cultivate beards or gardens. Pleasant folk of Kelvingrove point out that those hundred and fifty thousand—how well off they are! Free education, low rents, no rates, State relief—half of them, in fact, State pensioners. Besides, they enjoy life as they are—damn them, or they ought to. Always raising riots about their conditions. Not that they raise the riots themselves—it's the work of the communists—paid agitators from Moscow. But they've long since lost all hold. Or they ought to have——.

In those days of Nationalism, of Douglasism, (that in-
genious scheme for childbirth without pain and—even more
intriguing—without a child), of Socialism, of Fascism,
Glasgow, as no other place, moves me to a statement of
faith. I have amused myself with many political creeds—the
more egregrious the creed the better. I like the thought of a
Scots Republic with Scots Border Guards in saffron kilts—
the thought of those kilts can awake me to joy in the middle
of the night. I like the thought of Miss Wendy Wood leading
a Scots Expeditionary Force down to Westminster to reclaim
the Scone Stone: I would certainly march with that expedition myself in spite of the risk of dying of laughter by the way.
I like the thought of a Scots Catholic kingdom with Mr.
Compton Mackenzie Prime Minister to some disinterred
Jacobite royalty, and all the Scots intellectuals settled out on
the land on thirty-acre crofts, or sent to recolonize St. Kilda
for the good of their souls and the nation (except the hundreds streaming over the Border in panic flight at sight of
this Scotland of their dreams). I like the thought of the ancient Scots aristocracy revived and set in order by Mr.
George Blake, that ephor of the people: Mr. Blake vetoing
the Duke of Montrose is one of my dearest visions. I like the
thoughts of the Scottish Fascists evicting all those of Irish
blood from Scotland, and so leaving Albyn entirely deserted
but for some half-dozen pro-Irish Picts like myself. I like the
thought of a Scottish Socialist Republic under Mr. Maxton—
preferably at war with royalist England, and Mr. Maxton
summoning the Russian Red Army to his aid (the Red Army
digging a secret tunnel from Archangel to Aberdeen). And I
like the thought of Mr. R. M. Black and his mysterious Free
Scots, that modern Mafia, assassinating the Bankers (which
is what bankers are for). . . .

But I cannot play with those fantasies when I think of the
hundred and fifty thousand in Glasgow. They are a something that stills the parlour chatter. I find I am by way of
being an intellectual myself. I meet and talk with many

people whose interests are art and letters and music, enthusiasm for this and that aspect of craft and architecture, men and women who have very warm and sincere beliefs indeed regarding the ancient culture of Scotland, people to whom Glasgow is the Hunterian Museum with its fine array of Roman coins, or the Galleries with their equally fine array of pictures. 'Culture' is the motif-word of the conversation: ancient Scots culture, future Scots culture, culture ad lib. and ad nauseam. . . . The patter is as intimate on my tongue as on theirs. And relevant to the fate and being of those hundred and fifty thousand it is no more than the chatter and scratch of a band of apes, seated in a pit on a midden of corpses.

There is nothing in culture or art that is worth the life and elementary happiness of one of those thousands who rot in the Glasgow slums. There is nothing in science or religion. If it came (as it may come) to some fantastic choice between a free and independent Scotland, a centre of culture, a bright flame of artistic and scientific achievement, and providing elementary decencies of food and shelter to the submerged proletariat of Glasgow and Scotland, I at least would have no doubt as to which side of the battle I would range myself. For the cleansing of that horror, if cleanse it they could, I would welcome the English in suzerainty over Scotland till the end of time. I would welcome the end of Braid Scots and Gaelic, our culture, our history, our nationhood under the heels of a Chinese army of occupation if it could cleanse the Glasgow slums, give a surety of food and play—the elementary right of every human being—to those people of the abyss. . . .

I realize (seated on the plump modernity of *The Modern Scot* by the side of my investigator out on Loch Lomondbank) how completely I am the complete Philistine. I have always liked the Philistines, a commendable and gracious and cleanly race. They built clean cities with wide, airy streets, they delighted in the singing of good, simple songs and hunting and lovemaking and the worshipping of relevant

G

and comprehensible Gods. They were a light in the Ancient
East and led simple and happy and carefree lives, with a
splendour of trumpets now and again to stir them to amusing
orgy. . . . And above, in the hills, in Jerusalem, dwelt the
Israelites, unwashed and unashamed, horrified at the clean
anarchy which is the essence of life, oppressed by grisly fears
of life and death and time, suborning simple human pleasures in living into an insane debating on justice and right,
the Good Life, the Soul of Man, artistic canon, the First
Cause, National Ethos, the mainsprings of conduct, aesthetic
approach—and all the rest of the dirty little toys with which
dirty little men in dirty little caves love to play, turning with
a haughty shudder of repulsion from the cry of the wind and
the beat of the sun on the hills outside. . . . One of the greatest
tragedies of the ancient world was the killing of Goliath by
David—a ghoul-haunted little village squirt who sneaked up
and murdered the Philistine while the latter (with a good
breakfast below his belt) was admiring the sunrise.

The non-Philistines never admire sunrises. They never
admire good breakfasts. Their ideal is the half-starved at sunset, whose actions and appearances they can record with a
proper aesthetic detachment. One of the best-loved pictures
of an earlier generation of Glasgow intellectuals was Josef
Israel's *Frugal Meal* in the Glasgow Galleries. Even yet the
modern will halt you to admire the chiaroscuro, the fine
shades and attitudes. But you realize he is a liar. He is merely
an inhibited little sadist, and his concentrated essence of en-
joyment is the hunger and dirt and hopleessness of the two
figures in question. He calls this a 'robust acceptance of life.'

Sometime, it is true, the non-Philistine of past days had a
qualm of regret, a notion, a thin pale abortion of an idea that
life in simplicity was life in essence. So he painted a man or a
woman, nude only in the less shameful portions of his or her
anatomy (egregious bushes were called in to hide the genital
shames) and called it not *Walking* or *Running* or *Staring* or
Sleeping or *Lusting* (as it generally was) but *Light* or *Realiza-*

tion or *The Choir* or what not. A Millais in the Glasgow Galleries is an excellent example, which neither you nor my investigator may miss. It is the non-Philistine's wistful idea of (in capitals) Life in Simplicity—a decent young childe in a breech-clout about to play hoop-la with a forked stick. But instead of labelling this truthfully and obviously *Portrait of Shy-Making Intellectual Playing at Boy Scouts* it is called (of course) *The Forerunner*.

The bourgeois returns at evening these days to Kelvin-grove, to Woodsidehill, to Hillhead and Dowanhill with heavy and doubting steps. The shipyards are still, with rusting cranes and unbefouled waters nearby, in Springburn the empty factories increase and multiply, there are dead windows and barred factory-gates in Bridgeton and Mile End. Commercialism has returned to its own vomit too often and too long still to find sustenance therein. Determinedly in Glasgow (as elsewhere) they call this condition 'The Crisis', and, in the fashion of a Christian Scientist whose actual need is cascara, invoke Optimism for its cure. But here as nowhere else in the modern world of capitalism does the impartial investigator realize that the remedy lies neither in medicine nor massage, but in surgery. . . . The doctors (he hears) are gathered for the Saturday-Sunday diagnoses on Glasgow Green; and betakes himself there accordingly.

But there (as elsewhere) the physicians disagree—multitudes of physicians, surrounded by anxious groups of the ailing patient's dependents. A brief round of the various physicians convinces the investigator of one thing: the unpopularity of surgery. The single surgeon orating is, of course, the Communist. His gathering is small. A larger following attends Mr. Guy Aldred, Non-Parliamentary Anarcho-communist, pledged to use neither knives nor pills, but invocation of the Gospels according to St. Bakunin. Orthodox Socialism, ruddy and plump, with the spoils from the latest Glasgow Corporation swindle in its pocket, the fee'd physician, popular and pawky, is fervent and optimistic. Pills?—

Nonsense! Surgery?—Muscovite savagery! What is needed to remove the sprouting pustules from the fair face of commercialism is merely a light, non-greasy ointment (which will not stain the sheets). Near at hand stands the Fascist: the investigator, with a training which has hitherto led him to debar the Neanderthaler from the direct ancestral line of *Homo Sapiens*, stares at this ethnological note of interrogation. The Fascist diagnosis: Lack of blood. Remedy: Bleeding. A Nationalist holds forth near by. What the patient needs is not more food, fresh air, a decent room of his own and a decent soul of his own—No! What he needs is the air he ceased to breathe two hundred and fifty years ago—specially reclaimed and canned by the National Party of Scotland (and forwarded in plain vans.) . . . A Separatist casts scorn on the Nationalist's case. What the patient requires is: Separation. Separation from England, from English speech, English manners, English food, English clothes, English culinary and English common sense. Then he will recover.

It is coming on dark, as they say in the Scotland that is not Glasgow. And out of the Gorbals arises again that foul breath as of a dying beast.

You turn from Glasgow Green with a determination to inspect this Gorbals on your own. It is incredibly un-Scottish. It is lovably and abominably and delightfully and hideously un-Scottish. It is not even a Scottish slum. Stout men in beards and ringlets and unseemly attire lounge and strut with pointed shoes: Ruth and Naomi go by with downcast Eastern faces, the Lascar rubs shoulder with the Syrian, Harry Lauder is a Baal unkeened to the midnight stars. In the air the stench is of a different quality to. Govan's or Camlachie's—a better quality. It is not filth and futility and boredom unrelieved. It is haunted by an ancient ghost of goodness and grossness, sun-warmed and ripened under alien suns. It is the most saving slum in Glasgow, and the most abandoned. Emerging from it, the investigator suddenly realizes why he sought it in such haste from Glasgow Green:

it was in order that he might assure himself there were really and actually other races on the earth apart from the Scots!

So long I have wanted to write what I am about to write—but hitherto I have lacked the excuse. Glasgow provides it . . . . About Nationalism. About Small Nations. What a curse to the earth are small nations! Latvia, Lithuania, Poland, Finland, San Salvador, Luxembourg, Manchukuo, the Irish Free State. There are many more: there is an appalling number of disgusting little stretches of the globe claimed, occupied and infected by groupings of babbling little morons —babbling militant on the subjects (unendingly) of their *exclusive* cultures, their *exclusive* languages, their *national* souls, their *national* genius, their unique achievements in throat-cutting in this and that abominable little squabble in the past. Mangy little curs a-yap above their minute hoardings of shrivelled bones, they cease from their yelpings at the passers-by only in such intervals as they devote to civil-war flea-hunts. Of all the accursed progeny of World War, surely the worst was this dwarf mongrel-litter. The South Irish of the middle class were never pleasant persons: since they obtained their Free State the belch of their pride in the accents of their unhygienic patois has given the unfortunate Irish Channel the seeming of a cess-pool. Having blamed their misfortunes on England for centuries, they achieved inde-pendence and promptly found themselves incapable of securing that independence by the obvious and necessary operation—social revolution. Instead: revival of Gaelic, bewildering an unhappy world with uncouth spellings and titles and postage-stamps: revival of the blood feud; revival of the decayed literary cultus which (like most products of the Kelt) was an abomination even while actually alive and but poor manure when it died. . . . Or Finland—Communist-murdering Finland—ruled by German Generals and the Central European foundries, boasting to its ragged popula-tion the return of its ancient literary culture like a senile octogenarian boasting the coming of second childhood. . . .

And we are bidden go and do likewise:

'For we are not opposed to English influence only at those points where it expresses itself in political domination and financial and economic over-control, but we are (or ought to be) opposed to English influence at all points. Not only must English governmental control be overthrown, but the English language must go, and English methods of education, English fashions in dress, English models in the arts, English ideals, everything English. Everything English must go.'

This is a Mr. Ludovic Grant, writing in *The Free Man*. Note what the Scot is bidden to give up: the English language, that lovely and flexible instrument, so akin to the darker Braid Scots which has been the Scotsman's tool of thought for a thousand years. English methods of education: which are derived from Germano-French-Italian models. English fashions in dress: invented in Paris—London—Edinburgh—Timbuktu—Calcutta—Chichen-Itza—New York. English models in the arts: nude models as well, no doubt—Scots models in future must sprout three pair of arms and a navel in the likeness of a lion rampant. English ideals: decency, freedom, justice, ideals innate in the mind of man, as common to the Bantu as to the Kentishman—those also he must relinquish. . . . It will profit Glasgow's hundred and fifty thousand slum-dwellers so much to know that they are being starved and brutalized by Labour Exchanges and Public Assistance Committees staffed exclusively by Gaelic-speaking, haggis-eating Scots in saffron kilts and tongued brogues, full of such typical Scottish ideals as those which kept men chained as slaves in the Fifeshire mines a century or so ago . . . .

Glasgow's salvation, Scotland's salvation, the world's salvation lies in neither nationalism nor internationalism, those twin halves of an idiot whole. It lies in ultimate cosmopolitanism, the earth the City of God, the Brahmaputra and Easter Island as free and familiar to the man from Govan as the Molendinar and Bute. A time will come when the self-wrought, prideful differentiations of Scotsman, Englishman, Frenchman, Spaniard will seem as ludicrous as the infantile squabblings of the Heptarchians. A time will come when nationalism, with other cultural aberrations, will have passed from the human spirit, when Man, again free and unchained, has all the earth for his footstool, sings his epics in a language moulded from the best on earth, draws his heroes, his sunrises, his valleys and his mountains from all the crinkles of our lovely planet. . . . And we are bidden to abandon this vision for the delights of an archaic ape-spite, a brosy barbarization!

I am a nationalist only in the sense that the sane Heptarchian was a Wessexman or a Mercian or what not: temporarily, opportunistically. I think the Braid Scots may yet give lovely lights and shadows not only to English but to the perfected speech of Cosmopolitan Man: so I cultivate it, for lack of that perfect speech that is yet to be. I think there's the chance that Scotland, especially in its Glasgow, in its bitter straitening of the economic struggle, may win to a freedom preparatory to, and in alignment with, that cosmopolitan freedom, long before England: so, a cosmopolitan opportunist, I am some kind of Nationalist. But I'd rather, any day, be an expatriate writing novels in Persian about the Cape of Good Hope than a member of a homogeneous literary cultus (to quote again the cant phrase of the day) prosing eternally on one plane—the insanitary reactions to death of a Kelvingrove bourgeois, or the owlish gawk (it would speedily have that seeming) of Ben Lomond through its clouds, like a walrus through a fuff of whiskers.

For this Scottish Siva herself, brandishing her many arms of smoke against the coming of the darkness, it is pleasant to remember at least one incident. On a raining night six hundred and fifty years ago a small band of men, selfless and desperate and coolly-led, tramped through the wynds to the assault of the English-garrisoned Bell o' the Brae (which is now the steep upper part of High Street). It was a venture unsupported by priest or patrician, the intellectual or bourgeois of those days. It succeeded: and it lighted a flame of liberty throughout Scotland.

Some day the surgeon-leaders of the hundred and fifty thousand may take that tale of Bell o' the Brae for their text.

ABERDEEN

No foreigner can think of that vulgarization of Scots humour and the Scots lyric which Sir Harry Lauder has brought to such pitch of perfection without a bye-thought on a Scots city which would seem to breed, principally, if not entirely, Lauder-imitators. For the benefit of the English-reading public Aberdeen is the home of the typical 'Scotch' joke. In this the Scot is shown as ludicrously mean, he is the victim and perpetrator of a farcical and brainless greed. And most of the material for those tales and fantasies of so-called humour are exported from Aberdeen itself, as the editor of any light-hearted English periodical will confirm.

Now, a tale may be read, quite consciously and knowingly, as humour-fantasy, and yet have curious repercussions on the mind of the reader. So with Aberdeen: it is impossible that its streets can be thronged with reproductions of this odd caricature of humanity who parades in the jokes. Still—and the good Englishman and the good American display a kind of humorous contemptuous care in their dealings with an authentic Aberdonian, set foot in Aberdeen itself with wary grins on their faces. Recently I received a reply-paid envelope from an American publisher. In the course of the accompanying letter the publisher referred to the envelope (in a business-like fashion, without inverted commas, because the joke in this minor aspect has grown stale and passed into the ordinary vocabulary of American business) as an 'Aberdeen envelope.' Once, in Jerusalem, I struck up acquaintance with an intelligent and interesting Syrian. We talked ethnology; and in the course of the conversation I told him that I was born in Aberdeenshire in Scotland. He was amused and pitiful, though a little hazy. 'Aberdeen—it is the pariah place, is it not?'

These phenomena—Aberdeen's comic reputation and Aberdonian humour itself—are worthy of some investigation, just as the man who laughs too loudly and too long stirs curiosities in the mind of the sceptical bystander. Why so much laughter—and why that steely ring in the last guffaw? Here is an Aberdonian 'funny story":

'An Aberdonian died and gave instructions in his will that his body be cremated. This was done. The day after the cremation the widow heard a knock at the door. She opened it and saw a small message-boy standing on the doorstep holding out a package towards her. "What's this?" she enquired. "Your husband, Mem," said the boy, "—his ashes, you know." Slowly the widow took the package in her hand. 'His ashes? Oh, ay. *But where's the dripping?"'*

I choose this example deliberately as that of an Aberdonian story insufficiently padded. You laugh, but (if you have any imagination at all) you have a slight qualm. The grisliness below the humour is insufficiently concealed. You can smell the stench of that burning body, you can see the running human fats—with a dish in appropriate position to collect them. . . . You see too closely in this instance the grinning skull behind the large, jolly countenance of the laughing man; you may suspect him, outside the flare of lights in the bar and the help of alcohol, as one solemn and serious enough, uneasy, haunted by an unending apprehension of life as a bleak enough parade.

Bleakness, not meanness or jollity, is the keynote to Aberdonian character, not so much lack of the graces or graciousness of existence as lack of colour in either of these. And this is almost inevitable for anyone passing his nights and days in The Silver City by the Sea. It is comparable to passing one's existence in a refrigerator. Aberdeen is built, largely and incredibly, of one of the most enduring and indestructible and appalling building-materials in use on our planet—grey granite.

It has a flinty shine when new—a grey glimmer like a morning North Sea, a cold steeliness that chills the heart. Even with weathering it acquires no gracious softness, it is merely starkly grim and uncompromising. The architect may plan and build as he will with this material—with its variant, white granite, he may rear the curvetting spires and swooping curlecues and looping whirlimagigs of Marischal College—and not escape that sense of one calamitously in jail. Not only are there no furbelows possible in this architecture, there is amid it, continually, the uneasy sense that you may not rest here, you may not lounge, you cannot stand still and watch the world go by. . . . Else presently the warders will come and move you on.

To know that feeling in its full intensity the investigator must disregard the publicity posters and visit Aberdeen in November. Whatever the weather as his train crossed from Kincardineshire into Aberdeenshire, he will arrive at Aberdeen Station in sleet. Not falling sleet or drifting sleet, but *blown* sleet—blown with an infernal and unescapable persistence from all points of the compass, from the stretches of the harbour, from the Duthie Park, down Market Street. And through this steely pelt he will see the tower and lour and savage grimace of the grey granite all about him, curdling his nerve centres even as the sleet curdles his extremities. If he holds by Guild Street and Market Street up to the pride of Aberdeen, Union Street, he will discover how really vocal this materialization of an Eskimo's vision of hell may become. Aberdeen is, without exception, the most exasperatingly noisy city in the world. Paris is bad—but one accepts Paris, it is free, it is anarchistic, the cabmen are trying to kill each other—a praiseworthy pursuit—and Citröens were made by devils in hell and manned by chauffeurs from purgatory—and it is all very amusing. But Aberdeen is not amusing in its epitome, Union Street. This street is paved with granite blocks, and over these, through the sleeting downpour, trams rattle, buses thud, and (unescapable) four large iron-wheeled drays hauled by Clydesdale horses are being drawn at break-neck speed. There is no amusement in the thought of the drivers being killed: you can see in each gaunt, drawn face that the driver is doing it not for pleasure or the fun of life or because he is joyously and righteously drunk—he is doing it to support a wife, five children, a blind grandmother, and a sister in the Aberdeen Infirmary.

Aberdeen is the cleanest city in Britain: it makes you long for good, wholesome dirt, littered roadways and ramshackle buildings leaning in all directions, projecting warm brown sins and rich smutty reds through an enticing, grimy smile. Union Street has as much warmth in its face as a dowager duchess asked to contribute to the Red International Relief. If you escape the trams and the drays and the inferno where Market Street debouches on Union Street, and hold west up Union Street, you will have the feeling of one caught in a corridor of the hills. To right and left tower the cliffs, scrubbed, immaculate and unforgiving. Where Union Terrace breaks in upon Union Street there is an attempt at a public Garden. But the flowers come up and take one glance at the lour of the solicitors' offices which man Union Terrace, and scramble back into the earth again, seeking the Antipodes.

Union Terrace is beset with statues: the advocates stroll to their windows from plodding through briefs for the Sheriff Court and look out on King Edward to the right, Robert Burns in the middle and William Wallace to the left. Aberdeen may be forgiven much because of those statues. For her flinty granitic heart was moved to wisdom when she commissioned them, giving their subjects that due proportion and appearance which they bore in history: King Edward is merely vulgar, Burns pathetic and Wallace heroic. The investigator may do worse than consider the Wallace with care: round the plinth are written quotations from his speeches to the Army of the Commons of Scotland; lounging upon the plinth, yawning and bored (even in the sleet) are the tired and the old and the unemployed of Aberdeen in great number. Wallace fascinates them, you would say. He belongs to a past they dare not achieve, they have come to such horrific future as he never visioned.

In his right hand is a great sword; his outflung left hand points—to the nearby bulk, copola'd and gilded, of His Majesty's Theatre. But I think the gesture is unwarranted, for it is an excellent theatre, there are folk and institutions in Aberdeen far more worthy of gesture and sword. One wonders if the slum landlords of Correction Wynd or the Gallowgate, emerging from their cars to make their way to the padded fauteuils of His Majesty's, ever cast an uneasy glance at the great Guardian.

Probably not—unless some socialist orator is holding forth from the plinth. It is a favourite place of the orator, the communist orator for preference. Unemployed Aberdeen chews tobacco and listens vaguely and smokes vague cigarettes, and you can hear the orator at a great distance, the thin Aberdonian voice in the thin Aberdonian patois—full of long *ee's*, and conversions of *wh's* into *f's*. . . . Agitationally, in spite its unemployed, Aberdeen sleeps these days. A friend of mine once led a procession of the unemployed; the mounted police charged: and when they had passed my friend was found clinging far up in the branches of a tree. This is the reality that has succeeded those visions of the barricade that vexed young folk of my ilk in the War-time days: days that distance covers with a fine glamour, when the mob broke up the peace-time meeting in the Music Hall addressed by Ramsay MacDonald: and a party of them made to storm the platform: and a socialist pugilist pacified them, asking for a single representative to come up: and one belligerent young man ascended: and demanded to be led to Ramsay: and the socialist pugilist agreed: and took the young man behind the scenes and socked him in the jaw; and came dragging back the body as an exhibition of what Ramsay did to interrupters. . . . Or another meeting, with locked doors, which a company of the Gordon Highlanders attempted to storm: and broke down the upper half of the door, and climbed in one by one: and as they descended were met by a solemn, six-foot pacifist with the limbs of an aurochs and hands like hams: who solemnly and pitifully knocked each one unconscious: and then revived them and carried them upstairs to the meeting, on the soldiers' tearful promise that they *would* be good. . . . Or the founding of the Aberdeen Soviet when the news of the Bolshevik Revolution came through from Russia; and how I and a cub reporter from another paper attended the foundation meeting; and were elected to the Soviet Council, forgetting we were pressmen; and spent perspiring minutes with our chief reporters afterwards, explaining that we could not report the meeting being ourselves good sovietists. . . . *O tempora! O mores!*

Remote as the banners of the Army of the Commons. Yet (and to presume that the sleet is over, and you are now in your overcoat) if you turn rightwards from Wallace into that grouping and festering of mean streets that lie behind and beyond the Infirmary, surely it is impossible that these things have passed? There are odd little shops here, with revolutionary journals for sale? Instead, odd little shops which sell stockings and shirts and such-like necessitous intimacies on the hire-purchase system: and sue with great savagery the improvident purchasers. Fifteen years ago that young cub-reporter who, with myself, had been elected to the Aberdeen Soviet—we were so young and full of dreams we could not sleep o'nights. We prowled Aberdeen all the hours of the night, seeking not amorous adventure, but talking the moon into morning about jolly and heartsome and splendid things: life, death, the Revolution and the great green-cheeseness of the moon. . . . And the years went by, and I journeyed afar; and garnered a little in experience, including a keen distaste for that snarling cry of the machine-gun which sends a man clawing earthwards on his belly; and twelve years went by and I came again to Aberdeen; and for curiosity I wandered into its police court one morning; and a shameful woman had purchased knickers from the owner of a little chain of shops; and had neglected her payments, and was now being sued, poor proletarian with her red-chapped hands and her wrinkled, terrified face, and her poor, shifting eyes and her stammering voice. . . . I turned away my eyes and felt unreasonably sick. But the voice of the owner of the chain of shops brought back my attention as he spoke from the witness-box. And he was——.

With me the investigator turns to a thing more pleasant— Allenvale Cemetery, where the dead of Aberdeen lie in serried lines under immense granitic monuments. They move one to a wondering horror. Granite, grey granite, in birth, in puberty, adolescence, grey granite encasing the bridal room, grey granite the rooms of blear-eyed old age. And even in death they are not divided. . . . Lower middle-class Aberdeen comes here of a Sunday in its Sunday blue suit and yellow boots and dickie and bowler: and parades, and admires the monuments, and goes back to Aberdeen high tea.

High tea in Aberdeen is like no other meal on earth. It is the meal of the day, the meal par excellence, and the tired come home to it ravenous, driven by the granite streets, hounded in for energy to stoke against that menace. Tea is drunk with the meal, and the order of it is this: First, one eats a plateful of sausages and eggs and mashed potatoes; then a second plateful to keep down the first. Eating, one assists the second plateful to its final home by mouthfuls of oatcake spread with butter. Then you eat oatcake with cheese. Then there are scones. Then cookies. Then it is really time to begin on tea—tea and bread and butter and crumpets and toasted rolls and cakes. Then some Dundee cake. Then—about half-past seven—someone shakes you out of the coma into which you have fallen and asks you persuasively if you wouldn't like another cup of tea and just *one* more egg and sausage. . . .

And all night long, on top of this supper and one of those immense Aberdonian beds which appear to be made of knotted ship's cable, the investigator, through and transcending the howl of the November sleet-wind, will hear the lorries and the drays, in platoons, clattering up and down Market Street. They do it for no reason or purpose, except to keep you awake. And in the morning when you descend with a grey face and an aching head, they provide you with an immense Aberdeen breakfast; and if you halt and gasp somewhere through the third course they send for the manager who comes and questions you gravely as to why you don't like the food?—should he send for a doctor?

I'm presuming the investigator has taken a room in one of the hotels in Market Street. They are very good and cheap and never advertise, and this is their free advertisement in return for their unostentatious virtues. And their windows look out on Aberdeen Harbour, a wide, dull stretch round which I can never wander these days without a vague feeling that all is not well with the harbour, there is a definite something missing in the ships and shipping. And then I remember: the War-time camouflage when the ships rode bravely bespattered in painted zig-zags, and all kinds of odd people came wandering across the North Sea and were landed at Aberdeen from those pantomime vessels. M. Krassin was deported from England by way of Aberdeen and I attempted to interview him as he boarded his boat: he had a little beard and a twisted nose; and I spoke to him in halting Russian and he said kindly that he spoke English when he was allowed to—only he wasn't. And as I came away from that abortive interview I saw a soldier walking along the quays, an elderly man, a sergeant, in full equipment, with rifle and steel helmet. And he stopped and looked into the water, thoughtfully, and laid aside the rifle and helmet, and jumped

into the water. There he swam to and fro for a little and some
loafers threw him a rope and dragged him out. He shook himself, large, solemn, like a great dog, picked up the rifle and
helmet, and departed towards the station without saying a
word. . . .

Twice weekly in the summer season the London boat comes
into Aberdeen, and twice weekly departs. The Aberdonians
are an emotional people: they assemble in great multitudes
on the quay where the London boat is leaving. As the syrens
hoot they begin to cheer and wave handkerchiefs. About a
tenth of the two hundred waving from the shore have friends
or relatives on board. The rest are there moved by a curious
pity. I have seen an Aberdeen woman in tears as she waved
towards the departing boat, though she knew not a soul on
board. Some are even more enthusiastic. They pursue the
boat from quay to quay, bridge to bridge, waving and weeping, till they can pursue no further. The passengers stand and
wave and cheer in return, then light cigars and stroke their
tartan ties and tell how they climbed up Lochin-y-Gair.

Leftwards, Footdee sleeps with silent shipyards and factories these days, with great rusting cranes lifting their unmoving chains high in the air, and long cobbled walks silent
and nerveless enough. A kind of palsy has fallen here, the
investigator will note: the trawlers still come in of a morning
in long sweeping lines, with laden creels for the Fish Market,
but Footdee smells ill even these salt mornings, even this
stinging November morning when the wind has veered a
point and it has forgotten to sleet. This assuredly is the morning to survey the Beach.

The Beach, it is at once evident, was constructed by a
cretin brought up under the tuition of an imaginative, un-
reliable, but high-spirited gorilla. Behind it stretch the Links:
in front of it, the North Sea. Its buttressed walls rise and
swoop with a care admirable for the gambollings of the lesser
anthropoids, if somewhat at variance with the needs of a
more normal populace. To your right is the Amusements

H

Park; here the gorilla relaxed and scratched and was momentarily human, for here is a lovely scenic railways. The investigator, turning from the horror of the North Sea and the equal horror of the Beach, concludes that if he lived in Aberdeen he would spend his days on that scenic railway.

But this is Aberdeen by day. Aberdeen by night is a different city, thronged with a more subtle, a different folk. The watching granite relaxes on the façades of the great grey buildings, in the manners and customs of the folk in the streets. At eight o'clock on Friday night all Aberdeen assembles and parades in Union Street; and here the investigator stands aside and views with care the high cheek-bones in the brachycephalic heads of the males, that singularly dis-harmonic head that is so singularly Aberdonian. The proletarian wears a cap with a long check peak, the petit bourgeois wears the regulation bowler hat, the bourgeois walks bareheaded, for he is in plus-fours and his domed bald head is browned with the suns of the Links. There is an endless flow and unflow of the thin Aberdeen speech. But the bourgeois speaks English, and, strangely, speaks it successfully, acquiring depths and rhythm as he mislays the false, pale vowels and slurred consonants of his city. The women wear clothes indistinguishable from those of Paris or New York. But a strange fate haunts the Aberdonian woman. She cannot walk. Some go by with a duck-like waddle, some prance on squattering toes, some slouch with laggard steps. It is the granite sidewalks responsible, the investigator concludes, as the hours fade and the throngs fade with them, and down over the Town Hall the clocktowers tell it is one o'clock.

But for prostitutes, policemen, and journalists Union Street is deserted now. With a sough and a sigh the night-wind, edged as with a knife, is blowing along Union Terrace: King Edward stands freezing, bald-headed: down in the station a train chugs remotely, with a flying shower of sparks. In the glare of the night lights the tramlines swoop down towards Market Street like great snakes: in a remote shop-front a policeman is flashing his lamp. A young man in a slouch hat goes by, yawning: the *Journal* has been put to bed. Two girls consult the investigator on his needs for the night. He is regretful, with another engagement. They intimate, drifting away, a profound conviction in his illegitimacy. So to bed.

In the days when I first knew Aberdeen two names fascinated me—St. Machar and Kittybrewster. They lie at points remotely one from the other, the St. Machar Cathedral and the Kittybrewster district, but these the investigator (who has now purchased a fresh supply of woolly underwear) may not miss. St. Machar's Cathedral, they tell us, was builded first in the fourteenth century—there are still scraps of fourteenth-century architecture there. But towards the close of the seventeenth century the central tower fell in and smashed and demolished greatly chancel and transept, transforming the building from an active agency in dissemination of a cultural aberration to a seemly haunt for the archaeologist. St. Machar sleeps through it all undisturbed. But from youth the notion persists in my mind that he turns in uneasy remembrance now and again of the days when he and Kitty Brewster——.

Nor can any tell where Kitty lies. Perhaps beneath the smoke and soot and thundering trains of the Goods Station, lying, like good King Olaf, or Arthur in Avalon, waiting till they call her again and she wake and come forth and free the .world. Dreaming below that clatter of an industrialism gone mad, Kitty must yet hear on the early mart mornings sounds more familiar and loved—the lowing of the great cattle herds they drive to the sales there—smell, smell back through the centuries that odour of dust and dung and cowishness that maybe haunted the hills when she and Machar——.

But this is incredible romance. From earliest times Aberdeen has engaged itself in eschewing romance. Hardly had Kitty and St. Machar died in each other's arms (after a wild night's orgy on the Beach scenic railway) than Romance blew her trumpets through Aberdeen. It was the year 1411, and Donald of the Isles, gaunt, Highland and hairy, was nearing the city with an army of northland raiders. The citizens ran and busked themselves, piled into the tramcars at Castlegate and poured out in their thousands to contest the march of Donald. They met him at Harlaw, a misty morning, when the dew was white as hoar or grey granite on the whins, and arrayed themselves in long, dour ranks of spearmen against the usual Highland tactic. Donald flung forward the clansmen in sweeping lines of attack: Aberdeen stood fast through a long and bloody day and at night Donald marched back the remnants of his forces into the hills. This was a great turn of the tide in Scots history—and Aberdeen wrought it.

It was a city that remained incurably and gloriously anti-Highland. Stout business men from Mannofield and Cults may nowadays send their children to the High School in kilts and bonnets: in ancient times they would as soon have thought of sending them forth into the world in dishclouts and tompions. In the '45 the rest of Scotland might go Prince Charlie mad: Aberdeen stared out from its granite doorways with a dour startlement, then turned its back on the whole ill business. Freedom, the winds of romance, the crying of banners marching south—not for it, not for the flinty souls who matched their flinty dwellings. So instead it aided and abetted the men of Hanover, it feted and feasted the dour butcher Cumberland returning from Culloden field, and made him a guest of the Provost at No. 13 in the Guestrow—and there it stands unto this day to tell you if I lie.

But it is under orders for demolition—great sections of the older streets and wynds stand condemned, streets and wynds with antique names that move the antiquarian to suitable regrets when he considers their fate—the Upper Kirkgate, the Nether Kirkgate, the Gallowgate, the Guestrow. But I have no such regrets. Those gates to kirks and gallows: you think of a foetid sixteenth century stench and

the staring mobs watching some poor, tormented hind dragged out to the Gallows in Market Square—and you turn,
with relief and a new resolve, to face the glinting, flinting
structures that tower new-built up Union Street.

For if you cannot come to terms with the grey granite, you
must come to an understanding or else escape into Golf and
the Conservative Club, if you have the suitable status, or into
pub-crawling and the drinking of Red Biddies, that curious
Aberdonian stimulant, if you are of the plebs. The understanding is no easy thing. One detests Aberdeen with the
detestation of a thwarted lover. It is the one haunting and
exasperatingly lovable city in Scotland—its fascination as
unescapable as its shining mail.

But is there need to escape? There are moments when I
think of it as the essential—something to be apprehended and
in its apprehension to uncover new countries of stark and
glowing wonder, something lighted and shining with a fine
flame, cold and amber and gold, behind the flinty cliffs of
Union Street, the flinty cheekbones of the disharmonic faces
that press about you in an Aberdeen tram. I prefer to think
that the bitterly underpaid and wet and sogging fisherman
stumping up from the Fish Market after a night on the reel and
drummle of the tides has apprehended that granite quality
and made of it, warmed and kindly, his life quality ...
The investigator looks after him with a warmth and interest
in the grey of the sleeting November morning as he peers
from the stalactited window of his hotel bedroom and then
turns to consult a train time-table.

As for the women of Aberdeen ... it is strange the vagrant
associations the mind hinges on this word and that. About
half of the women of Aberdeen appear to rejoice in the name
of Grizel—and rejoice with justness, for my saner self tells me
it is a lovely and incisive name. But for some strange reason I
can never hear it pronounced without thinking of a polar bear
eating an Eskimo.

And that is all about Aberdeen.

THE WRECKER—

JAMES RAMSAY MACDONALD

Language, that 'perfected crying of apes and dogs' at which
Anatole France professed a whimsical astonishment in its
ability to debate the profoundities of metaphysics, has never
been merely a technique of expression for Mr. MacDonald.
Very early he was snared in the ancient debate between
Nominalist and Realist and very early (albeit unconscious of
the fact) took sides in that ancient argument. He has never
succeeded in penetrating behind words to thought: there is,
indeed, no evidence that he ever attempted this awesome
feat. Even in elementary manipulation of English one is conscious of a curious phenomenon: he is a clever, if rather unintelligent child, engaged in lifting sentences piecemeal from
some super-abacus frame and arranging them in a genteel
pattern. He is not engaged in displaying either James Ramsay MacDonald or his reactions of awe or hate or wonder or
love towards that bright glimmer between the shades of
sleep that we call the universe. He is merely engaged in
genuflection at the shrine of Words:

'Away to the north, across the Firth, rose the pale blue
hills of Sutherland and Ross: to the south lay the fertile
farms of Morayshire sloping up through green wood and
purple moorland into the blue tops of the Grampians, with
the ruined Palace of Spynie in the mid-distance; to the east
swept the sea, bordered by a wide stretch of yellow sand
bending away into the horizon, with hills in the background, the whole stretching out in peaceful beauty which

has won for it the name of the "Bay of Naples"....'

Note both the cleverness and the rigid adjectival conventionality: pale blue hills and fertile farms and peaceful beauty. It is the kind of thing that the dux in a little Scots school pens while the Dominie beams upon him (I know, having been such a dux myself, companioned by such a Dominie). It is pre-adolescent, it tells one nothing about either Mr. MacDonald's countryside or about his feelings towards it. It is the kind of guidebook chatter which raises your ire against an unknown (and probably inoffensive) landscape.

So with that philosophy of Socialism which Mr. MacDonald was wont to exfoliate in the days before, glancing downwards and backwards, he caught sight of the seemly shape his calves occupied inside the silk stockings of Court dress. Perhaps this Socialism had once a logic, as certainly it had once a fine, if anaemic, sincerity, a passionate pity if also an unimpassioned patience. In the mazes of Mr. MacDonald's vocabulary it behaves like a calf in an amateurish slaughter-shed, dodging with frightened moos the impact of innumerable padded bludgeons:

'Biologically "the negation of the existing state of things," its "inevitable breaking up," its "momentary existence" is impossible. Here we find, as we find everywhere in the Marxian method, a lack of real guarantee (although there are many verbal guarantees) that change is progress. The biological view emphasizes the possibilities of existing society as the mother of future societies, and regards idea and circumstance as the pair from which the new societies are to spring. It gives not only an explanation of the existing state of things, but of its giving birth to a future state of things. It also views every form of existence on its actual process of movement and therefore on its perishing—very different from perishable—side. It lays the very slightest emphasis on its "critical and revolutionary side", because it is mainly constructive and the idea of "clearing before building" is alien to its nature.'

This is a waste of wind and water, a seeping marshland under a fog. Note the power of the word 'biological' in the mind of Mr. MacDonald. It means one of a dozen things, and means none of them for long. Firstly, it is pure Darwinism in operation. Then it is Weismannism. Then (for all we know to the contrary) it is the epitome of the benign convolutings of Tantric Buddhism. We catch a faint glimpse through yellow fogs of verbosity of an idea that the great lizards of the Mezozoic suffered no deep or terrible calamity with the coming of the ice-caps. Did the stegosaurus freeze in his swamps and pass from the world for ever? Not at all. The stegosaurus looked about him and said: 'The cold comes on apace. I must discard my scales and grow me some hair.' And this the good stegosaurus did, mislaying scales, claws, reptilian intestines and reptilian nature, and was presently a mammoth.

This—if ever he has possessed a view, not merely a vocabulary—is Mr. MacDonald's view of the processes of biological evolution. *Cassell's Popular Educator*, he tells with pride, was 'his only university.' We may well believe the truth of this statement. That the great lords of the Mezozoic age did indeed die away completely and catastrophically, leaving to rise to greatness in the alien mammalian world their lesser and harried kin, not their own direct evolving descendants, is an elementary scrap of knowledge in which the good Cassell had perhaps no space to specialise. Yet lack of that knowledge has conditioned the being of what purports to be a 'scientific Socialism'—the creed which was presently foisted upon the British Labour Party, the creed which presently wrecked that party completely and disastrously.

In ascribing to Mr. MacDonald responsibility for bringing about (soulfully, with a radio-wide slurring of consonants) that wreckage, one is, of course, personifying many tendencies and many obscure gospels in the movement itself. Yet this hazy inability to grasp at the flinty actualities of existence, personal or universal, is in so many ways characteristically

Scots that to Mr. MacDonald more than to any other may
be ascribed the major share in this notable achievement. He
is as representationally Scots in his approach to politics as the
late Sir James Arthur Thomson was in his approach to biology, as Sir Arthur Keith is in his approach to ethnology.
They are as three investigators commissioned to three minute
and elaborate experiments in the weighing and sifting of
chemical constituents: and they approach their tasks uniquely clad in boxing-gloves and blinkers.

In the case of Mr. MacDonald, at least, it is both farcical
and tragic to note how much his inability to penetrate below
words is caused by the fact that the shape and setting of the
words are racially unfamiliar to him. English remains for him
a foreign language: its terms and expressions, its unique
twists of technique, he has followed and charted laboriously,
competently, and unintelligently. Yet, mazed in these pursuits, he has never learned to think like an Englishman, he
has never comprehended what Englishmen thought, he has
never comprehended essential meanings in English vocabularies or English minds. As a result, he has foisted antique
Scotticisms upon quite alien essentials, misapprehended the
meaning, origin and intention of a great social movement,
and (in ultimate prideful pose) stood aside to watch that
movement murdered. . . .

He is supposed to have Norse blood in his veins. It is ex-
tremely likely. One of his biographers, a babbling lady
greatly given to clothing her expressions in the raggedest of
verbal reach-me-downs, tells us that 'his homeland is
Morayshire, and Morayshire, north and east of the Grampians, breeds a race in which mingle the blood of the Highlanders and that of the Norse rovers from across the sea.'
His grandmother, by whom he was brought up, 'had seen
better days, and, even in the poorest circumstances, retained
the demeanour of a gentlewoman, a natural grace and dignity of manner.' Oh God, oh Lossiemouth! 'There he made
the acquaintance of some of the remarkable men of the

country through Samuel Smiles' "Life of a Scottish Natura-
list," Thomas Edwards of Banff, "Thomas Dick, the Thurso
Baker"—geologist. Above all, Hugh Miller influenced him
then. Hugh Miller's "Schools and Schoolmasters" was
among the first books he bought. The watchmaker also lent
him Scott and Dickens."

He appears to have flourished greatly in the sipping of this
pale scum from the surface of English letters. Young, handsome, genteel, he set out for London.

London for a while was unkind. It employed him as an
invoice clerk in a City warehouse at a salary of 12/6 a week.
We are assured that this was the foundation of his Socialism
and that he never forgot those terrible days. The 1931 cuts in
the pay of junior civil servants—cuts in many a case reducing
purchasing power to a lower level than 12/6 a week—were
authorized during a period of temporary amnesia.

It was 1888. Presently he became secretary to a Liberal
Parliamentary candidate; presently he had joined the Social
Democratic Federation. But the Federation had never
heard of Samuel Smiles or the dignity of labour or the
necessity (they stared, astounded Cockneys) for 'independent
thote.' Soon their soullessness had vexed the young Mr. Mac-
Donald from the ranks. He joined the Fabians, and, about
the same time, obtained a footing in journalism.

Meanwhile, Labour representations in the Liberal Party
was moulting forth its discontents. Keir Hardie had arisen as
the apostle of Independent Labour. The young MacDonald
watched this development carefully. At the Bradford Conference of 1893 Keir Hardie was instrumental in founding the
Independent Labour Party. A cautious year afterwards Mr.
MacDonald adhered to the new party.

It was the strangest of parties. Disgruntled Liberal intellectuals with Parliamentary leanings supported it; intelligent workmen supported it; sentimental anarchists supported it. It had all kinds of philosophies, all kinds of codes of
action. Round the problems of the class war it revolved like

a monkey in a cage, distrustful of the tail-nipping propensities of the central axle. In the election of 1895 it put forward twenty-eight candidates. Young Ramsay MacDonald stood for Southampton and was rejected with great unanimity, despite a voice already highly trained in the enunciation, terrifyingly, of those platitudinous nebulosities before which the simple Keir Hardie bowed his head, acknowledging MacDonald Labour's 'greatest intellectual asset.'

For a moment we may let temptation have its way, and turn to the lady biographer for a gem-cut paragraph. She is describing MacDonald of the Southampton election:

'If he appeared a knight in armour, he was hardly, for all his charm and intermittent humour, the glow of his vitality, the Merciful Knight. But at the right hour he met the right woman. A hand was laid upon him that softened the rigidity, mellowed and sweetened the vital strength.'

Predestined the hero of a novelette, Providence had not bungled in her choice. He travelled; he wrote disappovingly of the unstatesmanlike Boer War; and he had a weekend cottage at Chesham Bois. He was shedding the rougher cut lines of his Scottishness, though the unique accent remained undiluted. Cultured, curving of moustache, he looks out from the photographs of those days. The conviction of continuity of culture became fixed in his mind—the mind which could lump 'Cromwell, Milton, Hampden, Penn, Burke' as 'the best in the life of England'!

In 1900 the Labour Representation Committee came into being—the embryo Labour Party which returned two men to Parliament in the General Election of that year. MacDonald was elected secretary of the new organization, and worked with a fine assiduity in building it up. In the next election—that of 1906—he had his reward in two fashions— he himself was returned to Parliament by Leicester and twenty-eight other members of the Labour Party were returned as well. Mr. MacDonald became a skilled and outstanding Parliamentarian; more important, he became the chief theoretician of the Labour Party—of that group of men which claimed, and with some justice, to represent the true commons of Great Britain, the lowly, the oppressed, the Cheated of the Sunlight, the bitter relics of the savagery of the Industrial Revolution. He organized publishing ventures, issues of series of Socialist books and tracts; he engaged and won the attention of a vast audience beyond his immediate ken.

Three quotations from his published works:

'Socialism is no class movement. Socialism is a movement of opinion, not an organization of status. It is not the rule of the working class; it is the organization of the community.'

Surely it was very plain. The stegosaurus was on the move, shedding its vertebrate spikes, abandoning its carnivorous diet, and realizing, appalled, that hitherto its constituent cells had been quite unorganized.

'History is a progression of social stages which have pre- ceded and succeeeded each other like the unfolding of life from the amoeba to the mammal, or from the bud to the fruit. To-day we are in the economic stage. Yesterday we were in the political stage. To-morrow we shall be in the moral stage.'

It was all so plain. Peace to the Abbé Mendel and his dis- coveries of violent revolution, from stage to stage, within the sleek skin of evolution. To-day was the economic stage: our fathers lived quite without economic organization, subsisting on sea-kale and mushrooms. Despite this, they engaged in politics—an abandoned pursuit we have quite outgrown. To-morrow our children will inherit the moral stage—both we and our fathers being entirely without morals. . . . And the day after to-morrow the world would enter on a millenial dotage.

'Intelligence and morality indicate the goal by which the struggle to escape the existing purgatory is guided. Human evolution is a stretching out, not a being pushed forward.'

The much-tried stegosaurus, properly coaxed, would set about elongating its spine. . . .

To describe the opinions in such quotations as sub-human maunderings may be natural: it is also profoundly unjust. The Lossiemouth dux was writing good essays: he could, it seems, have written them almost in his sleep, and then stood by with a solemn smirk on his face while the Dominie read them. The Dominie was the British Labour Movement; and it put down each essay and gazed at the writer with a fresh upstirring from the wells of awe. . . .

Nevertheless, he was no more than epitome of the movement itself. From 1906 until 1914 there were strikes and disputes and wage-cuts: there were folk who starved to death, folk who lived mean and desperate lives, phthistic children who gasped out their last breaths in the slums of the Duke of Westminster—but the great trade unions were powerful and comparatively rich. Conditions pressed not too bitterly on the great mass of labouring men and women. There was no direct and brutal tyranny, and this philosophy of slow and gradual and easy change, when no blood would be shed and little exertion would be required and the repentant lion would turn to a lamb, suited admirably the temper of the padded times. In Germany, the other country with a gret and well-organized labour movement, Marxism, though not definitely repudiated, was watered down to innocuousness, the Day of Change remotely postponed to the era of Germany's grandchildren—those children who have now inherited Hitler.

Then the War came.

The Labour International fell (as Mr. MacDonald no doubt said) like a house of cards. Labour leaders lined up in platoons before the War Ministries of their various countries not to protest against war, not to threaten sabotage, not to proclaim the General Strike: but to clamour for salaried positions. That unique internationalist, Mr. H. G. Wells, erupted like an urgent geyser—'every sword drawn against Germany is a sword drawn for peace.' (Stout, chubby elderly men in comfortable beds could hardly sleep o'nights for dreaming of the gleaming swords.) Mr. Arthur Henderson became a Cabinet Minister. Miss Marie Corelli wrote a patriotic pamphlet of great richness and ferocity, *What can we do for England?*, and later was fined for hoarding sugar.

The way was clear for Mr. Ramsay MacDonald. He was offered a place in the Cabinet by a muddled Government anxious to conciliate this dangerous Parliamentarian. But the Government did not realise that, Parliamentarian or no Parliamentarian, this Scots Labour Leader, predestined the hero of a novelette, could no more break through the Author's plot than one of his favourite amoeba could escape its jelly-film. He refused the offer, proclaimed his opposition to the War, and went into the wilderness, dark, tremendous, and Luciferian.

He was to acquire great kudos with this action. His sincerity in opposing the War is undoubted; his sincerity from those early days in the genteel poverty of Lossiemouth to these modern days as an animated exhibit at the Geological Museum is undoubted. But there can be little doubt that, like Lucifer, he gathered a unique satisfaction from his position—the dauntless tribune (as a Victorian 'historical' novelist would have seen him, in genteel toga and side-whiskers) defying the tyrannical Senate and the brutalized plebs. And there can be as little doubt that (as ever) he quite failed to penetrate behind words to that vile reality that the War was. Addressing a conference in 1918 he spoke of the 'hot and bloody faces on the Somme, only fanned in death by the wings of the angel.' That tumult of fear and filth to Mr. Mac-Donald was no more than excuse for manipulation of the shoddy platitudes of minor poetasters.

In 1917 came the two Russian Revolutions: the first a proper and praiseworthy revolution, the stegosaurus paring its claws and going out to grass; the second—Mr. Mac-Donald looked on the second with an astounded, wurring disapproval. It was a quite different beast, not the old, friendly dinosaur at all—an aggressive, alien, froward beast, biologically unsound. In Great Britain a certain amount of sympathy was manifested for the brute by the Labour Movement. This Mr. MacDonald set himself to combat. By 1918, when Leicester refused to re-elect him to Parliament, the battle between Reform and Revolution in the Independent Labour Party was in full swing. By 1920 the revolutionaries had suffered a severe defeat and Mr. Mac-Donald, still in the wilderness, was building up afresh his war-shattered gospel of 'evolutionary Socialism.'

'The patriotism which expresses a share in common life felt and valued is of a totally different quality from that which expresses a share in common power. The latter is the patriotism that "is not enough," that issues in no fine national spirit, and no sane political judgement. It is a blinding pride, not an enlightening dignity. Therefore political education should begin by the cultivation of the tradition of the locality, and democratic government should be founded on the self-government of the local community. "My fathers' graves are there."'

What appeal had Lenin and the sovietism of the Third International compared with this clarion call to upbuild Socialism on the Parish Council heroisms of our fathers—our non-moral, non-economic, but bitterly political fathers?

'In ten years the work of the Bolshevist Government, freed from outside attacks and commanding the necessities of life, will bring Russia to where (and no further) five years of Labour Government in this country, backed by public opinion, would bring us; two years of Bolshevism in this country would bring us where Russia was a dozen years before the Revolution.'

That experiment in Labour Government was unfair. In the 1923 General Election, the Conservatives, though numerically superior to either Labour or Liberal representation, found themselves unable to secure Liberal support. Mr. Ramsay MacDonald was summoned to Buckingham Palace; he emerged from it the first Labour Premier. Labour burst into loud pœans.

They were mistimed. Earnest colliers poring over their *Daily Herald* learned astounded of the inclusion of the good and Conservative Lord Chelmsford in the Cabinet. There were other as astonishing personalities. In the Labour Speech from the Throne, a vague Niagara of bubbling sonorosities, nothing of any moment was promised. This was but just anticipation. Nothing was done. The Merciful Knight engaged in nine months' elaborate skirmishing with the Liberals—the radical, undignified, uneasy Liberals pressing him forward to all kinds and manners of dangerous experiments with the economic structure of our island. Mr. MacDonald fought them back at every point: he would consent to the clipping of not a single claw on the stegosaurus' hooves. Dazed Conservatives realized that here was the most Conservative Government since Lord Salisbury's; obstreperous Mesopotamians were bombed with great thoroughness by orders of the Under-Secretary for Air, the personal friend of the Premier, the pacifistic Mr. Leach. The communists —much the same collection of irreligious, vigorous blasphemous Cockneys as Mr. MacDonald had turned from in a frayed disgust in the eighteen-nineties—began to prove quite as obstreperous as the Mesopotamians. Unfortunately, they could not be bombed. What change was there in the stegosaurus, they cried—except that it ate more flesh? Labour cursed them gruffly, turning trusting eyes to its Premier. He would tell them how the best was really changing—he knew about it all, *he* knew, HE knew!

Unfortunately, he was rarely visible on the English horizon. He fled from conference to conference across the European scene; at rare intervals, returning to Parliament, he uttered profound appeals for national unity to save the peace of the world—a world injected with a trilling diapason of consonants and false vowels. In Court dress he displayed an exceptional leg. More and more it was becoming evident to him how necessary was the slow and gradual evolution of human society—retaining dignity, tradition, culture.

But evil men conspired. The communists had taken to appealing directly to soldiers on the subject of the stegosaurus. One of their propagandists was arrested. Labour —uneasy, moody Labour—rumbled in protest and Mr. MacDonald, bestirred from his sane and logical immersements in conference-creation, was reminded that he was a Labour leader. He was prevailed on to have Campbell released. Thereat the Liberals, soured of his tactics, voted out the first Labour Government.

In the succeeding election the stegosaurus lost all sense of honour—a frightened and unsavoury beast. It produced the famous Red Letter, pleasingly forged in Berlin, and proving that Mr. MacDonald took his orders from Moscow. For a moment it seems that Mr. MacDonald caught a glimpse of the reality of the beast he had played with and patted so long —the sterile and unlovely beast he had assured the Labour Movement was really a gentle female beast about to give birth to an unique offspring. Then the smashing defeat at the polls came and he abandoned beast and plebs for the wilderness of opposition. And never, during that period of opposition, did he look again on the horror of the dinosaur's countenance. It was merely a dream he had dreamt: the beast was a comely, if occasionally mistaken beast; and he would soon invite him to ride its back again.

Meanwhile wages sank. The hours of the miners were threatened. Labour, long unused to any other general action than the Parliamentary, sprouted a dangerous revolutionism. It proclaimed the General Strike. For Nine Days that strike paralysed and exhilarated Great Britain. There was a blowing up of a sudden comradeship, a sudden and astoundingly Marxian class-consciousness. The Government, appalled, determined to arrest the strike leaders. The strike leaders, appalled, determined to save their skins. They abandoned the strike and abandoned thousands of those they had called out to victimization and intimidation. Mr. MacDonald and Mr. Baldwin exchanged courtesies and congratulations in

the House of Commons, and sent out bulletins to the effect
that the dinosaur was itself again.

Labour turned to Parliamentary organization. As the year
of the next General Election drew near it flung all its
strength into securing a heavy Parliamentary representation
—to secure that way to reform and change which Mr.
Ramsay MacDonald and his colleagues had preached it since
the days of the L.R.C. Its hopes were not disappointed. It
returned over two hundred and fifty members to Parliament;
it returned Mr. MacDonald to the premiership; in conjunc-
tion with the small and radical group of Liberal M.P.'s he
was free to display to the doubting Stalin—the abandoned,
uncultured, unloquacious Stalin—how a Labour Government worked swift and efficient change the while a Godless
Bolshevist one did no more than stamble doggedly forward in
the dark.

The stegosaurus' health was far from sound: it complained
of internal pains. Breathlessly each morning the Labour
voter opened his *Daily Herald* to read the news of the beast's
safe delivery in the skilful hands of its midwife, Ramsay Mac-
Donald. But still the news delayed. Mr. MacDonald instead
began to issue bulletins—quite unexpected bulletins—about
the beast. Copulation and pregnancy were indecencies
foreign to the dinosaur's nature. It was a cultured, amiable
and happy beast—but for those pains. It was the duty of all
men and women of good will to pool their resources to save
the health of this happy, innocent animal. . . . Between whiles,
as in 1924, he sped rapidly about the European scene. He
crossed to America and held a conference with President
Hoover. Still the dinosaur languished. Mr. MacDonald laid
before his colleagues of the Labour Cabinet his plan to reduce
unemployed relief to provide fresh rations for the monster's
table. He did this with wrung withers, but the bankers, the
dinosaur's physicians, saw no other way to save its life. . . .

One abandons dinosaur (a very real beast) and simile with
regret. It may be admitted that MacDonald's colleagues,

refusing to agree with this final onslaught on the standard of that dumb, patient puzzled horde that had elevated them to Parliamentary position, abandoned the beast with regret as well, in spite of the feeble flare of revolutionary zeal they displayed when their late leader appeared—still Premier—at the head of his 'National Government,' backed by row on row of that enemy against which so long and so often he had swung his padded mace. But outside the House of Commons there arose a slow creaking and cracking and spiralling of dust—it was the Labour Movement crumbling to dust. At the 1931 General Election, leading the combined Liberals and Conservatives, Mr. Ramsay MacDonald completed his task of wreckage. On the morning of October the 29th, 1931, the country awoke to find that the pacifist of the War-time years had for once abandoned the padded bludgeon and smashed to atoms with a merciless blow that party and group which had raised him to power, which had followed him and his unique philosophy for a long twenty-five years.

The Labour Movement may win again to shadowy triumphs, but the spirit, the faith and the hope have gone from it. Time, impatient, has turned its back on new re-echoings of those thunderous platitudes which once seemed to ring prophet-inspired from a MacDonald platform. New armies are rising, brutal and quick, determinded, desperate, mutually destructive, communist and fascist. Mr. Ramsay MacDonald has completed to perfection the task set him by the play of historic movements and blind economic forces. He still hastens from conference to conference, solemn and creased; his voice still rings out those rolling periods; he poses, one foot on the step of his aeroplane, for the pressing photographer——.

But there is a greyness and chill come upon it all. One realizes that this is hardly a living human being at all, but a hollow simulacrum. One realizes with a start of enlightenment that indeed there was never life here at all, it was a fantasy, a play of the jaded Victorian sense, a materialization of some hazy lady novelist's dreams after reading Samuel Smiles as a bed book. Even so, there are moments when the presence touches raw nerves: this ghost delays so long on the boards of history, unhumorous, unappeasable. There is hardly a Scotsman alive who does not feel a shudder of amused shame as the rolling turgid voice, this evening or that, pours suddenly from his radio. We have, we Scots (all of us), too much of his quality in our hearts and souls.

THE ANTIQUE SCENE

The history of Scotland may be divided into the three phases of Colonization, Civilization, and Barbarization. That the last word is a synonym for Anglicization is no adverse reflection upon the quality of the great English culture. Again and again, in the play of the historic forces, a great civilization on an alien and lesser has compassed that alien's downfall.

Few things cry so urgently for rewriting as does Scots history, in few aspects of her bastardized culture has Scotland been so ill-served as by her historians. The chatter and gossip of half the salons and drawing-rooms of European intellectualism hang over the antique Scottish scene like a malarial fog through which peer the fictitious faces of heroic Highlanders, hardy Norsemen, lovely Stewart queens, and dashing Jacobite rebels. Those stage-ghosts shamble amid the dimness, and mope and mow in their ancient parts with an idiotic vacuity but a maddening persistence. Modern research along orthodox lines balks from the players, or re-names them shyly and retires into footnotes on Kaltwasser.

Yet behind those grimaces of the romanticized or alien imagination a real people once lived and had its being, and hoped and feared and hated, and was greatly uplifted, and loved its children, and knew agony of the patriotic spirit, and was mean and bestial, and generous, and sardonically merciful. Behind the posturings of those poltergeists are the lives of millions of the lowly who wiped the sweats of toil from browned faces and smelt the pour of waters by the Mull of Kintyre and the winds of autumn in the Grampian haughs and the sour, sweet odours of the upland tarns; who tramped in their varying costumes and speeches to the colour and play of the old guild-towns; who made great poetry and sang it; who begat their kind in shame or delight in the begetting; who were much as you or I, human animals bedevilled or uplifted by the play of the forces of civilization in that remote corner of the Western world which we call Scotland.

All human civilizations originated in Ancient Egypt. Through the accident of time and chance and the cultivation of wild barley in the Valley of the Nile, there arose in a single spot on the earth's surface the urge in men to upbuild for their economic salvation the great fabric of civilization. Before the planning of that architecture enslaved the minds of men, man was a free and happy and undiseased animal wandering the world in the Golden Age of the poets (and reality) from the Shetlands to Tierra del Fuego. And from that central focal point in Ancient Egypt the first civilizers spread abroad the globe the beliefs and practices, the diggings and plantings and indignations and shadowy revilements of the Archaic Civilization.

They reached Scotland in some age that we do not know, coming to the Islands of Mist in search of copper and gold and pearls, Givers of Life in the fantastic theology that followed the practice of agriculture. They found the Scots lowlands and highlands waving green into morning and night tremendous forests where the red deer belled, where the great bear, perhaps, had still his tracks and his caverns, where wolves howled the hills in great scattering packs, where, in that forested land, a danker climate than to-day prevailed. And amid those forests and mountain slopes lived the Golden Age hunters—men perhaps mainly of Maglemosian stock, dark and sinewy and agile, intermixed long ages before with other racial stocks, the stock of Cro-Magnard and Magdalenian who had followed the ice-caps north when the reindeer vanished from the French valleys. They were men naked,

cultureless, without religion or social organization, shy
hunters, courageous, happy, kindly, who stared at the advent
of the first great boats that brought the miners and explorers
of the Archaic Civilization from Crete or Southern Spain.
They flocked down to stare at the new-comers, to offer tentative gifts of food and the like; and to set on their necks the
yoke under which all mankind has since passed.

For the Archaic Civilization rooted in Scotland. Agriculture was learned from the Ancient Mariners and with it the
host of rites deemed necessary to propitiate the gods of the
earth and sky. Village communities came into being, the
first peasants with the first overlords, those priestly overlords
who built the rings of the Devil Stones on the high places
from Lewis to Aberdeenshire. And the ages came and passed
and the agricultural belts grew and spread, and the smoke of
sacrifice rose from a thousand altars through the length and
breadth of the land at the times of seedtime and harvest,
feast and supplication. They buried their dead in modifica-
tions of the Egyptian fashion, in Egyptian graves. There came
to them, in the slow ebb of the centuries, a driftage of other
cultural elements from that ferment of civilization in the
basin of the Mediterranean. They learned their own skill with
stick and stone, presently with copper, and at last with
bronze. But, until the coming of the makers of bronze that
Archaic civilization in Scotland, as elsewhere, was one
singularly peaceful and undisturbed. Organized warfare had
yet to dawn on the Western World.

How it dawned is too lengthy a tale to tell here in any
detail: how bands of forest-dwellers in the Central European
areas, uncivilized, living on the verge of the great settlements
of the Archaic communities and absorbing little but the worst
of their practices, fell on those communities and murdered
them was the first great tragedy of pre-Christian Europe. The
ancient matriarchies of the Seine were wiped from existence
and in their place, (and presently across the Channel) came
swarming the dagger-armed hosts of a primitive who, never

civilized, had become a savage. This was the Kelt.

We see his advent in the fragments of sword and buckler that lie ticketed in our museums; but all the tale of that rape of a civilization by the savage, far greater and infinitely more tragic than the rape of the Roman Empire by the Goth, is little more than a faint moan and murmur in the immense cañons of near-history. In Scotland, no doubt, he played his characteristic part, the Kelt, coming armed on a peaceful population, slaying and robbing and finally enslaving, establishing himself as king and overlord, routing the ancient sun-priests from the holy places and establishing his own devil-haunted, uneasy myths and gods through the efforts of the younger sons. From Berwick to Cape Wrath the scene for two hundred years must have been a weary repetition, year upon year, of invasion and murder, inversion and triumph. When Pytheas sailed the Scottish coasts it is likely that the Kelt had triumphed almost everywhere. By the time the Romans came raiding across the English Neck Scotland was a land of great barbaric Kelt tribes, armed and armoured, with a degenerate, bastardized culture and some skill in war and weapon-making. It was as capable of producing a ferocious soldiery and a great military leader like Calgacus as it was incapable of a single motif in art or song to influence the New Civilization of the European World.

Yet of that culture of those Picts or Painted Men, those Caledonians whom the Romans encountered and fought and marvelled upon, it is doubtful if a single element of any value had been contributed by the Kelt. It is doubtful if the Kelts ever contributed a single item to the national cultures of the countries miscalled Keltic. It is doubtful for the best of reasons: There is no proof that the Kelts, invading Britain, came in any great numbers. They were a conquering military caste, not a people in migration: they imposed their language and their social organization upon the basic Maglemosian-Mediterranean stock; they survived into remoter times, the times of Calgacus, the times of Kenneth MacAlpin, as nobles, an aristocracy on horseback. They survive to the present day as a thin strand in the Scottish population: half Scotland's landed gentry is by descent Normanized Kelt. But the Kelts are a strain quite alien to the indubitable and original Scot. They were, and remain, one of the greatest curses of the Scottish scene, quick, avaricious, unintelligent, quarrelsome, cultureless, and uncivilizable. It is one of the strangest jests of history that they should have given their name to so much that is fine and noble, the singing of poets and the fighting of great fights, in which their own actual part has been that of gaping, unintelligent audition or mere carrion-bird raiding.

The first serious modification of the basic Pictish stock did not occur until towards the end of the sixth Christian century, when the Northumbrian Angles flowed upwards, kingdom-building, as far as the shores of the Firth of Forth. They were a people and nation in transit; they exterminated or reduced to villeinage the Kelt-led Picts of those lands: they succeeded in doing those things not because they were braver or more generous or God-inspired than the Pictish tribes, but because of the fact that they were backed by the Saxon military organization, their weapons were better, and apparently they fronted a congeries of warring tribes inanely led in the usual Keltic fashion—tribes which had inter-warred and raided and murdered and grown their crops and drunk their ale unstirred by alien adventures since the passing of the Romans. The Angle pressed north, something new to the scene, bringing his own distinctive culture and language, his own gods and heroes and hero-myths. About the same time a tribe of Kelt-led Irish Mediterraneans crossed in some numbers into Argyllshire and allied themselves with, or subdued the ancient inhabitants. From that alliance or conquest arose the kingdom of Dalriada—the Kingdom of the Scots. Yet this Irish invasion had no such profound effect on the national culture as the coming of the Angles in the South: the Irish Scots were of much the same speech and origin as the Argyllshire natives among whom they settled.

With the coming of the Angles, indeed, the period of Colonization comes to a close. It is amusing to note how modern research disposes of the ancient fallacies which saw Scotland overrun by wave after wave of conquering, colonizing peoples. Scotland was colonized only twice—once fairly completely, once partially, the first time when the Maglemosian hunters drifted north, in hunting, happy-go-lucky migration; the second time, when the Angles lumbered up into Lothian. The Kelt, the Scot, the Norseman, the Norman were no more than small bands of raiders and robbers. The peasant at his immemorial toil would lift his eyes to see a new master installed at the broch, at the keep, at, later, the castle: and would shrug the matter aside as one of indifference, turning, with the rain in his face, to the essentials of existence, his fields, his cattle, his woman in the dark little eirde, earth-house.

The three hundred years after that almost simultaneous descent of Scot and Angle on different sectors of the Scottish scene is a tangle of clumsy names and loutish wars. Kings bickered and bred and murdered and intrigued, armies marched and counter-marched and perpetrated heroisms now dust and nonsense, atrocities the dried blood of which are now not even dust. Christianity came in a number of guises, the Irish heresy a chill blink of light in its coming. It did little or nothing to alter the temper of the times, it was largely a matter of politics and place-seeking, Columba and John Knox apart there is no ecclesiastic in Scots history who does not but show up in the light of impartial research as either a posturing ape, rump-scratching in search of soft living, or as a moronic dullard, hag-ridden by the grisly transplanted fears of the Levant. The peasant merely exchanged the bass chanting of the Druid in the pre-Druid circles for the whining hymnings of priests in wood-built churches; and turned to his land again.

But presently, coastwise, north, west, and east, a new danger was dragging him in reluctant levies from his ancient pursuits. This was the coming of the Norsemen.

If the Kelts were the first great curse of Scotland, the Norse were assuredly the second. Both have gathered to themselves in the eyes of later times qualities and achievements to which the originals possessed no fragment of a claim. The dreamy, poetic, God-moved Kelt we have seen as a mere Chicagoan gangster, murderous, avaricious, culturally sterile, a typical aristocrat, typically base. The hardy, heroic Norseman uncovers into even sorrier reality. He was a farmer or fisherman, raiding in order to supplement the mean livelihood he could draw from more praiseworthy pursuits in the Norwegian fjords. The accident of his country lying at the trans-Baltic end of the great trans-Continental trade-route had provided him with the knowledge of making steel weapons in great number and abundance. Raiding Scotland, he was in no sense a superior or heroic type subduing a lowly or inferior; he was merely a pirate with a good cutlass, a thug with a sudden and efficient strangling-rope. Yet those dull, dyspeptic whey-faced clowns have figured in all orthodox histories as the bringers of something new and vital to Scottish culture, as an invigorating strain, a hard and splendid ingredient. It is farcical that it should be necessary to affirm at this late day that the Norseman brought nothing of any permanence to Scotland other than his characteristic gastritis.

Yet that cutlass carved great sections from the Scottish coasts: presently all the Western Isles had suffered a profound infiltration of the thin, mean blood of the northern sea-raiders. In the east, the attacks were almost purely burglarious. The hardy Norseman, with his long grey face so unfortunately reminiscent of a horse's, would descend on that and this village or township, steal and rape and fire, and then race for his ships to escape encounter with the local levies. On such occasions as he landed in any force, and met the Picts (even the idiotically badly-led, Kelt-led Picts) in any force, he would, as at the Battle of Aberlemno, be routed with decision and vigour. Yet those constant raidings weakened the Eastern kingdom of the Picts: in A.D. 844 the Scot king, Kenneth MacAlpin, succeeded to the Pictish throne—it was evidently regarded as the succession of a superior to the estates of an inferior. Thereafter the name Pict disappears from Scottish history, though, paradoxically immortal, the Pict remained.

From 1034, when Duncan ascended the Scottish throne, until 1603, when James VI ascended the English throne, Scotland occupied herself, willy-nilly, in upbuilding her second (and last) characteristic civilization. Her first, as we have seen, was that modification of the Archaic Civilization which the Kelts overthrew; this second which slowly struggled into being under the arrow-hails, the ridings and rapings and throat-cuttings of official policy, the jealous restraints of clerical officialdom, was compounded of many cultural strands. It was in essentials a Pictish civilization, as the vast majority of the inhabitants remained Picts. But, in the Lowlands, it had changed once again its speech, relinquishing the alien Keltic in favour of the equally alien Anglo-Saxon. The exchange was a matter of domestic policy, a febrific historical accident hinged on the bed-favours wrung from his consort by the henpecked Malcolm Canmore.

The third of the name of Malcolm to rule in Scotland, his speech, his court, and his official pronunciamentos were all Keltic until he wedded the Princess Margaret, who had fled from the Norman invasion of England. A great-niece of Edward the Confessor, Margaret was a pious daughter of the Church and greatly shocked at the Keltic deviations from Roman dates and ceremonial incantations. She devoted her life to bringing the usages of the Scottish Church into harmony with orthodox Catholicism. She bred assiduously: she bred six sons and two daughters, and in return for the delights of the shameful intimacies which begat this offspring, the abashed Malcolm refrained from any hand in their christening. They were all christened with good English names, they were taught English as their native speech, they lived to grow up and Anglicize court and church and town. Of the two great women in Scots history it is doubtful if the most calamitously pathological influence should be ascribed to Margaret the Good or to Mary the Unchaste.

Yet this Anglicization was a surface Anglicization. English speech and English culture alike were as yet fluid things: it meant no cultural subjection to the southern half of the island. It begat a tradition, a speech, an art and a literature in the southern half of Scotland which were set in an Anglo-Saxon, not an English, mould, but filled with the deep spiritual awarenesses of the great basic race which wielded this new cultural weapon as once it had wielded the Keltic. It was a thing national and with a homely and accustomed feel, this language in which Wyntoun and Barbour and Blind Harry were presently telling the epic stories of the great War of Independence.

The effect of that war, the unceasing war of several centuries, was calamitous to the Scots civilization in the sense that it permanently impoverished it, leaving Scotland, but for a brief blink, always a poor country economically, and a blessing in that it set firmly in the Scots mind the knowledge of national homogeneity: Scotland was the home of true political nationalism (once a liberating influence, not as now an inhibiting one)—not the nationalism forced upon an unwilling or indifferent people by the intrigues of kings and courtesans, but the spontaneous uprising of an awareness of blood-brotherhood and freedom-right. In the midst of the many dreary and shameful pages of the book of Scottish history the story of the rising of the Scots under the leadership of William Wallace still rings splendid and amazing. Wallace was one of the few authentic national heroes: authentic in the sense that he apprehended and moulded the historic forces of his time in a fashion denied to all but a few of the world's great political leaders—Cromwell, Lincoln, Lenin.

It was 1296. Scotland, after a dynastic squabble on the rights of this and that boorish noble to ascend the Scottish throne and there cheat and fornicate after the divine rights of kings, had been conquered, dismembered and ground in the mud by Edward the First of England. He did it with a cold and bored efficiency, as a man chastising and chaining a slobbering, yelping cur. Then he returned to England; and the chained cur suddenly awoke in the likeness of a lion.

'The instinct of the Scottish people,' wrote John Richard Green, 'has guided it right in choosing Wallace for its national hero. He was the first to assert freedom as a national birthright.' His assertion roused Scotland. The peasants flocked to his standard—suddenly, and for perhaps the first time in Scots history, stirred beyond their customary indifference over the quarrels of their rulers. Here was something new, a leader who promised something new. Nor did he only promise: presently he was accomplishing. At the head of a force that bore the significant title of the 'Army of the Commons of Scotland' Wallace met and routed the English in pitched battle at Cambuskenneth Bridge in 1297, was offered the crown of Scotland, refused it, and instead was nominated Guardian of Scotland, a great republican with the first of the great republican titles, albeit he called himself a royalist.

For a year it seemed his cause would sweep everything before it. The laggard nobles came to join him. Presently the Army of the Commons of Scotland was being poisoned by the usual aristocratic intrigues, though still the troubled peasants and townsmen clung to their faith in the Guardian. The news came that Edward in person was on the march against Scotland. Wallace assembled all his forces and met the invader at Falkirk. The Scots cavalry, noble-recruited, noble-led, strategically placed to fall on the ranks of the English archers and rout them at the crucial moment, fled without striking a blow. Wallace's great schiltrouns of heroic peasant spearmen were broken and dispersed.

Wallace himself sailed for France, seeking aid there for his distracted country. In 1304 he returned, was captured by the English, tried and condemned as a traitor, and hanged, castrated, and disembowelled on Tower Hill. This judicial murder is one of the first and most dreadful examples of that characteristic English frightfulness wielded throughout history against the defenders of alien and weaker peoples. More serious than Wallace's personal fate, it murdered that fine hope and enthusiasm that had stirred the Army of the Scots Commons on the morning of Falkirk. In a kind of despairing hatred, not hope, the Scots people turned to support the rebellions of the various shoddy noble adventurers who now raised the standard against the English. By intrigue, assassination, and some strategical skill one of those nobles, Robert the Brus, had presently disposed of all his rivals, had himself crowned king, and, after various reverses and flights and hidings and romantic escapades in company with spiders and Lorne loons, succeeded in routing the English at the Battle of Bannockburn. With that victory the Scots royalties came to their own again, however little the Scots commons.

Yet, in the succeeding centuries of wars and raids, dynastic begettings and dynastic blood-lettings, the commons of Scotland showed a vigour both un-English and un-French in defence of the rights of the individual. Villeinage died early in Scotland: the independent tenant-retainer came early on the scene in the Lowlands. In the Highlands the clan system, ostensibly aristocratic, was never so in actuality. It was a communistic patriarchy, the relation of the chief to his meanest clansman the relation of an elder blood brother, seldom of a noble to a serf. The guildsmen of the towns modelled their policies on those of the Hansa cities and Augsburg, rather than on the slavish subservience of their contemporaries in England. Presently the French alliance, disastrous from a military point of view, was profoundly leavening the character of Scots culture, leavening, not obliterating it. Scots built and carved and sang and wrote with new tools of technique and vocabulary to hand. The

Scots civilization of the fifteenth and sixteenth centuries absorbed its great cultural impulses from the Continent; as a sequence, Scots literature in the fifteenth century is already a great literature while in contemporary England there is little more than the maundering of a poetasting host of semi-illiterates. Despite the feuds and squabbles of noble and king, there came into being a rude plenty in Scotland of the fifteenth and sixteenth centuries. The reign of James the Fourth was, economically and culturally, the Golden Age of the great Scots civilization. Its duration was brief and its fate soon that which had overtaken the Golden Age of the happy Pict hunters three thousand years before.

The end of James the Fourth at Flodden in 1513, the dark end to the greatest raid of the Scots into England, plunged the country into fifteen years of mis-government, when this and that clownish noble attempted to seize the power through this and that intrigue of palace and bed-chamber. The Golden Age faded rapidly as marauding bands of horse clattered up the cobbled streets of the towns and across the fertile Lowland crop-lands. By the time the Fifth James assumed the power Scotland was a distracted country, the commons bitterly taxed and raided and oppressed, the ruler in castle and keep a gorged and stinking carrion-crow. James, the Commons' King, the one heroic royalty in Scots history, faced a hopeless task with the broken and impoverished commons but half aware of his championship. He put down the nobles with a ruthless hand, defied the monk-murdering Henry VIII of England, established the Court of Session and the Supreme Court of Justice; he might well have re-established the economic prosperity of his father's reign but for the English invasion of the country in 1542. The nobles refused to join the army he raised—the pitiful Church army routed at Solway Moss. Dying at Falkland Palace a few days later James, God's Scotsman as he has been well called, heard of the birth of a daughter. 'It cam wi' a lass and 'twill gang wi' o lass,' he said, speaking perhaps of his own

dynasty; unforeseeing the fact that it was the Scots civilization itself that that daughter was to see in early eclipse.

That eclipse was inaugurated by the coming of the tumul-
tuous change in Christian ritualism and superstitious practice dignified by the name of Reformation. Into its many
causes in Western Europe there is no need to enter here.
Nobles hungered to devour Church lands; churchmen were
often then, as later, cowardly and avaricious souls; the
Church, then as often, seemed intellectually moribund, a
dead weight lying athwart the minds of men. So, in apparent
dispute as to the correct method of devouring the symbolic
body of the dead god, symbolically slain, hell was let loose on
the European scene for a long two hundred years. Men
fought and died with enthusiasm in the cause of ceremonial
cannibalism. In Scotland the Reforming party had been
growing to power even in the age of the Fifth James. During
the long minority of his daughter, Mary Queen of Scots, it
was frequently in possession of the reins of power: in 1557 it
gathered together its forces and signed a National Conven-
tion for the establishment of the Reformed Faith.

Two years afterwards the ecclesiastic, John Knox, returned from a long exile in England and on the Continent.
Knox had served as a slave on the French galleys for eighteen
months after the assassination of Cardinal Beaton in 1546, he
had definite and clear beliefs on the part the Reformation
must play in Scotland, and in the years of his exile he had
wandered from haunt to haunt of the European revolutionaries (much as Lenin did in the first decade of the twentieth
century) testing out his own creed in converse and debate
with Calvin and the like innovators. Once again a Scotsman
had arisen capable of apprehending the direction of the
historic forces, and determined to enchannel those for the
benefit of a Commons' Scotland. The nauseous character of
his political allies in Scotland did not deter him from the
conflict. In the triumphant Parliament summoned in 1560 the
Protestants under his direction established the Reformed

K

Church, forbade the mass, and practically legalized the wholesale seizure of Church property. Knox's intentions with regard to the disposal of that property were definite and unshakable: it would be used for the relief of the poor, for the establishment of free schools, for the sustentation of a free people's priesthood. But, though he had foreseen the direction of the historic forces thus far, history proved on the side of his robbing allies, not on his. The Covenant left the Commons poorer than ever and Knox an embittered and sterile leader, turning from his battle in the cause of the people to sardonic denunciations of the minor moral lapses of the young Queen.

He was a leader defeated: and history was to ascribe to him and his immediate followers, and with justice, blame for some of the most terrible aberrations of the Scots spirit in succeeding centuries. Yet Knox himself was of truly heroic mould; had his followers, far less his allies, been of like mettle, the history of Scotland might have been strangely and splendidly different. To pose him against the screen of antique time as an inhibition-ridden neurotic (as is the modern fashion) who murdered the spirit and hope of an heroic young queen, is malicious distortion of the true picture. The 'heroic young queen' in question had the face, mind, manners and morals of a well-intentioned but hysterical poodle.

Her succession by the calamitous Sixth James, who was summoned to the English throne in 1603, was the beginning of the end of the Scots civilization. That end came quickly. Not only had temporal power moved from Edinburgh to London (for at least a while) but the cultural focus had shifted as well. There began that long process of barbarization of the Scots mind and culture which is still in progress. Presently it was understood to be rather a shameful thing to be a Scotsman, to make Scots poetry, to be subject to Scots law, to be an inhabitant of the northern half of the island. The Diffusionist school of historians holds that the state of Barbarism is no half-way house of a progressive people towards full and complete civilization: on the contrary, it marks a degeneration from an older civilization, as Savagery is the state of a people absorbing only the poorer elements of an alien culture. The state of Scotland since the Union of the Crowns gives remarkable support to this view, though the savagery of large portions of the modern urbanized population had a fresh calamity—the Industrial Revolution—to father it.

Yet, though all art is no more than the fine savour and essence of the free life, its decay and death in Scotland was no real mark of the subjection and decay of the free Scottish spirit: it was merely a mark of that spirit in an anguished travail that has not yet ceased. Presently, gathering that unquenchable force into new focus, came the Covenanting Times, the call of the Church of Knox to be defended as the Church of the Commons, of the People, bitterly assailed by noble and King. That the call was justified we may doubt, that the higher councils of the Church government themselves were other than sedulously manipulated tyrannies in the hands of the old landed Keltic gentry may also be doubted. But to large sections of the Lowland Scots the Covenant was not so much a sworn bond between themselves and God as between their own souls and freedom. They flocked to its standards in the second Bishops' War, they invaded England. For a time the Covenanting Scots Army at Newcastle dictated English policy, ruled England, and almost imposed on it the Presbytery. Thereafter, in the sway and clash of the Parliamentarian wars, it suffered collapse under the weight of its own prosperity and rottenness. Cromwell forcibly dissolved the General Assembly of the Scots Church in 1653, incorporated Scotland in the Commonwealth, and marched home leaving a country under English military governance—a country chastised and corrected, but strangely unbroken in spirit. Scotland and the Scots, after a gasp of surprise, accepted Cromwell with a wary trust. Here, and again, as once in those brief days when the standards of the

Guardian of Scotland unfurled by Stirling Brig, was something new on the Scottish scene—English-inspired, but new and promising. If they laboured under dictatorship, so did the English. If their nobles were proscribed and persecuted, so were the English. If their frontier was down, trade with England and the English colonies was free. . . . It was a glimpse of the Greater Republicanism; and it faded almost before Scotland could look on it. The Second Charles returned and enforced the Episcopacy on the Scots, and from 1660 until 1690 Scotland travailed in such political Terror as has few parallels in history.

The People's Church gathered around it the peasants—especially the western peasants—in its defence. At Rullion Green the Covenanting Army was defeated, and an orgy of suppression followed. Covenanters were tortured with rigour and a sadistic ingenuity before being executed in front of their own houses, in sight of their own women-folk. In the forefront of this business of oppression were the Scots nobles, led by Graham of Claverhouse, 'Bonny Dundee.' This remarkable individual, so much biographied and romanticized by later generations, was both a sadist and a criminal degenerate. He was one in a long train of the Scots nobility. He had few qualities to recommend him, his generalship was poor and his strategy worse. Torturing unarmed peasants was the utmost reach of statesmanship ever achieved by this hero of the romantics. Where he met an army—even a badly organized army as at Drumclog—he was ignominiously defeated and fled with the speed and panic of the thin-blooded pervert that he was. His last battle, that of Killiecrankie, he won by enlisting the aid of the Highlanders against those whom they imagined to be their enemies. His portrayed face has a rat-like look in the mean, cold eyes; his name has a sour stench still in the pages of Scottish history.

That last battle of his marked almost the end of the Church persecutions: the Kirk of Scotland emerged with the Revolution from its long night into a day of power and pomp. So

doing, following an infallible law of history, it shed the enthusiasm and high loyalty of all generous souls. From 1690
onwards the history of the churches in Scotland is a history of
minor and unimportant brawling on questions of state support and state denunciation, it is an oddly political history,
reflecting the dreary play of politics up to and after the Union
of the Parliaments, the Union which destroyed the last out-
ward symbols of the national civilization.

Whatever the growing modern support for repudiation of
that Union, it is well to realize that the first tentative moves
towards it came from the side of the Scots Parliament, if not
of the Scots people. As early as 1689 the Scots Parliament
appointed commissioners to treat for an 'incorporating
union,' though nothing came of it. Scottish trade and Scottish industry was very desperately hampered by the English
Navigation Act, in which Scots were treated as aliens; and
also by the fact that the Scots lacked any overseas dominion
on which to dump their supluses of wealth and population—
though indeed, except in the farcical economics of that time
(ours are no less farcical) they had surpluses of neither. The
first attempts at Union came to nothing: the Scots turned
their energies to founding a colony in Darien.

The attempt was disastrous: the Spaniards, already in possession, and aided and abetted by powerful English influences, beat off the settlers. News of the disaster killed
among the Scots people any desire for union with the auld
enemy; nor indeed did they ever again support it. The Union
was brought about by as strange a series of intrigues as history is aware of: England ingeniously bribed her way to
power. There was little real resistance in the Scots Parliament except by such lonely figures as Fletcher of Saltoun. On
May 1st, 1707, Scotland officially ceased to be a country and
became 'that part of the United Kingdom, North Britain.'
Scotsmen officially ceased to be Scots, and became Britons—
presumably North Britons. England similarly lost identity—
impatiently, on a scrap of paper. But everyone knew, both at

home and abroad, that what really had happened was the final subjugation of the Scots by the English, and the absorption of the Northern people into the polity and name of the southern.

There was a smouldering fire of resistance: it sprang to flame twice in the course of the first half-century. In 1715 the Earl of Mar raised the standard for the exiled Jacobite King. He received a support entirely unwarranted by either his own person or that of the puppet monarch whose cause he championed. At the strange, drawn battle of Sheriffmuir the Jacobite rebellion was not so much suppressed as suddenly bored. It was as though its supporters were overtaken by a desire to yawn at the whole affair. They melted from the field, not to assemble, they or their sons, for another thirty years.

This was with the landing of Prince Charles Edward in the Highlands in 1745. Scotland—Scotland of the Highlands, great sections of Scotland of the Lowlands—took him to the heart. The clans rose in his support, not unwillingly following the call of their chiefs. Here was relief from that crushing sense of inferiority that had pressed on the nation since the first day of the Union: here was one who promised to restore the Ancient Times—the time of meal and milk and plenty of the Fifth James; here was one who promised Scotland her nationhood again. In after years it became the fashion to pretend that the vast mass of the Scots people were indifferent to, or hostile to, this last adventure of the Stewarts. But there was no Scotsman worthy of the name who was not, at least at first, an enthusiast and a partisan.

Charles marched from victory to victory: presently he was marching across the Borders with an ill-equipped army of Highlanders and Lowland levies, seeking the support promised him by the English Jacobites. He sought it in vain. To the English Jacobite, to all the English, it was plain that here was no exiled English king come to reclaim his throne: here was something long familiar in wars with the northern

enemy—a Scots army on a raid. Charles turned back at
Derby, and, turning, lost the campaign, lost the last chance
to restore the ancient nationhood of Scotland, lost (which was
of no importance) himself.

His final defeat at Culloden inaugurated the ruthless
extirpation of the clan system in the Highlands, the extirpation of almost a whole people. Sheep-farming came to the
Highlands, depopulating its glens, just as the Industrial
Revolution was coming to the Lowlands, enriching the new
plutocracy and brutalizing the ancient plebs. Glasgow and
Greenock were coming into being as the last embers of the
old Scots culture flickered and fuffed and went out.

There followed that century and a half which leads us to
the present day, a century through which we hear the wail of
children in unending factories and in night-time slums, the
rantings of place-seeking politicians, the odd chirping and
cackling of the bastardized Scots romantic schools in music
and literature. It is a hundred and fifty years of unloveliness
and pridelessness, of growing wealth and growing impover-
ishment, of Scotland sharing in the rise and final torturing
maladjustments of that economic system which holds all the
modern world in thrall. It was a hundred and fifty years in
which the ancient Pictish spirit remembered only at dim
intervals, as in a nightmare, the cry of the wind in the hair of
freemen in that ancient life of the Golden Age, the play of
the same wind in the banners of Wallace when he marshalled
his schiltrouns at Falkirk.

LITERARY LIGHTS

One of the most praiseworthy—praiseworthy in its enter-
tainment value—efforts of the critic has always been his
attempt to leviate himself out of himself by the ingenuous
method of hauling with great passion upon his own bootlaces.
In the words of Mr. Alan Porter 'The critic, before he sets
down a word, must beat himself on the head and ask a
hundred times, each time more bitterly and searchingly,
"And is it true? Is it true?" He must analyse his judgement
and make sure that it is nowhere stained or tinted with the
blood of his heart. And he must search out a table of values
from which he can be certain that he has left nothing uncon-
sidered. If, after all these precautions and torments, he is
unable to deliver a true judgement, then fate has been too
strong for him; he was never meant to be a critic.'

The present writer was assuredly never meant to be a
critic. He has attempted no feats of manipulative surgery
upon either his personality or his judgement. He confesses
with no shame that the dicta of criticism laid down by Mr.
Porter appear to him analogous to the chest-beating posturings of a righteous baboon prior to its robbing an orchard.
Flippancy apart, the researches of Bekhterev and Pavlov
should have disposed once and for all of such archaic beliefs
as the possibility of inhibiting a reflex by incantation. Indeed,
it did not require reflexological research (of which the average critic has never heard—or, if he has, imagines it has
something to do with the torturing of dogs and Mr. Bernard

Shaw) to dispose of this nonsense regarding 'heart' and 'head'. To commit hari-kari may be an admirable and hygienic exercise, but is an operation seldom survived by even the remoter portions of the extra-intestinal anatomy.

Far more serious doubts assail the non-professional critic when he enters upon the study of such a subject as (reputed) Scots letters. If he enters this great library from the open air, not through an underground passage from the book-lined gloom of a study, the piles of stacked volumes are dismaying in their colour and size and plentitude. Only here and there does he recognize a name or a title; the books tower to dim ceilings, are piled in great strata, have the dust of the last few years gathered yet thickly enough upon them. How may he pass judgement? The books he has missed—the books he has never read! What relative importance have the few names and titles in his memory to the hidden values in this great library?

For, in the pressing multitudes of reputedly Scots books which pour from the presses, there may have been a new Melville, a new Typee, a Scots Joyce, a Scots Proust? Nothing impossible in any of those suppositions. The book may have appeared, it failed to be noticed, (as hundreds of good books have failed to be noted,) it was poorly advertised, had inadequate publicity, was overshadowed by the simultaneous publication of a great name—and moulders now its representative copies in two or three libraries while the remainder of the stock—not even 'remaindered'—has returned to the printer for repulping. There is nothing to say that this has not happened very often.

Even if the critic passes a judgement with some fair knowledge of the factors—how of the unpublished books? There may be manuscripts circulating the publishers' offices that sing a new, clear splendid note in letters—sing it so loudly that no publisher's reader can abide the beat of the music in his ears. . . . This is not only possible, but very probable. It was as true of the past as it is of the present, though both gods and machines were of a different order three hundred years ago. Yet even then it is possible that poets dwarfing Shakespeare remained unpublished and unplayed for lack of suitable influences, suitable patronage; and their manuscripts, with the wisdom and delight of the shining minds that begat them, have long mouldered to dust.

The new and unknown Scots writer facing the publishing, printing world has the usual chances and mischances to face in a greater measure than his English compeer. Firstly, in almost every case, he must seek publication in London. Scots publishers are surely amongst the sorriest things that enter hell: their publicity methods are as antique as their format, their houses are generally staffed by those who in Bengali circles would write after their names, and as their chief qualification, 'failed B.A.' (or slightly worse, 'M.A. (St. Andrews)'). He must consign his manuscript to alien publishers and the consideration of largely alien readers.

For, however the average Scots writer believes himself Anglicized, his reaction upon the minds of the intelligent English reader (especially of the professional reader) is curiously similar to that produced by the English poems of Dr. Rabindranath Tagore. The prose—or verse—is impeccably correct, the vocabulary is rich and adequate, the English is severe, serene. . . . But unfortunately it is not English. The English reader is haunted by a sense of something foreign stumbling and hesitating behind this smooth façade of adequate technique: it is as though the writer did not *write* himself, but *translated* himself.

Often the Scots writer is quite unaware of this essential foreignness in his work; more often, seeking an adequate word or phrase he hears an echo in an alien tongue that would adorn his meaning with a richness, a clarity and a conciseness impossible in orthodox English. That echo is from Braid Scots, from that variation of the Anglo-Saxon speech which was the tongue of the great Scots civilization, the tongue adopted by the basic Pictish strain in Scotland as its chief literary tool.

Further, it is still in most Scots communities, (in one or other Anglicized modification,) the speech of bed and board and street and plough, the speech of emotional ecstasy and emotional stress. But it is not genteel. It is to the bourgeois of Scotland coarse and low and common and loutish, a matter for laughter, well enough for hinds and the like, but for the genteel to be quoted in vocal inverted commas. It is a thing rigorously elided from their serious intercourse—not only with the English, but among themselves. It is seriously believed by such stratum of the Scots populace to be an inadequate and pitiful and blunted implement, so that Mr. Eric Linklater delivers *ex cathedra* judgement upon it as 'inadequate to deal with the finer shades of emotion.'

But for the truly Scots writer it remains a real and a haunting thing, even while he tries his best to forget its existence and to write as a good Englishman. In this lies his tragedy. He has to *learn* to write in English: he is like a Chinese scholar spending the best years of his life in the mystic mazes of the pictographs, and emerging so exhausted from the travail that originality of research or experiment with his new tool is denied him. Consequently, the free and anarchistic experimentations of the progressive members of a free and homogeneous literary cultus are denied him. Nearly every Scots writer of the past writing in orthodox English has been not only incurably second-rate, but incurably behind the times. The Scots discovery of photographic realism in novel-writing, for example—I refer to *Hatter's Castle*, not the very different *House with the Green Shutters*—post-dated the great French and English realists some thirty or forty years. But to the Scot Dr. Cronin's work appeared a very new and terrifying and fascinating thing indeed; to the English public, astounding that anything faintly savouring of accuracy, photographic or otherwise, should come out of Scotland, it was equally amazing. At such rate of progress among the Anglo-Scots one may guess that in another fifty years or so a Scots Virginia Woolf will astound the Scottish scene, a Scots

James Joyce electrify it. To expect contemporary experimentation from the Anglo-Scots themselves appears equivalent to expecting a Central African savage in possession of a Birmingham kite to prove capable of inventing a helicopter.

Consciousness of this inferiority of cultural position within the English tradition is a very definite thing among the younger generation of Anglo-Scots writers of to-day. Their most characteristic organ, *The Modern Scot*, is a constant reiteration of protest. Owned and edited by one of those genial Englishmen in search of a revolution who have added to the gaiety of nations from Ireland to Uganda, *The Modern Scot* has set itself, strictly within the English tradition, to out-English the English. As one who on a lonely road doth walk with fear and dread, very conscious of the frightful fiend who close behind doth tread, it marches always a full yard ahead of extremist English opinion—casting the while an anxious backward glance. It decries the children of 'naturalism' with a praiseworthy but unnatural passion, championing in their place, with a commendable care for pathology, the idiot offspring begat on the modern literary scene in such numbers from the incestuous unions of Strindberg and Dr. Freud. It is eclectic to quite an obscure degree, is incapable of an article that does not quote either Proust or Paul Einzig, and raises an approving voice in praise of the joyous, if infantile tauromachic obsessions of Mr. Roy Campbell. Its motif-note, indeed, is literary Fascism—to the unimpassioned, if astounded, eye it would seem as if all the Fascist undergraduates of Scotland these days were hastening, in pimples and a passion for sophistication, to relieve themselves of a diarrhoetic Johnsonese in the appropriate privy of *The Modern Scot*. The entire being of the periodical, however, is rather an exhibitory, or sanitary, exercise, than a contributing factor towards authentic experimentation.

With a few exceptions presently to be noted, there is not the remotest reason why the majority of modern Scots writers should be considered Scots at all. The protagonists of the Scots literary Renaissance deny this. They hold, for example, that Norman Douglas or Compton Mackenzie, though they write in English and deal with un-Scottish themes, have nevertheless an essential Scottishness which differentiates them from the native English writer. In exactly the same manner, so had Joseph Conrad an essential Polishness. But few (except for the purpose of exchanging diplomatic courtesies) pretend that Conrad was a Polish writer, to be judged as a Pole. He wrote brilliantly and strangely and beautifully in English; so does Mr. Norman Douglas, so does Mr. Cunninghame Graham. Mention of the latter is peculiarly to the point. Mr. Graham has, I believe, a large modicum of Spanish blood in his veins, he writes much of Spanish or Spanish-American subjects, and his word-manipulation is most certainly not of the English orthodox. But we have still to hear of Spain acclaiming him one of her great essayists.

The admirable plays of Dr. James Bridie—such as *Tobias and the Angel* or the unforgettable *Jonah and the Whale*—have been hailed in Scotland as examples of modern Scots drama. They are excellent examples—but not of Scots drama. They are examples of how an Englishman, hailing from Scotshire, can write excellent plays. Mr. Edwin Muir writes poems of great loveliness; so does Mr. Roy Campbell; both are of Scots origin: ergo, great Scots poetry. Dumas père had negro blood in his veins and wrote excellent romances in French: ergo, great negro romance.

That such a position is untenable is obvious. Modern Scotland, the Gaels included, is a nation almost entirely lacking a Scottish literary output. There are innumerable versifiers, ranging from Dr. Charles Murray downwards to Mr. W. H. Hamilton (he of the eldritch glamour); there are hardly more than two poets; and there is no novelist at all. To be oneself a provincial or an alien and to write a book in which the characters infect one's literary medium with a tincture of dialect is not to assist in the creation or continuation of a separate national literature—else Eden Philpotts proves the great, un-English soul of Dartmoor and Tennyson in *The Northern Farmer* was advocating Home Rule for Yorkshire. The chief Literary Lights which modern Scotland claims to light up the scene of her night are in reality no more than the commendable writers of the interesting English county of Scotshire.

Let us consider Mrs. Naomi Mitchison. She is the one writer of the 'historical' novel in modern English who commands respect and enthusiasm. Her pages are aglow with a fine essence of apprehended light. *The Conquered* and *Black Sparta* light up the human spirit very vividly and truly. And they are in no sense Scots books though written by a Scotswoman. Their author once wrote that had she had the command of Scots speech possessed by Lewis Grassic Gibbon she would have written her Spartan books (at least) in Scots. Had she done so they would undoubtedly have been worse novels —but they *would* have been Scots books by a Scots writer, just as the worst of Finnish peasant studies *are* Finnish peasant studies, infinitesimal by the side of Dostoieffski or Tolstoi, but un-Russian in language and content.

Another writer hailed as a great Scots novelist is Mr. Neil Gunn. The acclamation is mistaken. Mr. Gunn is a brilliant novelist from Scotshire who chooses his home county as the scene of his tales. His technique is almost unique among the writers of Scotshire in its effortless efficiency: he moulds beauty in unforgettable phrases—there are things in *The Lost Glen* and *Sun Circle* comparable to the best in the imaginative literature of any school or country. He has probably scarcely yet set out on his scaling of the heights. . . . But they are not the heights of Scots literature; they are not even the pedestrian levels. More in Gunn than in any other contemporary Anglo-Scot (with the exception, perhaps, of George Blake, in a very different category from Gunn, and the finest of the Anglo-Scots realists) the reader seems to sense the haunting

foreignness in an orthodox English; he is the greatest loss to
itself Scottish literature has suffered in this century. Had his
language been Gaelic or Scots there is no doubt of the space
or place he would have occupied in even such short study as
this. Writing in orthodox English, he is merely a brilliantly
unorthodox Englishman.

Once again, a writer who has been hailed as distinctively
Scots, Mrs. Willa Muir. So far she has written only two
novels—*Imagined Corners* and *Mrs. Ritchie*—and both show a
depth and distinction, a sheer and splendidly un-womanly
power which stir even the most jaded of enthusiasms. They
suffer, perhaps, from the author's learnings and erudition-
gatherings in the dull hag-forests of the German psycho-
analysts, just as Neil Gunn's *Sun Circle* suffers from a crude
and out-dated concept of history and the historical processes.
But that psychoanalyst obsession is the common leprosy over
all contemporary European imaginative literature, and Mrs.
Muir's strength of spirit and true integrity of vision may yet
transcend it. She has promise of becoming a great artist. But
a great English artist. The fact that she is Scots herself and
deals with Scots scenes and Scots characters is (to drive home
the point ad nauseam) entirely irrelevant from the point of
view of Scots literature: if she were a modern Mexican writing in Spanish and her scene was Mexico and her peasants
spoke bastardized Nahuatl, would we call it a triumph of
Aztec letters?

Mr. John Buchan has been called the Dean of Scots letters.
Mr. Buchan writes mildly exhilarating romances in the vein
of the late Rider Haggard (though without either Haggard's
magnificent poetic flair or his imaginative grasp), commendable essays on a variety of topics, uninspired if competent
biographies of Sir Walter Scott, the Marquis of Montrose,
and the like distinguished cadaverlitter on the ancient
Scottish scene. He writes it all in a competent, skilful and
depressing English: when his characters talk Scots they do it
in suitable inverted commas: and such characters as do talk

Scots are always the simple, the proletarian, the slightly ludicrous characters.

Mr. Buchan represents no more than the great, sound, bourgeois heart of Scotshire. He has written nothing which has the least connection with Scots literature except a few pieces of verse—if verse *has* any connection with literature. In compiling *The Northern Muse*, however, a representative anthology of Scots 'Vernacular' poetry, he turned aside from other pursuits to render a real service to what might have been his native literary language. Yet even in that service he could envisage Braid Scots as being only a 'vernacular,' the tongue of *a home-reared slave*.

Mrs. Catherine Carswell is among the most interesting of the Anglo-Scots. Her *Life of Robert Burns* was one of the most unique and innocently mendacious studies of the subject ever attempted; her *Savage Pilgrimage* (which met such a sad fate in the teeth of the enraged Mr. Middleton Murry) contributed as little to our knowledge of D. H. Lawrence as it contributed greatly to our knowledge of its author. With such a personality and philosophy much more may be heard of Catherine Carswell: that the philosophy of her school appears a strange and repulsive one, as strange an aberration of the human spirit as history has ever known, merely adds a pathological to a genuine literary interest in her development. Scots letters represses its death-rattle to wave her on with a regretful relief.

Prior to writing *Hatter's Castle*, *Three Loves*, and *Grand Canary* Dr. A. J. Cronin descended five hundred collieries on tours of inspection. As a consequence he is notable for a kind of inky immensity, and an interestingly Latinized barbarization of the English language. While *Hatter's Castle* had a Scots scene its characters were gnomes from the sooty deeps of the less salubrious regions of myth: though acclaimed as great and realistic portraits. In *Three Loves* Dr. Cronin showed a disposition to prove uneasy on the Scottish scene; in *Grand Canary* he escaped it entirely, taking his place (probably a permanent place) among the English writers of an order comparable to Miss Mannin or Mr. Gilbert Frankau. He is also the author of a history of aneurism.

Sir James George Frazer, a Scotsman by birth, is the author of the immense *Golden Bough*, a collection of anthropological studies. The author's methods of correlation have been as crude and unregulated as his industry and the cultivation of his erudition have been immense. The confusion of savage and primitive states of culture commenced by Tylor and his school has been carried to excess in the works of Sir J. G. Frazer. From the point of view of the social historian attempting to disentangle the story of man's coming and growth upon this planet he is one of the most calamitous phenomena in modern research: he has smashed in the ruin of pre-history with a coal-hammer, collected every brick disclosed when the dust settled on the débris, and then labelled the exhibits with the assiduous industry of a literary ant. His pleasing literary style in that labelling is in orthodox English.

Mr. Eric Linklater is a lost Norseman with a disposition to go Berserk amidst the unfamiliar trappings of literary civilization. This disposition came to a head in *The Men of Ness*, a story of the vikings and their raids into the regions of stern guffawdom and unpronunciability. It is a pity that this disposition should be let loose by the author of *Juan in America*,—in the genre of Mark Twain's *Tramp Abroad*, and one of the most acute and amusing picaresque studies ever perpetrated by the literary farceur. It would be even more regrettable if Mr. Linklater hampered his genius by an uneasy adherence to a so-called Scots literary Renaissance.[1]

Miss Muriel Stuart is one of the very few great poets writing in non-experimental English. She has a comprehension and a lyric beauty almost unknown to this English day: the deep passion of her poems in *Christ at Carnival* shines the more finely in that they lack the ornate imagery of Francis Thompson.

[1]This fear has been pleasingly dispelled with the publication of the excellent *Magnus Merriman*.

L

One of the most magic lines in a memory prolific in the waste amusement of collecting magic lines (as is the present writer's) is her '*A thin hail ravened against the doors of dark.*' Miss Stuart, of Scots origin, has been hailed as a great Scots poet, She is as little Scots as Dante.

Yet Miss Stuart's genius brings us at last to consideration of the two solitary lights in modern Scots Literature. They rise from men who are writers in both Scots and in English— very prolific and controversial writers, men occupied with politics and economic questions, poets in the sense that life, not editors or anthologists, demand of them their poetry. But for the fact that this paper has been devoted largely to an argument that should have needed no enforcing, the work of these two would have occupied almost all the space under such heading as Literary Lights. One of these two is Hugh MacDiarmid and the other Lewis Spence.

MacDiarmid's poetry in Braid Scots came upon a world which had grown accustomed to the belief that written Scots was a vehicle for the more flat-footed sentiments of the bothy only; it came upon a world pale and jaded with the breathing and rebreathing in the same room of the same stagnant air of orthodox English. He demonstrated, richly and completely, and continues to demonstrate, the flexibility and the loveliness of that alien variation of the Anglo-Saxon speech which is Braid Scots. The first of MacDiarmid that the present writer encountered was something which still lingers in his mind (unreasonably, considering the magnificent *To Circumjack Cencrastus* or the sweeping majesty of the *Hymns to Lenin*):.

> 'Ae weet forenicht i' the yow-trummle
> I saw yon antrim thing,
> A watergaw wi' its chitterin' licht
> Ayont the on-ding;
> An' I thocht o' the last wild look ye gied
> Afore ye dee'd!

> There was nae reek i' the laverock's hoose
>   That nicht—an' nane i' mine;
> But I hae thocht o' that foolish licht
>   Ever sin' syne;
> An' I think that maybe at last I ken
>   What your look meant then.'

This is probably, in Mr. MacDiarmid's own view, no more than light versification. But it is certainly not English versification; the prisoner behind the polished walls has escaped and engaged himself in the moulding of a curious façade. Mr. Mac-Diarmid, like all great poets, has his in and out moments—some of them disastrous moments; his care to set this planet aright has laid waste some of his finest poems—but, working in that medium of Braid Scots which he calls synthetic Scots, he has brought Scots language into print again as a herald in tabard, not the cap-and-bells clown of romantic versification.

Of an entirely different order, but a genius no less genuine, is Mr. Spence in his Scots poetry. To show the width and sweep of Braid Scots from MacDiarmid to Spence, it is necessary to quote only:

> 'Time that has dinged doun castels and hie toures,
> And cast great crouns like tinsel in the fire,
> That halds his hand for palace nor for byre,
> Stands sweir at this, the oe of Venus's boures,
>
> Not Time himself can dwell withouten floures,
> Though aiks maun fa' the rose shall bide entire;
> So sall this diamant of a queen's desire
> Outflourish all the stanes that Time devours.'

How far these two are isolated phenomena, how far the precursors of a definite school of Scots literature is still uncertain: they have their imitators in full measure: in William Soutar the Elijah of MacDiarmid may yet have an Elisha. When, if ever, the majority of Scots poets—not versifiers—

begin to use Braid Scots as a medium that dream of a Scots literary renaissance may tread the *via terrena* of fulfilment, enriching (in company with orthodox English) the literary heritage of that language of Cosmopolis towards which the whole creation moves.

An experiment of quite a different order from MacDiarmid's writing in synthetic Scots, or Spence's in deliberate excavation in the richness of the antique Scots vocabularies, may be noted here. As already stated, there is no novelist (or, indeed prose writer), worthy of the name who is writing in Braid Scots. The technique of Lewis Grassic Gibbon in his trilogy *A Scots Quair*—of which only Parts I and II, *Sunset Song* and *Cloud Howe*, have yet been published—is to mould the English language into the rhythms and cadences of Scots spoken speech, and to inject into the English vocabulary such minimum number of words from Braid Scots as that re-modelling requires. His scene so far has been a comparatively uncrowded and simple one—the countryside and village of modern Scotland. Whether his technique is adequate to com-pass and express the life of an industrialized Scots town in all its complexity is yet to be demonstrated; whether his peculiar style may not become either intolerably mannered or de-generate, in the fashion of Joyce, into the unfortunate un-intelligibilities of a literary second childhood, is also in question.

For the Gaels, one cannot do better than quote James Barke, the author of *The World his Pillow* and *The Wild MacRaes*, and himself a remarkable Anglo-Gael:

'In Scotland to-day there exists no body of Gaelic culture. In the realms of imaginative literature—in fiction and drama —there is little or no original work in evidence; and what does exist is of poor quality and vitiated by a spineless sentimentality.

'In verse alone the modern Gaelic writer would seem to find a suitable medium for expression—Donald Sinclair (died recently); Duncan Johnston of Islay; John MacFadyen.

MacFadyen, I believe, has it. But here too the output is small and fragmentary and, in quality, perhaps best compared to the Poet's Corner of the provincial press.

'There is no one to-day in any way approaching the stature of the great Gaelic poets: Alasdair MacMhaighistir Alasdair and Duncan Ban MacIntyre—or even Alexander Mac-Donald or Ewan MacColl.

'The reason for the poverty of contemporary Gaelic culture is not difficult to state.

'When the Young Pretender and his Highland forces were defeated on Culloden Moor in 1746, there followed a ruthless military occupation of the Highland. The clan system was broken up and all forms of Gaelic culture were suppressed. The ownership of partly communal land passed into the hands of a small group of private individuals. The land was soon cleared of its human population. With the exception of a few impoverished crofting communities the native Gael became subservient to the dominant land-owning class.

'First military suppression and dictatorship, then economic suppression were the cause of the decay of the Gael and his native Gaelic culture. From the field of Culloden to the first National Government economic, and consequently racial, decay has continued steadily. In the modern capitalist state the Gael finds himself an anachronism—almost an extinct species. The few of them who are articulate turn, therefore, to a hopeless backward looking, backward longing. A decayed economic system, can produce only a decayed culture.

'The present attempts to revive this culture are necessarily doomed to failure. In its hey-day, Gaelic culture was surprisingly beautiful and vital. As part of Scotland's cultural heritage it will survive for its richness and beauty. But a people can no more live on the glories of the past than it can survive on the memories of its last meal.

'The death rattle of Gaelic culture may be amplified by all sorts of bodies and committees. They delude themselves, however, in thinking that by so doing so they are performing an act of resurrection. . . .

'Fionn MacColla, in English, it may be noted, is far away the finest example of the Gaelic influence. In a very profound sense, his English is the finest Gaelic we have.'

Sic itur ad astra.

RELIGION

Definition is the better part of dissertation. Before one sets to a sketch of Religion in Scotland it is well to state what Religion is not. It is not altruism, it is not awe, it is not the exercise of a super-conscious sense. It is not ethics; it is not morality. It is neither the evolution of primitive Fear into civilized Worship nor the deified apprehension of an extra-mundane Terror.

Instead, a Religion is no more than a corpus of archaic science. The origin of Religion was purely utilitarian. Primitives—the food-gatherers, the ancient folk of all the ancient world—knew no religion. Their few and scattered survivors in this and that tiny crinkle of our planet are as happily irreligious as our own remote ancestors. They are without gods or devils, worship or cities, sacrifices or kings, theologies or social classes. Man is naturally irreligious. Religion is no more fundamental to the human character than cancer is fundamental to the human brain.

Man in a Primitive condition is not Man Savage. Confusion of those two distinct cultural phases has led to the ludicrous condition of anthropology and ethnology at the present day—the confusion which produces such eminent Scotsmen as Sir Arthur Keith capable of asserting that racialism is the life-blood of progress. Of a like order and origin are the wordy 'theses' of the various psycho-analyst groups which follow Freud and Jung. Psycho-analysts are our modern supreme specialists in the art of slipshod research.

A Viennese Jew has been haunted from early years by the desire (inhibited) to cut his father's throat. The psychoanalyst, excavating details of this laudable, but abortive intention, turns to such gigantic compendiums of irrelevantly-indexed myth and custom as Sir James G. Frazer's *Golden Bough*. Therein he discovers that parricide was common to Bantu, Melanesian, aboriginal Australian. Ergo, common to primitives: ergo, a fundamental human trait. . . . The fact that Bantus, Melanesians and Australians are not primitives, but savages, peoples who have absorbed religious and social details from alien cultures and transformed their economic organization in harmony with that absorption is either unapprehended or dismissed as unimportant: and we reach back to smear the face of Natural Man with the filth of our own disease.

Particularly is this the case with regard to Religion; and particularly is the truly utilitarian nature of Religion manifested in that long life of three centuries which the Scots people led under the aegis of the Presbyterian churches.

Religion for the Scot was essentially a means of assuring himself life in the next world, health in this, prosperity, wealth, fruitful wombs and harvests. The Auld Kirk in Scotland is the greatest example of an armchair scientific Religion known to the world since the decay of the great State cults of Egypt and Mexico. In the case of all three countries the Gods were both unlovely and largely unloved; and in the case of all three definite discomforts of apparel and conduct were undergone in return for definite celestial favours manifested upon the terrestrial scene. One of those innumerable (and generally nauseating) pulpit stories illustrates this:

'A town minister was on holiday in the country, and consented to act one Sabbath in place of the local incumbent. While he was robing himself in the vestry he was approached by some of the elders, farmers all, and tactfully desired to remember in his prayers a supplication for rain—there had been a considerable drouth. Accordingly, he ascended the pulpit, and in the course of the service prayed that 'the windows of Heaven might be opened to cheer the thirsty ground, and fulfil the earnest hopes of the husbandman.'

'Scarcely had he finished than a flash of lightning was observed through the kirk windows. The growl of thunder followed; and in a few minutes such a downpour of rain as was speedily levelling to the ground the standing crops, and leaving the cornfields ruined and desolate. Ascribing this disastrous phenomenon [very reasonably] to the minister's prayer, one of the farmers remarked as he tramped away through the rain: "That poor fool may be well enough in the town, but God Almighty! the sooner he's out of the country the better for everybody".'

Behind those couthy tales of ministers and kirks, beadles and elders, sessions and sextons, a system operated with a ruthless efficiency for three long centuries. In Scotland the human mind and the human body were in thrall to what the orthodox would call a reign of religion, what the Diffusionist historian recognizes as the reign of a cultural aberration, what the political student might apprehend as a reign of terror. The fears and hopes of long-defunct Levantines, as set forth in the Christian Bible, were accepted as a code of conduct, as a science of life, and foisted upon the Scottish scene without mercy and greatly without favour. This is an attempt at impartial statement, not an expression of anti-Christianity. Had they been the codes of the Korân or the Rig-veda the scene would doubtlessly have been even more farcical objectively, if in subjective essence the same.

Late seventeenth and eighteenth century Scotland saw the domination of the code at its most rigorous. Not only was the Sunday (meticulously then, as still in the meeting-houses of the Free Kirk, misnamed the Sabbath) a day of rigid and

inexorable piety, but the week-days as well were under the
control and spying activities of kirk-session and minister,
beadle—and indeed any odd being with a desire to vex the
lives of his fellow-men. The Sunday in particular was sancti-
fied to an exclusive care with the rites and wraths of the
Scottish Huitzilopochtli—war-god and maize-god in one. In
the *Social Life of Scotland in the Eighteenth Century* a slightly
modernized cleric says of the kirk-officers, beadles and
deacons:

'There was not a place where one was free from their in-
quisitorial intrusion. They might enter any house and even
pry into the rooms. In towns where the patrol of elders or
deacons, beadle and officers, paced with solemnity the deserted causeway eagerly eyeing every door and window, craning
their necks up every close and lane, the people slunk into the
obscurity of shadows and kept hushed silence. So still, so
empty were the streets on a Sunday night that no lamps were
lighted, for no passengers passed by, or if they did they had
no right to walk.'

This was the state of affairs everywhere, not only in small
and obscure parishes. Elders and deacons were empowered
to visit where they liked, to assure themselves that families
were engaged in unsecular interests. If admittance were refused them to a house they could (and very frequently did)
invoke the civil magistrates' aid for breaking in forcibly. They
could impose innumerable fines and penalties. The power of
life and death was in the hands of this great priesthood, the
guardians and functionaries of the science. A minute of the
Edinburgh kirk-session (from *The King's Pious Proclamation*
(1727)) says:

'Taking into consideration that the Lord's Day is profaned
by people standing in the streets, vaguing in the fields and
gardens, as also by idly gazing out at windows, and children

and apprentices playing in the streets, warn parents and threaten to refer to the Civil Magistrates for punishment, also order each Session to take its turn in watching the streets on Sabbath, as has been the laudable custom of this city, and to visit each suspected house in each parish by elders and deacons, with beadle and officers, and after sermon, when the day is long, to pass through the streets and reprove such as transgress, and inform on such as do not refrain'.

During the week the minister might notify any member of his congregation that he intended to visit him in his own house and hold a 'catechizing' of his family. This 'catechizing' consisted of a play of question and answer on knowledge of the Christian Scriptures, the Christian Code of the Good Life, and the Christian Code of Eternal Punishment. Everyone was questioned in rote—the master, the mistress, the children, and all the servants within the gates. Those who failed to answer according to the code might be rebuked or punished, according to the nature of the offence; those who failed to put in an appearance at those ceremonies of droned affirmation and incantation might be very bitterly prosecuted. Until well towards the nineties of last century the officials of the Scots priesthood were the real rulers of the Scots scene, they were Spartan ephors, largely elected by the people and keeping the people under a rigorous rule. And then the rank blossomings of Industrialism loosened their hold, weakened their status, and freed Scotland from the nightmare of their power.

It is obvious that any people under the rule of such rigorous and robidding code—belief in a joyless but necessary agricultural God, belief in a joyless but necessary ceremonial ritual—would develop strange abnormalities of appearance and behaviour. It is evident in the ancient scene in Mexico, for example, where every year thousands of human beings were sacrificed to the Gods of the earth and rain, that a few more hundred years of evolution along the same lines would have wrought a biological deviation from the human norm: the ancient Mexicans, but for the fortunate arrival of Cortes, would have aberrated into a sub-species of *Homo Sapiens*. The same may be said of the Scots. Left alone and uninvaded, they might have passed entirely beyond the orbit of the normally human but for the coming of the Industrial Revolution. This brought Scotland its slums and its Glasgow, its great wens of ironworks and collieries upon the open face of the countryside; but its final efflorescence broke the power of the Church and released the Scot to a strange and terrible and lovely world, the world of science and scepticism and high belief and free valour—emerging into the sunlight of history from a ghoul-haunted cañon.

There is still a Church of Scotland—ostensibly more powerful then ever, having recently amalgamated with its great rival, the United Free Church. There are still innumerable ministers of the Kirk to be met with in the leafy manse walks, the crowded Edinburgh streets, the gatherings of conferences and associations and the like. There is still the trickle of the kirkward folk on a Sabbath morning in summer, when the peewits hold their unending plaint over the greening fields and the young boys linger and kick at the thistles by the wayside, and young girls step daintily down whin-guarded paths and over the cow-dung pats by this and that gate. There is still the yearly Assembly of the Kirk in Edinburgh—the strangest of functions, with the High Commissioner some vague politican generally discreetly unintelligible and inevitably discreetly unintelligent; with elderly clergymen acclaiming War 'for the good of the nation,' the sword the weapon of Christianity, the economic crisis an Apollyon to be moved by prayer. There are still old women and men who find sustenance and ease and comfort in the droned chantings of the risen God, in symbolic cannibal feastings upon the body of the dead God at time of Communion. . . .

But it is little more now than a thin and tattered veil upon the face of the Scottish scene. This ostensibly powerful Kirk, twin-headed, is riven with the sorriest of all disputes—a quarrel over meal and milk. For the old United Frees will not give up their own ministers and kirks in favour of the Auld Kirk ministers and kirks; nor vice versa. So in most parishes there are still to be found two churches in close proximity, staffed by ministers preaching exactly the same doctrine, ministers preaching to congregations of twenty or so in buildings erected to house a hundred. But the ministers themselves—of manse and walk and street and conference—are of strangely different quality and calibre to those who manned the Kirk in the mid-eighteenth century.

There are few such pleasant people as the younger ministers of Scotland. Pleasant is the one possible adjective. They are (the most of them) free-hearted and liberal, mild socialists, men with pleasant wives who blush over the books of such writers as myself, but read them nevertheless and say pleasant things about the pleasant passages. But the older generation differs from the younger very greatly. It has run to girth and very often to grossness. It grins with unloosened vest. Its congregation grins dourly in comprehension. It is, in the country parishes, the understood thing that the middle-aged, genial minister generally 'sleeps with' his housekeeper —a proceeding, I remember, which greatly astonished my innocent youth, for why should a man like the minister want to sleep with anyone when he had a big, fine bed of his own? The most luscious of filthy tales (with women the butt and object of each and the sex-act the festering focal point) I have ever heard were from the lips of a highly respected and reputable minister of the Church of Scotland who still preaches to an exclusive congregation in one of the Four Cities. The minister a minister at the beginning of the present century had been greatly freed from the fears and tabus that formerly inhered in the functioning of his office, but had obtained no such measure of mental freedom and enlightenment as his younger colleague of to-day.

And that kirkwards trickle of the folk is delusive as well. Here you behold not the fervid Presbyterian but the bored (if complacent) farmer and his wife attending a mild social function. They are going to church because there is nothing much else to be done on a Sunday; they can meet a neighbour there and ask him to supper; the wife will survey with some interest a neighbouring wife's hat or the advances yet another neighbour is making in exhibition of her stages of pregnancy. The old fires and the old fears are gone. Men and women sit and listen with a placid benignancy to sermons as varied in opinion and scope as are the political reaches between fascism and communism . . . and they are quite unstirred. It is something quite unconcerned with their everyday life of factory and field and hope and fear, it is something to amuse the wife and good for the children. . . . Why good? They are vague.

And though some of those children reluctantly holding kirkwards, reluctantly seated in those unpadded pews and staring with desperate earnestness at the buzzing busyness of a fly seeking to escape through the panes of a glazed window, may indeed have strange fears and dark terrors upon them, fears that awaken them screaming in the nights with this horrific God thrusting them into sizzling pits of fire because of some minor lapse of the previous day, fears that make lonely wood walks a terror, every screech of an owl the cry of some devil or gnome from the pages of Christian myth, yet their numbers are probably few. It is still a terrible and a dreadful thing that the minds of a nation's youth should be twisted and debased by those ancient, obscene beliefs and restraints; yet, good democrats, we may rejoice that it is now only the minds of the minority—the intelligent minority—that so suffer. And they are growing up into habitation of a world that will presently look back upon even the emasculated rites of the Kirk of Scotland as insanely irrelevant to human affairs as the Black Mass.

Nor does the yearly General Assembly resemble (as once)

the Sanhedrin of the Jews. To a large extent it is the excuse and occasion for much tea-drinking and the exchange of views on theological scholarship, rose-growing, and the meaner scandals. Its public speeches have an unexciting monotone of supplication and regret: the young are leaving the Kirk, how may they be reclaimed? The tides of irreligion and paganism are flooding in upon us: how may they be stayed? A similar tidal problem once confronted King Canute. It is recorded that he used denunciation with singular lack of success, and modern experience appears to verify the historical precedent. The pedestrian who pauses midway across a meadow and seeks to stay a charging bull by alternately denouncing its brutish appearance and calling upon it to forgo its essential bullishness is unlikely to survive the occasion for a sufficient length of time to draw up an unimpassioned monograph on the subject.

Occasionally (as has been noted) the Assembly abandons the pagans and turns to consideration of such pressing matters as unemployment, war, and the economic system. In the case of the first and the last it is, (very naturally and to some extent blamelessly, for it is the assembly of ministers of a State Religion) impotent. More diversity of talent and opinion greets the subject of war. Padded elderly gentlemen with cheerfully carmine cheeks and grey whiskers uphold the Sword as the Weapon of Righteousness, used aforetime by Scotland in defence of her liberties: may not Scotland need the Sword again? A sad commentary on the relation of the Assembly to contemporary military science lies in the fact that no opponent appears to have suggested the archaic character of the sword in modern warfare. Why not the Saw-Toothed Bayonet of Salvation? Why not the Gas of God? . . . Vexed from that humble impartiality which is his aim the investigator toys with a vision of the plump, rosy parson in the dirty grey pallor of a gas attack—Lewisite for preference. He sees the rosy cheeks cave in, the eyes start forth like those of a hamstrung pig, the mouth move vomiting as the gas bites into lung-tissues. He turns with a vagrant sigh from that vision: that sight in actuality would almost be worth another War.

That many of the old and the middle-aged of both sexes find comfort in the Kirk and its ceremonies is undeniable. And this brings us to a fine human essence in the relationship of Kirk and people that may not be abandoned on recognition of the archaic nature of the rites of Communion and the like. That comfort was and is sometimes very real. The bitterly toilworn and the bitterly oppressed have been often sustained and cheered and uplifted for the cheerless life of the day to day by the lovely poetry of the Bible, the kindly and just and angrily righteous things therein. They have found inspiration and hope in the sayings and denunciations of some Jewish prophet long powder and nothing, but one who, like them, had doubted life because of its ills and cried on something beyond himself to redress the sad balance of things, to feed the hungry and put down the oppressor. The humble and the poor have found the Kirk and kirk life not only a grinding and a mean oppressiveness, they have found (and find) ministers who are cheerful and helpful beings, with or without their theology, knowledgeable men in medicine and times of stress, champions against lairds and factors and such-like fauna. They have found in the kirk itself, in the blessed peace and ease of a two hours rest in the pews, listening to the only music they ever hear, refreshment and good feeling. If it has chastised the free and rebellious and wrought many bitter things upon the Scots spirit the Kirk has yet atoned in those little ways.

For they are little ways. A contented helot is not a freeman; a bitterly-oppressed and poverty-stricken serf is still a serf though you tell him tales in an idle hour and bind his worse hurts and sooth his worse fears of night and the dark that comes down on us all. The Kirk of Scotland, the Religion of the Kirk of Scotland, on its credit balance has done no more than that. It has tamed and clipped and sometimes soothed: it has used the sword often enough: after 1600 it used upon the people of Scotland themselves. Its policy and its code in the seventeenth and eighteenth centuries produced that Scot who was our ancestor: the Scot who had mislaid original thought for a dour debating of fine theological points, who was more concerned to applaud the spirited conduct of Elijah with the bears than to guard his own economic freedom, who at twenty, married, looked on the clean lusts and desires of the marriage bed as shameful and disgusting things; who tormented in a pit of weariness his young children, Sabbath on Sabbath, with the learning by rote of dull and unintelligible theological chatter from a book that can be as painfully wearying as it can be painfully enthralling; who looked forward to 'catechizings' with a clownish zest or a clownish fear; who mislaid beauty and tenderness and love of skies and the happy life of beasts and birds and children for the stern restraints, the droning hymns and the superhuman endurances demanded of the attendants at Kirk service; whose social life revolved round the comings and goings, sayings and preachings, rebukings and praisings of priests who were often dull and foolish and froward men, often good and dull and bewildered men; who, a logician, passed a sinner to the grave and therefore to hell and those zestful burnings beloved of the Presbytery.

Naturally there were sceptics throughout that era, very cautious but biting sceptics:

'There was a Cameronian cat
　A-seeking for its prey,
Went ben the hoose and caught a moose
　Upon the Sabbath day.

The Elders, they were horrified
　And they were vexèd sair,
Sae straight they took that wicked cat
Afore the meenistair.

M

The meenistair was sairly grieved
And much displeased did say:
'Oh, bad perverted pussy-cat
    Tae break the Sabbath day!

'The Sabbath's been, frae days o' yore,
    An Institution:
Saw straichtway tak' this wicked cat
    Tae Execution!'

Release from the secular power of the Kirk, or secular en-
forcement of the Kirk's displeasure, had effects on the Scots
similar to those that sunlight and wine might have on a
prisoner emerging from long years in a dank cellar. Freedom
had been forbidden him: he became the conscienceless
anarchist in politics, in commerce, in private affairs. Love of
women and the glorying in it had been forbidden him: the
modern Scot, escaping that tabu, is still fascinated and horrified by sex. He has seen it swathed in dirty veils of phrase and
sentiment so long that now he would expose it for the ludicrous and lewd and ridiculous thing he conceives it must be:
Scots in conversation, Scots novelists in their books these
modern days are full of details of sex and the sex-act, crude
and insanitary details. . . . They have escaped the tabu and
sought the reality and stumbled into a midden on the way.
An aphasia of the spirit has descended on the Scot so that he
can see only the foul in a thing that is neither foul nor fair,
that is jolly and necessary and amusing and thrilling and
tremendous fun and a deadly bore and exhilarating to the
point of making one sing and dreadful to the point of making
one weep. . . .

This is where the effects of Presbyterianism join issue with
the effects of the other Religions which dwindlingly survived in Reformed Scotland. Catholicism was more mellow
and colourful and poetic: it was also darker and older and
more oppressed by even more ancient shames. It produced

an attitude of mind more soft than the Presbyterian: and also infinitely more servile. Sex has always been a tabu and shameful thing to the Catholic mind, a thing to be *transmuted*—in the fashion of gathering a lovely lily from its cheerful dung and transmuting it into a glassy ornament for a sterile altar. Episcopalianism is in a different category. From the first it was more a matter of social status than of theological conviction; it was rather a grateful bourgeois acknowledgement of Anglicization than dissent with regard to the methods of worshipping a God. A typical Episcopalian was Sir Walter Scott—shallow and sedulous, incurably second-rate, incapable (so had his spirit-stuff been moulded) of either delineating the essentials of human character or of apprehending the essentials of human motivation. The Episcopalian Church in Scotland gave to life and ritual mildly colourful trappings, a sober display: it avoided God with a shudder of genteel distaste.

The modern Free Church member is the ancient Presbyterian who has learned nothing and forgotten nothing. As certain unfortunate children abandon mental development at the cretinaceous age of eight, Free Church doctrine, essentially un-Christian, abandoned development with the coming of the Kelts. It is a strange and disgusting cult of antique fear and antique spite. It looks upon all the gracious and fine things of the human body—particularly the body of woman—with sickened abhorrence, it detests music and light and life and mirth, the God of its passionate conviction is a kind of immortal Peeping Tom, an unsleeping celestial sneak-thief, it seeks to cramp and distort the minds of the young much as the ancient Maya sought to mould the brainstuff of *their* young by deforming the infants' heads with the aid of tightly-strapped slats of wood. As fantastically irrelevant to contemporary Scottish affairs as the appendix is to the human body, its elimination may be brought about rather by advances in social hygiene than by surgical operation.

Debating those elementary facts with regard to Religion

in Scotland the present writer before this time has met with
the surprising complaint: 'And what is going to happen now?
What are you going to put in the place of Religion?' The
question shows some confusion of mind. The present writer
had no hand in bringing about the decay of Religion; nor,
alas, is he likely to have any hand in planning its succession.
That succession lies with great economic and historical
movements now in being—movements which may bring to
birth the strangest of progeny on which we may look aghast.
Of the future of Religion ultimately the historian can have
little doubt: he sees its coming in ancient times, in the world
of the Simple Men, as a cortical abortion, a misapprehension
of the functions and activities of nature interlarded and interwoven with attributes mistakenly applied to human rulers.
He sees its passing from the human scene—even the Scots
scene—in the processes of change, immutable and unstay-
able. But—

But there may be long delays in that passing. Another
abortion of inactive brains—that of Fascism—looms over a
tormented world, a creed of the *must* jungle brute, the cowardly degenerate who fears the fine steely glimmer of the
open spaces of the heavens, the winds of change, the flow and
cry of strange seas and stars in human conduct and human
hope—who would drag men back into economic night, into
slavery to the state, into slavery (all slaveries aid his purpose)
to the archaic institutions of Religion. What has happened in
Italy and Germany may happen in Scotland. The various
Scots nationalist parties have large elements of Fascism
within them. There is now a definite Fascist Party. If ever
such philosophy should reach to power then again we may
see deserted streets of a Sabbath, crowded kirks, persecutions
and little parish tyrannies, a Free Kirk ministers's millenial
dream. If such should be the play of chance it is to be hoped
that the historian (albeit himself on the way to the scaffold
or the pillory) will look on the process with a cool dispassion,
seeing it as no more than a temporary deviation, a thing that

from its nature cannot endure. Man has survived this disease far too long either to perish in its last bout of fever or permanently retire into delirium tremens.

One sees rise ultimately (in that perfect state that is an ultimate necessity for human survival, for there is no sure half-way house between Utopia and extinction) in place of Religion—Nothing. To return to clinical similes, one does not seek to replace a fever by an attack of jaundice. One seeks the fields and night and the sound of the sea, the warmth of good talk and human companionship, love, wonder in the minute life of a water-drop, exultation in the wheeling Galaxy. All these fine things remain and are made the more gracious and serene and unthreatened as Religion passes. Passing, it takes with it nothing of the good—pity and hope and benevolence. Benevolence is as natural to Natural Man as hunger. It is an elementary thalamic state, a conditioned reflex of mental and physical health.

Yet, because men are not merely the victims, the hapless leaves storm-blown, of historic forces, but may guide if they cannot generate that storm, it might be well to glance at this last at those members of the various Scots priesthoods who affirm their liberalism, their belief in change, their faith that in a purified Christianity is the strait and undeniable way to that necessary Utopia. One cannot but believe that this is a delusion:

> 'Thou, in the day that breaks thy prison,
>   People, though these men take thy name,
> And hail and hymn thee rearisen,
>   Who made songs erewhile of thy shame,
> Give thou not ear; for these are they
>   Whose good day was thine evil day.
>
> Set not thine hand upon their cross.
>   Give not thy soul up sacrificed.
> Change not the gold of faith for dross

Of Christian creeds that spit on Christ.
Let not thy tree of freedom be
Regrafted from that rotting tree.'

But, if the investigator should stoop to point a moral, he
would do so rather in the tale of the Laird of Udny's fool
than in heroic rhyme. Of Jamie Fleeman, the reputed fool of
the parish, many a tale is told; and the best is that which
relates how, of all kirks in Scotland, Udny suffered the
worst from sleepy congregations. Hardly had the sermon
begun than heads began to nod. One Sunday the minister—
a new minister—looked down in the course of his discourse
and saw only one member of the congregation awake, and
that Jamie Fleeman.

Halting his sermon the minister exclaimed: 'This sleeping
in church is intolerable. There's only one man awake; and
that man's a fool!' 'Ay, ay, minister, you're right there,'
called up Jamie in reply. 'And if I hadn't been a fool I'd have
been sleeping as well.'

MITCHELL: ARBUTHNOTT
SCHOOL ESSAY BOOK
(SELECTIONS)

Editor's note

The survival of the earliest manuscripts of the writer who
came to be known as Lewis Grassic Gibbon is due to the
happy foresight of a village schoolmaster. Alexander Gray,
Leslie Mitchell's dominie at Arbuthnott School, was a life-
long friend as well as an important formative influence in the
boy's development and interest in a literary career. Mr Gray
who died in 1968 affirmed that these exercise books con-
taining the essays were the only ones he ever kept, and
he kept them for more than fifty years.

There is a variety and vitality in these pieces which make
them not only biographically pertinent but interesting in
their own right. They show remarkable imagination for a
thirteen year old boy who had never been away from that
lonely Mearns landscape. Already there is evidence of a deep
awareness of his own land, and of a search for words to record
it. A perceptive eye and an ear for a telling phrase are noticeable and there are early intimations in style and material of
the later efforts of both English and Scottish 'cousins'.

The following selections from 'Essay Book kept by James
Leslie Mitchell, Arbuthnott School, 1914' form part of the
story of the emergence of a writer.

[1] Mr. Alexander Gray died at Stonehaven in June 1968.

ARBUTHNOTT

On a fine, clear, sunny day, anyone at Arbuthnott School (if he has any sense of beauty in him at all), cannot help being enchanted with the beautiful scenery around him. In front stretches a sea of green, intersected here and there with small square fields, or a winding road disappearing in the waving masses of foliage. The view of the 'Silver Bervie', and the old antiquated church is cut off, but above the huge pines, and waving beeches, may be seen a solitary column of smoke, from Arbuthnott House. Turn to the east, down the long white winding road, past the dark clump of trees, to where lie the various fields, moors, and hills, belonging to the farms of Kirkton, Pitcarles, and Allardice. Beyond these, one may catch a glimpse of the town of Bervie, with its smoking factories, and a few fishing-boats dotting the sea beyond—To the north the view is more limited, except where the distant hills may be seen, covered with yellow broom.

THE HARVEST

Everything around seemed to acclaim harvest. The wide fields of waving corn, gleaming yellow in the morning sunshine, the sharp click! click! of the binder, the voice of the driver calling his horses, who seem greatly to relish a few mouthfulls of ripe grain and the busy workmen rapidly 'stooking' (I think that's the way you spell it) the sheaves— all of them acclaim the same thing. Zip! Zip! the rain begins to descend with the suddenness of a summer shower, but it soon passes, and the farmer, much relieved to see that it was only a 'bit shoorey' informs the men to 'stick in' again. That is generally the way the first cutting proceeds. Then comes the leading, and although I admire the thistle as Scotland's emblem, I can't say the same of it in connection with 'bigging' a cart.

BERVIE

There are two things especially noticeable about Bervie; the unlimited confidence of the inhabitants in their own ability; and secondly their pride in being townspeople of a Royal Burgh. How it became a royal burgh there is no very accurate account; although most of the 'citizens' have a vague notion that it was through a certain King David (but which King David, no one even professes to guess) who when wrecked off the Bervie coast, was rescued by some of the villagers and in return made Bervie there and then a Royal Burgh. But, still, there are a good many attractions about Bervie, especially the Bridge, which though not very long, is of considerable height. Indeed I think I once heard an urchin affirm that 'It wis the highest in Scotlan'.' The most unpleasant thing about Bervie is its smoking wincey factories, and its ear-splitting horns; the latter especially to the workers.

AUTOBIOGRAPHY OF A RIVER

Thank goodness! I've arrived here at last, although the salt waters of the Pacific do not exactly suit me! What am I? I'm what mortals call an obscure tributary of my big brother the Amazon. I'm several hundreds of years old, but well I remember the day—no it was at night—I sprang out of one of the Andes Mountains. Down the rocks I went! until I found the dry hollow where a cousin of mine had flowed, long before. At first my journey lay through a mountainous district, called Peru, where I witnessed mortals (or men) fighting against each other, some of whom wore armour, and had guns, others which were dressed in skins, ornamented with gold (they were, I afterwards learned, called Span-iards and Incas). On I went past huts, houses, and temples, being here and there, reinforced by a distant relation. Just as I was about to enter a huge forest, a curious beast called an alligator, waddled down to my bank, and made a grab at one of my tenants, a cowfish! One day as I was passing through a part of Amaxonia (Brazil) a dug-out canoe, filled with four men, stark naked, had the impertinence to cross over me, without leave, too! Angry at the intrusion, I caught the boat in my arms, and flung it against a rock, where it was dashed to pieces. I fear I would but weary you, mortal, for men (and women) are easily wearied, if I were to tell you all the thrilling things I saw and did. For I have passed through deep, dark, canyons, flooded the swampy lowlands, and carried both the Cashimbo's canoe, and the Portugese steamboat, but one thing I'm always disappointed in—I don't know my name!

POWER

What an irresistible feeling of power, comes over one—at least it has with me—when, on a calm, clear night, you gaze up at the millions of glistening worlds and constellations, which form the Milky Way. . . . 'Tis then—and then only— that one can realize the full power of the Creator . . . and the truth of the wild dream of the German poet; 'There is no beginning—yea, even as there is no end!'

Again, in the case of the earthquake that mighty up-heaval of Nature, still unsatisfactorily accounted for—as is the cause of volcanic eruptions—what mighty evidence of power there is in that demon, which wrecks all Man's paltry works —of hundreds of years—in a few minutes!

The power of mesmerism possessed by some persons is astounding—and dangerous. Anyone who possesses this uncanny gift, can—except in the case of an individual with a very strong will—force him, or her to conceive almost anything, at his command.

ARBUTHNOTT CHURCH

Forty years ago! What changes, Arbuthnot, 'midst thy 'shaggy woods' since I, a little boy, used to steal the minister's apples, and munch them by the Bervie's side! But where was the old school? I jumped off my cycle (not however with the agility with which I used to race down the hill, on the old 'clank-and-growl', which was the envy of my schoolmates and the pride of my heart) and proceeded to investigate. Through the open gate I passed, and sauntered slowly through the old churchyard. Alas! many a grave, and many a stone, had been added, since last I was there. Still, however I recognised many of the monuments, especially the small dilapidated stone which I had wondered at so often, when a child. 'In memory of C.G.C. and also of her husband John Douglas Grant Miltone, merchant, Inbervie.'—'He did his duty' . . .(!) There was little change in the church itself, except the wing which had been burned and of which I had already heard. Still the belfry was in the same place, and well I remembered the ear-splitting noise that same bell had!

MITCHELL:
UNPUBLISHED POEMS
(SELECTIONS)

Editor's note

Leslie Mitchell's poetic aspirations were of surprisingly long duration. He had written long poems before he was seventeen, and continued his attempts to write poetry after he had become a successful prose writer. It must be recognised that in this field the ambition outweighed the achievement. He was unsuccessful as a poet—indeed no poem was accepted for publication. Yet there was promise enough to prompt J. C. Squire when editor of *The London Mercury* to write: 'I can see that this fellow has stuff in him and will write prose; the poems just fall short.'

The faults and flaws in Mitchell's poetry are obvious, but they do contain at least a foretaste of his later 'poetry in prose'. Those selected from a fairly extensive unpublished collection have been chosen mainly on account of the significance of theme or style on the writer's development.

Comparisons between *Vision* and the closing paragraphs of *Grey Granite* and between the poem *Spartacus* and the later novel of the same name are particularly fascinating, but there are other parallels of interest.

IN EXILE

Chill through the dull, white night
The bare trees shiver,
Where long, dead, crackling grasses stand
Along the river.

Strident the voice of frogs
In marshes by;
And from the far sand-dunes
A jackal's wailing cry.

A little wind moans low
Amongst the eaves,
And showers with sudden taps
Dead almond leaves.

Sleepless, I lie and hear
The mid-night call;
Hear the quick, breathless hush
Ere pattering rain-drops fall.

You in my thoughts the while,
Tender and dear:
With all the darkness warm and exquisite
Your Dream-Self near,

(When all the unhappy times
Are dead and gone:
Dream-lips I'll kiss no more, O Shadow Love!
But your dear own.)

Out of the darkness, softly shod, you come
With perfumed hair;
Hands that are warmly trembling to the touch,
And bosom bare.

And bending low (as once of old you did)
With slender grace,
Like dew to thirsting desert sands, I feel
Your kiss upon my face.

And know, when comes the first still glint of dawn,
Grey-barred and clear—
Your soul has crossed the sund'ring leagues of sea
And loved me here!

LUDD
FEBRUARY 1922

THE LOVERS

5th June 1926

The thousand lamps of the stars shall be ours,
    And the wind's voice singing, and the sun's light,
Music of earth shall haunt our dreaming hours.
    We'll sleep and wake, turn in the kindly night.

Each unto each, and know the other there,
    And kiss in dreams, and sleep with even breath:
We've paid to peace in pain and sick despair,
    We've made to Life the sacrifice of Death.

We shall pass on: of those we shall forget
    In the press of years, in newer sadness.
Yet sometimes, when the lights of night are set,
    Then shall we remember them with gladness,

For that they gave, and bring in tears again,
    The love that makes our hearts remember then.

RONDEL

Ere youth be dead we'll ride the road again,
  The winding windward ways of Sunstone men—
Under torn stars, a moon volcano red,
  Clangour of ringing storm on mountain head—
    Ere youth be dead.

Ere youth be dead we'll ship by saffron seas,
  By shoreless sands and lost Symplegades—
Where through in ancient years the Argo sped
  Behind the dove that flashed and dipped and lead—
    Ere youth be dead.

Ere youth be dead we'll dread their love and lust—
  The dead world's springtime in the blowing dust,
The drying voices of the summers fled—
  Drink Lethe's draught and feed on dreams for bread
    Ere youth be dead.

VIGNETTE

The land was drowned in drowsy scent, I mind,
  Of clover, that last evening, and the hedge,
Drooped in the glare: The river's eddies spun
  And slept amidst the sedge.

Nothing we said, for we had naught to say:
  Quietly you wept: the curlews called; the brown
Slow night came on: I stood with tearless eyes
  And watched the sun go down.

N

VISION

We who have seen it when the scented year
Fades, and the leaves are touched of Autumn's hand,
And, quieter than a dream of summer days,
Death comes unto the russet, fruitful land:
When out against the windy skies of eve
A lap-wing wheels with wild and eery call,
And in the fir-wood's fern-strewn fortresses
      The sunset's shadows fall,

Thereafter walk as those with eyes unsealed,
Knowing that we behold the Hand of Change
Made manifest; and far by utmost line
Of sky and sea and cliff and bracken range,
The Vision, touched, intangible, hath passed,
Setting a sign for eyes of gods and men:
That that which is shall fade and die and fall,
      And Springtide comes again!

A LAST NIGHTFALL

      Swiftly,
Out of the mystery of waters,
The spuming night-tide
      Climbs;
      Abruptly,
Far in the brown dusk-stillness
A village night-bell
      Chimes;
      Right
Overhead, through heav'n's rent bars,
      Night
Like a bellying beast,
      Hangs,
Fanged with stars.

                    Here,
Where the grey rocks shake,
And the homing breakers
                    Beat,
                    Fear
Hath fled before Death
And our salt-sad kisses,
                    Sweet!
                    Nigh
Is the tide, and Life's light
                    Put by
As a candle quenched,
                    A ghost
Lost in the night.

DUST

I have drunk deeply of the ancient wine,
    Wandered a summer in the Sumer land,
Heard in the dusk the bells of Cretan kine
    And maidens song across the Cnossan strand,
Seen, where the grotesque temples groped to God,
    The sculptor-scribe who carved the Runic plan
Of suns and sames and serpents intertrod,
    On terraces of Toltec Yucatan.

I hear new voices down the English morn,
    And alien laughter by the lakeland meres,
And altars reared to faiths undreamt, unborn,
    Far in the seed-time of the sleeping years—

I see the Christ, an outcast, stand forlorn,
    A dream, a tale, a wonderment of tears.

SPARTACUS

O thou who lived for Freedom when the Night
   Had hardly yet begun: when little light
Blinded the eyes of men, and dawntime seemed
   So far and faint—a foolish dream half-dreamed!
Through the blind drift of days and ways forgot
   Thy name, thy purpose: these have faded not!
From out the darkling heavens of misty Time
   Clear is thy light, and like the Ocean's chime
Thy voice. Yea, clear as when unflinchingly
   Thou ledst the hordes of helotry to die
And fell in glorious fight, nor knew the day
   The creaking crosses fringed the Appian Way—

Sport of the winds, O ashes of the Strong!
   But down the aeons roars the helots' song
Calling to battle. Long as on the shore
   The washing tides shall crumble cliff and nore
Remembered shalt thou be who dauntless gave
   Unto the world the lordship of the slave!

MITCHELL:
SHORT STORIES
(SELECTIONS)

Editor's note

Following his discharge from the Royal Army Service Corps in March 1923 Leslie Mitchell attempted to earn his living as a freelance journalist. This spell as a civilian was a disastrously unsuccessful one—in retrospect he wrote: 'For six months I nearly starved to death.'

The solution was to rejoin the Services—on the last day of August 1923 Mitchell enlisted as a clerk in the Royal Air Force. His literary ambitions had not been dimmed by adversity, and he determined to use his spare time for writing. Within a year he achieved success through the medium of a short-story competition in *T.P.'s and Cassell's Weekly*. He won first prize with the story *Siva Plays The Game* which was printed in the issue for October 18, 1924.

In announcing the result the Editor observed:
The adjudicators are unanimous in awarding the first prize to Leslie Mitchell, Headquarters No. 6 Group, Royal Air Force, Kenley, Surrey, for his story entitled *Siva Plays The Game*. Mr. Mitchell submitted two other MSS—all three, by the way, bearing the modest and laconic instruction 'if unacceptable, please destroy'—and while they were unable to include either of these others in their final selection, the adjudicators declare their confident belief that in Mr. Mitchell has been found a new author with a future before him as a writer of short stories.

Despite this appreciation, and the 'confident belief' that the future so fully justified the main interest of the reprinted story is historical rather than literary—it was in effect the author's first published work.

The optimism of the adjudicators was not a guarantee of immediate success, and there was a bitter struggle and prolonged delay before any other of Mitchell's stories appeared in print. His experience with *For Ten's Sake* was typical. It had been rejected by many magazines before being commended by H. G. Wells, and even after the great man's approval it was submitted to and declined by 'more magazines than I had ever heard of' to use Mitchell's own words.

Eventually the story went to Dr. Leonard Huxley whose reaction was simply expressed. 'Mr. Wells is right. Yours is an excellent story, excellently told.' In due course *For Ten's Sake* appeared in the *Cornhill Magazine* and was followed by a cycle of twelve stories on the general theme *Polychromata*. These were reprinted later in the volume *Calends of Cairo* with a preface by Dr. Huxley and an Introductory Note by H. G. Wells.

Mitchell drew on his Middle East experiences for these tales, but his Cairo background is heightened and elaborated to the point of incredibility and fantasy on more than one occasion. Compensation for the general air of unreality is found in glimpses of an experiment in reproducing the idioms of native speech which achieved greater success in his later Scottish work.

SIVA PLAYS THE GAME

If George Menteith Elvar de Selincourt had written this
story before he went to the Sahara and fell into the second
last chapter of one of his own best-sellers, he would have
opened out somewhat in the following fashion:

Dusk was falling upon the ancient town of Siva—a brown,
Oriental dusk, scented and wonderful. To east and west the
mysterious Sahara was a-play with ruddy shadows, so that
the whole effect reminded the solitary traveller of a shaken
sea of blood. Far up, from the blue minarets of a mosque, a
muezzin stretched out his arms and called the Faithful to
prayer, to the unceasing witness that God was One.

'Allah il allah! Allahu akhbar! . . .'

Inevitably.

*　　　*　　　*

The dirty brown huts of the Sivan oasis were sweltering in
the evening heat. From one of them uprose the strains of a
cracked and ancient gramophone—to the accompaniment
of the heart-broken howls of such pariah dogs as wandered
near. In his sweetmeat dukkan by the Southern Gate the
Sheikh Ohmed Kheyn slumbered perspiringly, what time
his daughter Zöe, veiled and bored, attended to casual
customers.

Such daubs for the setting. Meantime, three miles away
to the north, poetic justice, a camel, and Selim Hanna had

succeeded in bearing George Menteith Elvar de Selincourt within view of it.

Garlanded all over with prickly heat, the noted English novelist halted his camel, wiped his brow, pursed his distinctly shoggly little mouth and regarded Siva with loathing.

Now, it is a fact capable of proof that when one creates a world which others take on trust—even though that world's being is resultant only on the incestuous union of a Baedaker and a foreign phrase-book—belief in the creation's actual existence is almost inevitable for its own author. So at least with George. When the leaping sales of 'Purple Sands' (38th ed), 'The Yellow Silence' (40th ed.), and other popguns of a similar calibre had at length provided him with wealth beyond the paring of any publisher's avarice, he had set out to visit the lands he had portrayed to such profit. Result: before him, Siva; behind, far off the beaten tourist track, three weeks in which the whole Cosmos had seemed to deliberately plan his disillusionment.

If you get the mentality of the man, he felt actually insulted. For Arabs were neither hawk-nosed nor handsome; as a rule their faces appeared to have been flattened with shovels, and their bodies were covered with festering sores. Moreover, they were neither grave nor fanatical; on the contrary they seemed generally as uproarious as Welshmen at an Eisteddfod or Scotsmen at a haggis-orgy—and quite as unintelligible. His guide Selim read Haeckel and spoke disparagingly of the Prophet's knowledge of biology. And no wonderful maidens sang at eve beside the pillars of a civilization buried in the sand . . .

Which was all exceedingly upsetting.

'Khawaga,' the voice of Selim, who sat on his camel a little way off and regarded the home of his fathers dispassionately, broke in on George's blurred musings. 'We would better get a move on, what?' George felt that to be the last straw.

*   *   *

Siva that night went en fête, the wherefore being that Selim Hanna, son of the Sheikh Ohmed Kheyn, had come back from his travels.

From birth Selim had been of an inquiring and inquisitive turn; so when, eight years before his return as the dragoman of the Khawaga Jorj, he had stolen a camel and set out to see the world, no one had been particularly surprised or grieved—excepting the man who owned the camel, and Selim's half-sister, Zöe. The mother of the latter had been a Greek, bartered from Khartoum to Kano in the Mahdi's heyday, and from thence purchased by the Sheikh Ohmed. Zöe's somewhat romantic disposition, which had caused her to admire the audacious Selim, was undoubtedly a trait from her mother.

Spite her romanticism, however, Zöe found the returned Selim not at all the hero of her memories. He was paunched, had blackened teeth, and insisted on putting aside her veil and kissing her in a fashion that was somehow frightening.

'Little sister, you should have found a husband long ago,' he said, holding her at arm's length and surveying her with eyes that held a glint of something other than brotherliness.

Thereat the Sheikh Ohmed, maundering over his nargileh, broke into complaint of Zöe's fastidiousness. She had refused all kinds of good offers, rejecting even the rich and worthy Saïd Donia, who had wanted another wife to help in the selling of the camel-dung which Siva used as fuel. Also, in'-sh'allah! there was—

Selim, his eyes still fixed on Zöe, broke in patronisingly. 'If you leave her to me, there will be an end of whims. A koorbash and a woman make good play.'

Zöe's heart struggled up into her throat.

Fortunately, the first of the visitors arrived then, and Selim temporarily forgot his sister in a recountal of his wanderings, an entirely immodest eulogy of himself, and a lengthy exposition of his exceeding importance as dragoman to the Khawaga Jorj. The latter, according to Selim, was a famous

Inkliz scribe, who, though he had never previously visited the sands and deserts, in his own land gathered unto himself boundless wealth by writing lying tales of them. Some of these tales Selim, who had mastered the barbarous animal-tongue of the Giaours, had himself read, and from them proceeded to relate various extracts to an appreciative and frequently hilarious audience. . . .

Most interested of all was Zöe.

*   *   *

Meanwhile the unfortunate George had put up in Siva's one caravanserai. He ate a supper which seemed to consist mostly of goatgut and garlic; and then, accompanied by a headache and a stupefied stomach, betook himself to his room. But even there he could find no peace. All the insects in Siva—horse, foot, and artillery—seemed to be campaigning on his string bed. Also, at the other end of Siva, assembled for what he had gathered was a kind of beastly 'At Home' in honour of his guide, raucous voices rose and fell, and a gramophone played maddeningly on a single record for three solid hours. . . .

'You have i-slep' well, Khawaga, dammit? What orders?'

It was next morning. George, in a suit of riddled pyjamas, sat up in bed and glared at the unshaven face which Selim blandly obtruded round the corner of the door. The sight was nauseating. George gulped and then broke loose. 'You——!' Even the conventionally unconventional heroine of 'The Yellow Silence' would, I imagine, have been shocked had she stood near the guide and listened to George. Upon the freethinking head of Selim was rained vituperation and reproach. How soon could they leave this stinking hole and set out on the return journey? Where were the wonders, surpassing those of his own books, of which Selim in Cairo had assured him? Did he think anyone could ever again write of the desert, after having seen and smelt this Siva's abominableness?

A quarter of an hour later, Selim, somewhat stupefied,

retired in bad order to the dukkan. There, after having looked up George's last word in the English dictionary and failed to find it, he proceeded to arrange his thoughts. While so engaged his roving and resourceful eyes fell speculatively on Zöe.

By the beard of the Sheykh Haeckel!

Forty-eight hours after his arrival in Siva, Romance, which George had thought dead for ever, came out of the darkness and hit him in the face, literally.

It was night time—a greasy Sivan night that might have been made of melted butter. In its sticky warmth George sat in his room, attempting to write. Every now and then he raised his hand and smote at bloated Saharan mosquitoes— mosquitoes such as the hero of 'Purple Sands' (38th ed.) had never dreamt of, far less fought pitched battles with.

A footstep sounded outside the goatskin flap which did duty as a window. George raised his head, and as he did so something damp and soggy hit him full between the eyes.

For a moment he sat gasping and then picked the thing up. It was a woman's garment, and, spite the intimacies of his novels, one that caused him to blush. Attached to it was a dirty note. George moved nearer to the light and found the pencilling to be in English.

'Come to my help. In Siva I have heard you to be. I am a white girl who was daughter to a professor Hellene whom many years ago Arabs capture. This night I am to be married to old Sheikh in white house in Shari es Souk by the great gate. For me a faithful dying friend this write I have no english. Oh my hero save me save me she burst into tears. This is my gage and showing it at the door may you pass.'

It was unsigned.

I take off my hat to George Menteith Selincourt with the 'Elvar de' thrown in. He did not, as you or I would, stop to consider the grammar of the letter, or to speculate who had 'burst into tears.' No, one moment, thrilled and amazed, he sat petrified, then sprang to the door and yelled for Selim who was generally about at that hour. His dragoman, whose sympathies he knew he must at once enlist, answered with commendable promptitude.

And, as he dived under the charpoy for his entirely useless and ornamental revolver, George himself, all his characters boiled down into Romance incarnate, knew a feeling of justification more sweet than he had ever dreamt possible.

For Siva was living up to first expectations—in fact, was playing the game.

*   *   *

Six months later, under the wide veranda awning of Heliopolis House Hotel, George sat at a little marble-topped table and scribbled busily. Now and then he raised his eyes and looked at his wife sitting opposite. After every such glance he scribbled with renewed inspiration.

Mrs. Selincourt regarded him dreamily. Clear white was her skin, her features Hellenic, and her English already almost intelligible. In front of her lay a half-filled sheet of paper in the looping Arabic scrawl.

George could not read Arabic, but was untroubled by the fact. His wife was writing one of her frequent letters to the 'faithful dying friend'—not yet defunct—in far-off Siva; the same who had indited the appeal for help on the night he had, with Selim's aid, romantically rescued this wife of his. Still could George's pulses stir with occasional thought of that hectic night's aftermath—the flight over the desert under the white stars; Sollum, where, being deeply and incurably in love, he had hastily married the 'daughter of the professor Hellene'; lastly, the parting with the faithful dragoman, who had gone south into an unbroken silence, with the declared intention of attempting to appease the Sivan choler with part of George's munifence. . . .

'Darleen!'

George looked up.

'Yes, dear?'

'Will . . . give-a me piastres for me freend in Siva?'

'Perhaps five hondred—I—yes?'

'All right. You can send it by the next caravan before we go to Europe.'

'Zank—' His wife smiles at him; and then, remembering much careful tuition, adds '—s.' She begins to write thoughtfully.

*   *   *

Storytellers have certain privileges. They can read any of their characters' private correspondence and feel no shame.

So while George ploughs triumphantly through the sixth chapter of 'My Saharan Romance—A Story of Real Life,' we will lean over his wife's shoulder, and, having the gift of tongues, read what she writes;

' . . . And, my Selim, I cannot send you much this time. Nor much hereafter. For Jorj would begin to suspect, and, though he is a fool. I love him a little. He has not beaten me yet.

'I care not if my father and you are angry because you cannot win through me great wealth from the trick you played Jorj. You read how to do it in his foolish books, and I was glad, for I hated the dukkan. And now in the quiet I know within me strange stirrings of woman's fulfilment, and soon I go far to the English land. Also Jorj, though he is a fool, I love a little, and with him I am free. He has not beaten me yet.

'Kiss the saint's tomb by the southern gate for me, though I do not worship the Prophet now, being wife of Jorj, who, though a fool, I love a little.

'Your sister,
        'Zöe'.

One wonders if, after all, George Menteith Elvar de Selincourt hadn't the best of it.

FOR TEN'S SAKE

It was Easter Day.

Under the feet of the watcher on the Hill of Burial the earth suddenly shook, quivered for a moment as might one in a nightmare, and then slowly subsided.

Mevr, the Hell-Gate of the East, lying asleep in the afternoon heat, scarcely stirred from its siesta; since its foundation in the days of Asoka as a meeting-place of the Central Asian caravans it had known the shocks of minor earthquakes. Like an obscene, sated animal it sprawled under the vacant grey eyes of the watcher. The heat-haze shimmered above it; northwards, its streets straggled towards the dim bulking of the Kablurz Beg; westwards, across the dun tundra, wound the white tract to Persia and far Iraq; eastwards, another caravan route vanished on the horizon towards Baluchistan.

As so many streams they seemed, these roads; streams flowing into the dark cesspool of Mevr and emerging from it —cleansed. Behind, in the City of the Plain, the caravans left their floating scum to fester and reek under the brassy noonday sky, under the sickened stars, under the seemingly endless patience of God. . . .

The vacantness vanished from the eyes of the watcher: they blazed with the hatred of the fanatic, the mono-maniac. A tall, gaunt figure, he rose from beside the dark mound where he had been crouching and out-reached thin, clutching hands.

'How long, O Lord?'

So, for a moment, he stood, threateningly, weird in his shabby black, a prophet of wrath above Merv. Then the dullness returned to his eyes; his glance grew wandering and fell on the mound at his feet. Suddenly he dropped to his knees; in his throat came a dry sob.

'Oh, Dick, Dick! Mevr might have spared at least you. . . . Janet it took, me it will take, but you——. Oh, my son! . . .'

Farther up the Hill of Burial two grave-robbers, Abdul Khaled and Osman the Nameless, had also been squatting on their haunches and looking down on Mevr. The cry of the man below reached their ears and they peered down at his black-coated figure. Then Osman (who was nameless in that, being a Turk, he was known merely by a contraction of Osmanli) spat expressively and contemptuously.

'It is the Englishman, the mad hakim, making prayers by the grave of his son,'

Abdul grunted. He was a soured man, for their day's work had so far disgorged nothing of value—not even a skeleton hand bearing a ring. In'sh allah! the greed of relatives these days was growing to unbelievable bounds, so poorly were kindred disposed of. The mad hakim did not interest him, except professionally.

'The grave of this son of his may contain some trifle of value,' he suggested.

The Nameless One shook his head. 'No unbeliever buries even a brooch with his dead. Did we not but yesterday spend two hours over the resting-place of that accursed Russian pig—may his bones poison the jackals who have since doubtlessly come to scrape them, seeing we did not fill in the pit!—and find nothing?' He rose up wearily, a burly brute, bestial faced, with squinting, red-rimmed little eyes. 'We'll seek a night's lodging at Miriam's. Eh?'

The fat Abdul had uttered a sudden gasp of pain. Now, clutching at his side, he rolled over on the turf. Then he tore something from the dirty djibbeh which enveloped him and flung it a yard or so away. Osman saw hit the ground a small green viper, yellow underneath, upturned, broken-backed, writhing.

'Allah! It is the end.' Abdul began to beat the ground with his feet and suddenly composed himself and drew a knife from his belt, for it is better to die by the bite of steel than the slow virus of the green-backed viper. Osman tore away the knife.

'Wait. I will call the hakim.' Forthwith, waving his arms, he shouted down the hill to the far, black-coated figure. In a little the latter stirred, stood upright. Down the windless air was borne Osman's shout.

'Haste, effendi. My brother has been bit by a yellow scorpion!'

For a moment the old man, who had once been Richard Southcote, M.D., stared up at the gesticulating Turk. Then returned to his eyes the same light as had been there when he had risen and threatened Mevr. He laughed, laughed aloud, ringingly, unemotionally, so that Osman dropped his arms and stared, and presently saw the hakim deliberately turn his back and walk down the hill towards Mevr. From the ground Abdul groaned.

'Give me the knife, Nameless.'

The bestial-faced Turk stared down at his fellow-scoundrel. His hands began to shake. Then, abruptly, he dropped by Abdul's side and tore away the stained djibbeh. His intention was evident. Abdul shrank away.

'Fool! Not that! It is death!'

The Turk's great hands gripped him. 'Peace! I drink worse poison every day in the Street of Ten!'

With that, he bent his trembling lips towards the little oozing incision on the brown hide of Abdul the grave-robber.

II

As the mad hakim entered Mevr from the Hill of Burial,

o

the fœtid city began to stir to life. In a narrow alley beggars squabbled querulously, stealing the chance alms dropped amongst their blind. The old man passed unseeingly amidst the sprawl of diseased, wasted bodies. In front he heard a shouting and commotion and the beat of a little drum. Coming to the great bazaar of the Suq es Iraq he was in the midst of a familiar scene.

A caravan—lines of laden, dusty camels and thirstily vociferous drivers—had newly arrived from Bokhara. The dust arose in clouds, babel of many tongues filled the air. From the near-by streets the vile things which had once been women were already flocking into the Suq. They mingled with the caravan drivers. One, a ragged harpy with a shrill voice, Southcote saw wheedling at a black-bearded camelier, already drunk and sitting, cup of arrack in hand. Suddenly, with an insane ferocity, the ruffian leapt to his feet and smote the woman a blow that cracked her jaw. She fell with a scream of pain, and wild guffaws of merriment broke out. Loudest of all laughed the two Persian gendarmes who patrolled the bazaar. The camelier stared vacuously down at the woman. . . . It was, set against its background of heat and dust, a scene that might have been filched from hell.

The old man looked about him with smouldering eyes. Slowly he made his way towards the centre of Mevr. Presently he found himself passing by the entrance to that which stank in the nostrils of even the City of the Plain—the entrance to the vile Street of Ten, a loathsome resort of thieves and murderers, where were practised unnameable vices of which even Mevr talked under breath, where no gendarme had ever dared patrol, where of a morning the knifed and rifled bodies of the night's victims were flung out into the reeking gutters of sunrise, whence, two years before to a day, young Dick Southcote had been brought, a bruised and lifeless and dreadful thing, to his father's house.

As Southcote passed there stood by the entrance to the

Street of Ten two whom he—and, indeed, all Mevr—knew by repute. One, pock-marked, lithe, white-clad, was a murderer who killed openly, with bravado, who sold the services of his knife to any who sought them; the other, Selim of Damascus, was a spy of the desert robbers, warning them of unarmed caravans, sharing in the loot of massacred trains.

Yet in Mevr they went scatheless. No gendarme dared lay hands on those whom, it was openly rumoured, the Governor himself had hired upon occasion. Indolently, insolently, they lounged in the hot afternoon sunshine. About them, from the cotes near by, pigeons wheeled with a blue flirr of wings.

Two horsemen, Europeans both, came trotting past the entrance to the Street of Ten. To the lounging scoundrels they nodded, under the pigeon-cloud ducked. Then in front of them, disappearing up a side street, they caught a glimpse of the bent figure of Southcote.

'The old man has been visiting his son's grave.' It was the short, burly man who spoke. He was the German Consul, not long transferred from Alexandria, but finding Mevr congenial and reminiscent of East African days.

'Then he has been visiting the foulest spot in Mevr.' The thin, debauched-looking Greek in white ducks who was known as 'Mitri', called himself a doctor, and had a reputation so unsavoury that the German raised amused eyebrows at his remark, looked after Southcote with a twisted grin. 'Poor fool! And to think, Herr Consul, that that crazed Englishman had once a European reputation!'

'So?' The German was indifferent. He had pulled out his watch, looked at it, and was now mopping his moist forehead. 'Twixt his horse's ears 'Mitri' was surveying Mevr with the owlishness of one unsoberly reminiscent.

'European. He was "Earthquake" Southcote. In Italy and Syria he spent years in seismological studies, was decorated by the English Society, and was famous. These things I know, for I learned them from his son.'

'Ah yes, the son.' The German, newcomer though he was had heard something of the Southcote story. 'And how came this—Academician and his son to Mevr?'

'Because this place is in the Central Asian earthquake belt. The Doctor Southcote came to study it, and brought his wife and son, who was a boy of eighteen. The wife died of malaria six months after they came. Though a scientist, the old Southcote was a Calvinist with a God waiting round the corner ready to be unpleasant. In such manner he took the death of his wife. Six months after that, when his son was killed, he became a madman and now abides in Mevr he knows not why.'

'You knew him once?'

'Mitri' stared unwinkingly ahead. 'I knew the son. Pfuu! . . . Me the old Southcote looked on as a native, and hated me on some Old Testament authority; me he considered an evil influence on his son.'

The German chuckled greasily. 'Mitri' abruptly reined up his pony. They had come to the Midan. The Greek pointed leftwards.

'You will be late for your festa, Herr Consul. And the Governor's desires are his belly's.

'Auf wiedersehen.'

'Auf wiedersehen.'

'Mitri' slowly rode down the rightward wall of the Midan. An 'evil influence?' He?

Something dreadful came in his face. Then, with a twisted grin, he looked down at his shaking hands—the hands which had strangled the life out of Dick Southcote.

III

Coming towards the tumble-down native house which he and Janet had furnished three years before, the mad hakim encountered Ahmed, the water-seller and scavenger. The latter was slinking along in the gutter in his usual fashion.

Though it was late in the day, his bleared eyes were of a habit fixed on the ground, for from the pockets of such numerous drunkards as speckled the early morning gutters of Mevr he gathered the wherewithal to augment his scanty legitimate earnings. At the old Englishman's approach he glanced up swiftly and shiftily. Dull, tortured eyes met dull, evil ones. Upon his thigh Ahmed made with two crossed fingers an obscure sign—the age-old sign wherewith the East wards off the evil eye.

Southcote's face twitched unhumorously. Ahmed was well known to him. He paused in the doorway and looked after the scavenger, broodingly. Impersonated in the foul carrion-grubber was Mevr itself. . . .

Entering from the street, he made his way to the room which was study, laboratory, and dispensary in one. The dingy walls showed streaked with a steamy damp, the furniture was ragged and thick with dust, for, beyond seeing to meals, the old Iraqi woman who acted as housekeeper did nothing. Southcote laid aside his hat, sank into a chair by the window, and there, upright and still, sat staring bleakly and unseeingly. Minutes went by. On a ledge of the window which tunnelled the thick wall a golden-eyed lizard flittered to and fro. The house was utterly quiet.

Presently Southcote moved. Under his heel something crunched. He glanced down and saw that the floor was strewn with broken glass. Then, catching a glimpse of a broken photo-frame under the table, he bent, gaspingly, and picked it up. It was a photograph of Dick, shaken from a ledge by the recent tremor.

Beside it, flung to the floor by the same cause, was a small, black-bound book. That Southcote let lie. With thin, unsteady fingers he smoothed the crumpled cardboard of the photograph. From a narrow, slatted window the sunlight streamed in and dappled the pictured face of the boy who lay beneath the mound on the Hill of Burial. Over the youth and freshness and the gladness in the young eyes the mad hakim sat and yearned, as a thousand times he had done. Dick, the strong, the light-hearted, his murdered boy. . . .

Two years to a day since the murdered lad had been carried into this very room: two years to a day since that black morning when something inside his brain had seemed to crack as he called down God's vengeance on the City of the Plain. Certain of its coming, certain of the doom that would fall on Mevr, he had ever since waited, his hatred of the foul place growing upon him month by month so that he shunned the native populace and the moving scum of the caravans, refusing help to the hurt even when they came to his door begging it. Never dependent on practice for a livelihood, he avoided even the few whites of Mevr because of that otherness of purpose for which he knew that God had designed him.

Once, when Kuchik Khan was sweeping down from the north with his army raised on Soviet gold, it had seemed to Southcote—unconsciously grown Eastern, un-European, a fanatic at once egotistic and sublimely selfless—that the hour was nigh, that in fire and rapine was God about to cleanse the earth of Mevr as once before He had cleansed the world with the sword of Tamerlane. But Kuchik's army had melted away, and Mevr breathed again, and Southcote, with vacant staring eyes, had climbed the Hill of Burial and looked to the skies and prayed for even such patience as God's own. . . .

But now, sitting with the crumpled photograph in his hand, an aching misery came upon him. He was only the mad hakim, dreaming a dreadful vengeance, living an insane hope. Of Dick was left nothing more than the captured beauty of his pictured face.

Upon that face he had never noted—as any stranger would at once have done—the heavy, sensual mouth, the contraction about the eyes which, spite the youthfulness of the latter, spelt viciousness. To the father they were the eyes of murdered hope, staring unavailingly, in a black world that knew not retribution.

It was the first moment of doubt within Southcote's last two years, and, in the instant of it, the ground shook under his feet. Upon the floor the little pieces of glass danced: the walls groaned ominously: a cup fell and smashed.

It was the second tremor within an hour.

IV

Into the eyes of the mad hakim had come an unwonted interest. Now he laid aside the photograph and rose to his feet. From the table he picked up a box of matches, made his way from the still quivering room, turned to the left, descended a flight of stone stairs. On a landing some eight feet below ground-level he stopped by the entrance to a small doorway and lit a candle which stood on a stone ledge.

The door opened easily at his touch. The candle lit up the smaller cellar of the house. In one corner was a chair and table; in the centre of the room an instrument embedded in the floor, held down by iron clamps, and rearing itself up, a cluster of thin glass rods, to a graded aluminium dial and pointer.

The Southcote Seismometer is a scientific toy, a mathematicians's dream gone astray in the realisation. In seismological works its possibilities are constantly referred to and its absolute unreliability demonstrated. As an instrument the purpose of which is accurately to gauge and foretell a many hours' distant earthquake it is recognised as a magnificent failure.

Yet there, in front of the old man in that stifling cellar in Mevr, was that seismologist's dream, the Improved Southcote, standing as it had been left on the day of its first installation, exactly two years before.

Candle in hand, Southcote approached it. Every day— single surviving habit of the one-time scientist—he came down into the cellar to clean the mechanism and make readings. Mevr, situated as it was, seldom failed to register

some forthcoming or passing tremor. On the twelve grada-
tions of the dial the pointer more often than not hovered
between zero and one.

Southcote flecked some dust from off the instrument, and
then bent to read it.

The pointer quivered above nine.

V

For a moment, after his first amazed start, the old man was
merely the scientist, calm and deft. He tested the apparatus,
searching for flaws, altered gauges, diminished the mercury
pressure in one of the long glass rods, and then changed back
again to normal. Promptly, with the last move, the pointer
swung again to nine. Then it began to creep up the dial
towards ten. . . .

And then, equally suddenly, the scientist died in Richard
Southcote. Realisation smote him like a breath of fire. Back
to his eyes flashed their uncanny glow, only with it was now
triumphant assurance as well.

Mevr was doomed!

In less than a hour, uprising out of the earth, its fate, swift
and awful, would leap upon it. Richard Southcote's prayers
had been answered, his faith and his patience justified. Far in
the bowels of the earth an awful force, more stupendous than
that of the San Francisco earthquake, was minute by minute
gathering to rise and smite and utterly blot out in torrents of
falling masonry and crashing landslides the Hell-Gate of the
East.

VI

Quietly the mad hakim left the cellar and went to the
room above. There his preparations were simple. Alone of
Mevr had he been warned, alone knew of the impending
doom. And from the Hill of Burial he would watch, as ah

God! how often had he watched and prayed, that doom over-take it.

He picked up his hat, glanced round the bare, dismal room, and turned, God's witness as he knew himself, to leave the house and Mevr for ever. Then his eye fell on the book which had lain on the floor beside the photograph of his son.

It had been Jenny's Bible. He picked it up, mechanically seeking to reset it in its shattered binding, to smooth its soiled edges. As he did so, with a strange deliberation it opened in his hands.

'Peradventure there be fifty righteous men within the city. Wilt Thou also destroy and not spare the place for the fifty righteous men that are therein?

'... And He said, I will not destroy it for ten's sake.'

Outside, through the drifting heat-waves, came the dron-ing purr that was the voice of Mevr; within his house the mad hakim stood and reread of the mercy promised to another City of the Plain.

'... And He said, I will not destroy it for ten's sake.'

If there should be ten righteous men in Mevr——.

Suddenly Southcote's laughter cracked the silence. The Bible, hurled against the wall, showered the floor with flimsy leaves. . . .

Underfoot, in Mevr, and for the third time that afternoon, the ground shook.

VII

It was near sunset. Out of the east the massing clouds drove swiftly towards the City of the Plain. A thin wind blew.

Through the deserted Suq es Iraq a mule clattered. Its rider was an old man with smouldering eyes. Squatting in an alley-way were two beggars, and one of them leant out to peer after the rider.

'God! Saw you the mad hakim? His face——'

'I see only the sky,' said the other, uneasily. 'There is death in it.'

Upon the foulness of Mevr, in its brutal pleasures and its
jaded vices, began to descend some such feeling. A strange
quiet held the city. And overhead, steadily, unwonted storm-
clouds massed.

Hastening from the doomed city to the Hill of Burial, the
mad hakim looked down the street towards the Southern
Gate and saw it thronged with the stalls of the afternoon's
chaffering. The way was blocked.

Southcote pulled up his mule. One other way out of the
city remained for him to take—through the street unvisited
and loathed, the place where his son had been murdered.
Was it not fitting that he should pass through there?

At the thought he shuddered and turned his mule. Then
he glanced up at the sky. He must hasten.

Right down through the narrow opening he drove his
mount, betwixt open cesspools, under the evil lower of over-
hanging, crumbling balconies. And then, above his head, in
Persian in the Arab script, he read an ancient inscription:

THE STREET OF TEN

VIII

What was that? Some dim associations of numbers clashed
in his mind. He half-halted the mule, and the beast, clumsily,
swung to one side——.

'Curse you!'

The mad hakim looked down. Almost under the mule's
feet sprawled a naked brown child. Its mouth was open, its
eyes pierced upwards a surprised terror. . . . Came a stamping of unshod feet in the dust, a lean arm outreached, and the
brown mite whisked away. Ahmed the scavenger, weeping
salvage in his arms, and cursing with the resourceful ob-
scenity of the East, glared up at Southcote.

Dazedly the old man met his eyes. Within his brain, as at
the stroke of a bell, he heard some voice count.

'*One!*'

The mule plunged on. The street twisted leftwards. On the sidewalk a man and woman moved lurchingly.

An everyday sight in the tainted city; some woman of the streets leading a customer to her house. Yet, passing, it seemed to the mad hakim that somewhere, before, he had seen those two——.

An unnameable impulse made him look back. The man was the black-bearded camelier of the Suq es Iraq: the woman, she whom Southcote had seen with him fell to the ground. Came the ruffian's shamed voice:

'Courage, little sister. I will not leave you,'

And again, within Southcote, spoke an unknown voice:

'*Two!*'

With the mad hakim rode some haunting presence. Up to the sky he looked again. The sun had vanished. The overhead wind was a thin scream. A lowering greyness had fallen on Mevr. Far thunder rumbled. From the path of the mule a strange group arose and staggered aside.

It was a man, bent almost double under the inert body of another. Southcote pulled his beast up, heard a voice that was not his own question:

'What ails the man?'

From under the weight of the Turk, Abdul the graverobber looked up at the Englishman with red-rimmed eyes.

'He is my brother. I was stung of a viper. You would not come when he cried your help on the Hill of Burial. He sucked the poison from my wound. Now he dies.'

Haggardly the old doctor stared. Within him, ever since entering the vile stew where his son had been murdered, had arisen an awful doubt. Now it clamoured in his brain. Ahmed, the camelier, these grave-robbers——.

Crash! went the thunder. For a moment, blindingly, a dagger of fire quivered down the Street of Ten. Southcote's terrified mule bucked and pawed at the air. . . .

IX

When he came to himself he seemed to be peering through a red mist. In his back was a terrible pain. He tried to move and lay unmoving.

The red mist cleared. A crowd of faces were peering down at him. The mule had flung him violently against a great corner-stone.

He tried to moisten his lips; failed; made a desperate effort to sit up; lay still. . . . And then, yet seeing clearly, hearing distinctly, he understood.

Paralysis. Death.

And upon his tortured brain at the thought, wearily, there came great peace.

X

In Damascus, twenty-three years before, a querulous old man had died, cursing the son who had disgraced his name, and who stood by his bedside, dry-eyed and scornful, to the last. In life the old man had availed little; in death he left a memory that had consequences unguessable.

Through the crowd Selim of Damascus pushed his way and knelt by the side of the mad hakim, and gathered him in his arms. As he strained to lift the limp body, one touched him on the shoulder.

'I will take his feet, brother.'

It was Ali, the murderer-bravo.

'For he is old, Selim.'!

Together they lifted him. Homeless themselves, they looked around them doubtfully. Then a woman's voice called nearby.

'In here.'

In the doorway of a house of shame stood a weary-faced woman, beckoning. Overhead the thunder rumbled as Selim and Ali bore the body of Southcote into the dark entrance of the house of Miriam the harlot. She guided them down a corridor into a large room where, on a bed, another woman lay moaning and fever-flushed. The heat of the place was stifling.

At a table a man was pouring a dose from a medicine bottle. He looked up. Miriam nodded.

'I bring another, "Mitri." He was thrown by his mule.'

She motioned to the two men. Southcote they laid on a pile of rags which did duty as another bed. Miriam knelt behind him and raised his head. 'Mitri' came across the room, halted suddenly, stood swaying unsteadily.

'My God! Southcote!'

So, for a minute, 'Mitri' standing as if petrified, Selim and Ali lingering in the doorway, the harlot kneeling, weary-faced. Then, drunkenly, 'Mitri' spoke.

'Do you know who this is, Miriam?—The father of Anah's seducer; the father of the thief who ruined the daughter whom you reared to be other than you are; the father of the man who made your daughter—that.' He pointed to the wasted woman upon the bed, and ceased, and swayed a little upon his feet.

Outside the lightning flashed. Miriam looked up with weary, unchanging eyes.

'I know it is the mad hakim—the father of Dick, whom you killed because always you loved Anah and I prayed you to do it. But our hate helped nothing, friend. Anah dies, remembering only the dead lover whom she tried to save. . . . You must help this old man. And God will judge.'

By the side of the Englishman 'Mitri' knelt unsteadily. As he did so the old eyes opened, and slowly from them a tear trickled down the still face.

XI

A living soul in a dead body he had lain, the while blinding revelation came upon him. Dick, the son for whom he had cursed Mevr—Dick, a seducer and thief; Dick, righteously killed by the drunken 'Mitri.' . . .

For a little, listening to their voices, that alone had been upon him, and bitter as death was the taste of the knowledge. And then, printed as in letters of fire across his vision, he saw the passage in Jenny's Bible.

'Peradventure there be fifty righteous men within the city. Wilt Thou also destroy and not spare the place for the fifty righteous men that are therein?

' . . . And He said, I will not destroy it for ten's sake.'

Blindly, blasphemously, he had rejected what was surely a command. Righteousness? Who were the righteous? Who, in the shadow-show of life, might lift him a light whereby to judge and condemn his fellows? Yet he, vengeful and hating, had done so, the while the harlot and the thief, the drunkard and the murderer, reached to unguessed heights of pity and forgiveness, heroism and shamed kindliness. . . .

Righteousness? As a silver thread he saw it now, winding through the lusts and cruelties, the filth and crime of every life in Mevr. And of Hope and Faith and Charity was it woven. Before him he saw the scavenger, the two grave-robbers, the camelier, the murderer and the thief, 'Mitri,' Miriam, Anah—those in whom, unguessed of him, had lain the seeds of righteousness—passing in the vomiting doom of Mevr, the doom of which he alone had been warned, the doom he was helpless now to avert. . . .

Was that God's will? Up at 'Mitri' he stared, and remembered that voice which had counted within himself as he witnessed the unguessed heroisms of the Street of Ten. Surely he heard it speak again. . . .

Kneeling beside him, they saw the sweat start out on his forehead, heard him breathe as one in a nightmare, saw the glare in his eyes. Then, with an awful effort, he sat upright, heedless of their attempt to restrain him. His head swam.

For an awful fear had suddenly gripped him. Was his vision false? By some new law other than that which had doomed the Cities of the Plain could righteousness indeed be reckoned?

Aloud, in the stifling room—desperately, with sudden inspiration—he began to count. Ten righteous. . . . From Ahmed the scavenger to the murderer of his son. . . .

. . . *If there should be but Ten.* . . .

And there were but NINE.

Again, peering round the dusking room, he counted. Then, in the shadows about the doorway, between Ali the murderer and Selim the thief, he saw stand for a moment One whom he had never known, One with bleeding hands and feet and hidden face.

*   *   *

A quarter of an hour later the bells of warning clanged out over Mevr, and from house to house the watchmen cried the message brought to the Governor from a brothel in the slums. Out into the safety of the plains and the falling dusk of that Easter Day, just as the first tremors of doom shook the City of the Plain, streamed the multitudes of fugitives.

And through the multitudes a murderer and a thief, two of those reckoned in the sum of the righteous Ten, carried Southcote to safety.

DAYBREAK

The little cluster of bell-flowers—From Scotland? But it has travelled far! I may smell it? . . . God mine, it is heather!

It cloaks your mountains in purple this time of year, does it not? Never have I seen it before; but I have smelt this smell. I have smelt it blowing on a wind from those mountains I have never trod, a breath of that autumn I have never known. . . .

Eh? In imagination? But no, in reality—here in our Cairo, almost the year ago to-day.

II

And the tale begins, if I must tell it, not here at all. It begins in the far Scotland that sent you the heather, with Roger Mantell on the autumn walking tour up through your Urals.

He was the young journalist in London, this Roger, and very poor, as is proper for the journalist. Something of your own height and appearance he had, with that brownness of hair and eyes that indistinguishes the Englishman, and a certain far-awayness of outlook that made of him the not too-good journalist. History was his passion, and he had taken the walking-tour to plan the writing of a book. This book was to refute the foolish Spengler—him who believes all history goes in cycles, like the mad dog chasing its tail.

And one night-time, very late, passing through a village

amongst those hills, he heard a girl singing a peasant song—
so sweet and strange and beautiful in the dark that he halted
and listened. And the song was this:

> 'Oh, the memory and the ache
>   They have stown the heart fra me,
> And there's heather on the hills
>   In my ain countree.'

All next day, though many miles away, he found memory
of singer and song haunting him. So pressing was it that he
turned about and went back to lay this ghostly thing. Outside the village school he heard the voice again.

Then, in growing amazement at himself, he rented a room
at the village inn, in three days obtained introduction to his
singer, and within the week, though his history had not pro-
gressed even in the draft beyond so-hairy Eoanthropus, was
planning nothing of greater import than to steal the singer
from the hills.

Her father had been the village schoolmaster and she was
teacher of the school. And because he had been a poet this
dead father of hers had called her Dawn. To watch her stand
against the sunrise, as many a morning she did when they
tramped the hills together and the mists were rising, caught
the amazement ever again in the throat of Roger. Slight and
slim and dark and quick, this singer of the hills, with clear
eyes, grey and grave, but with the little twinkle-lights deep
down in them. She had a pale, clear skin with the faint
blood-flush. She detested the poor Spengler and could run
like a deer.

Indeed, though one who had lived in the hills all her life,
she was of the most modern—one of that woman's miracle-
generation that knows nothing of the reserves and hesitations
and tantalisations. She had the body of a gracious boy and
the mind of an eager Greek.

If Roger first loved her for her voice, I think she loved him
at first sight, protectingly, because of that far-awayness of his

P

look. Under painted skies, children in a world transformed, they walked that autumn. Roger had been the unawakened tourist, but Dawn took him out into mornings of wonder when, in the silence, he would hear the sun come audibly up from the east, hear the earth stir and move as from its sleep. Or into fervid noons, to lie on a mountain-side and listen to the drowsy under-song of bees rising and falling on the never-coming wind. And the brown night would creep over this land of Dawn's as one very ancient who went home from toil. . . .

It seemed to him that she had deeper kinship with those things than he would ever fathom. 'I don't believe you are human at all,' he said to her once. 'You're out of the hills and the sunrise.'

She laughed at him, and then was grave, in that fashion that somehow had power to wring his heart absurdly. 'I never remember my mother. She died when I was born. And my father was always lost in his books. I carried all my desperate wrongs and fears to the hills.' She sat with cheek in hand and looked across the sun-hazed valleys. 'I think they love me, those hills, almost as much as I love them.'

'How can they help it?' said Roger, her lover.

III

In the little time they were deciding when they would marry and how many children they would have, and whether it would be better to wait until Roger made the thousand a year or.only eight hundred. Not till there was security and certainty were they to mate. . . . At the least, that was Roger's planning, and Dawn, this so-amazing Greek boy who was more than boy, sat and looked at him and her hills, I think perhaps with the twinkle-tapers lighting her grey eyes.

For he had come in the first months of the autumn. Day by day it deepened around them. Purple grew the mountains and under the long heats of day climbed to heaven in a

shimmering blaze. Out of the earth rose all the songs of
fruition and ending, and that second week there was a moon
that came and never seemed to set. They could not keep their
beds, these two, but stole out to meet each other in the white
radiant wonder.

Till one night—this but the guess-work of mine—they
kissed each other and in their kiss was already a wild regret.
The hours are on wings, on wings! beat the shadows that
were night-birds. Now, now! beat their own hearts. . . .
Perhaps Dawn held him at arms length, and laughed at him
with a little breathlessness. 'But, Roger! . . . A thousand a
year!'

And then, whatever his answer, in some such hour of the
earth-magic they came to their decision.

One night, under a moon that trembled on the wane, but
waited for them still, they climbed together up into the hills
and the radiance, and not a bird that called in the shadows
but was their friend, and there was none of the need to say
good night.

IV

But no moons endure for ever, and presently Dawn was
with Roger in a little flat in London and those days on the
hills dimmed till they were of a dream.

I have never seen your London or known its life, but it
seems they went to live there in the season of the fogs which
rise from a blind little river amidst the streets. They began
their life in a half-twilight, with the million under-murmurs
of other life a still roar about them. In the morning Roger
was gone to the office of his gazette; often he did not return
until midnight. For many weeks they would see each other
only at night-time, each wearied and a little tired. . . .

And in the little was the amazement, I think, and silent
tears shed in the darkness that love could ever tarnish so. For
they came to look on each other searchingly, even on the

wild occasion angrily—Dawn to see her dreamer of the hills visionary and unpractical, immersed in his book and the refutations of cyclic catastrophe, irritable over the refractory phrase or the inadequate reference. And to Roger it sometimes seemed that he was tied, by all unreasonable bonds, to a boy quickly bored and swift to anger, one whose eyes could light with other than mirth, one whose laughter could ring cruel and very clear. . . .

But these are things inevitable? They are not the less heart-breaking. Sometime, both knew, they would come to the adjustments and live with lesser friction. They would, in their English phrase, 'settle down.' But the ache in the dark of love, a thing so shining, to look forward to the settle-down!

Yet was that never to be, for a day came when they looked at each other in unbelief and the settle-down fled out into the blinded streets and romance rang her bugles for them again. The great secret was theirs, theirs partnership in the abiding mystery. . . .

But who am I to speak of it or understand? We of the unmarried are emotionally unborn, even though, wistfully, we catch a glimpse of understanding. This child of theirs was to be—oh, that hero that every child may be!—a captain of the hosts of the morning, Dawn and Roger in one, doer and dreamer, one who was to confound all erring Germans and bear the torch of vision yet another league up the Defile through which march the hosts that have climbed from the beast.

And they named him, and dreamt of him and hoped for him; and the months fell away, into spring warming London, into summer, till there came the day when Dawn must pass through her hours of agony and Roger doubt his vision of history. For there arose the complications and the bringing of a surgeon. . . .

In the end was the child born dead, and for the little it seemed that Dawn herself would die.

V

But she lived, returning to life wan and a stranger from a desolate land. She must bear no more children, nor must she stay the winter in England, the doctors said.

Roger—a Roger grown practical at last—took her north to the brief summer-autumn of her hills. So soon as he could leave her he went back to London again. In a week he was sending her the news that he had found a gazette willing to send him abroad for a year, to Egypt, to act as the correspondent and write a series-impression of Cairo and the Nile-country.

VI

So they came to our Polychromata, those two. On the voyage Dawn grew again the Greek boy, and her laughter came back, and the little twinkle that changed and yet abided in her grey eyes. They came from the ship at Alexandria and found a *pension* at Kubbah. From there they set to search for a house.

At the length, up on Nile-bank to the north of Gezireh Island, they came one afternoon on that at sight of which Dawn cried 'Oh Roger!' in the tone that stirred in him always a memoried cry from a day of agony. They stopped and looked at the desired possession and laughed eagerly, and kissed like the children they were.

For that was the supreme wonder of their days—their love that had flamed anew. As never before it flamed. But the burning is the wrong simile. It burgeoned and blossomed, strange and sweet, not the love of the first early days nor yet the compassionate passion of the dark London time. It was something that made of their first wild desire a childish greed, of the settle-down necessity a humour and a fantasy. . .

They surveyed the empty house by Nile-bank and went back to Kubbah in the apprehension that it would be gone by morning. But the next day they found the agent, rented

'La maison Saniosu,' and engaged two Egyptian servants. It jutted out upon the Nile, the house, old and of crumbling stone, mantled with a brown creeper that reached down its tendrils to the water. It was two stories in height and had a high-walled garden also skirted by the Nile.

They had taken it furnished, so after a few necessary purchases in the bazaars, and in the intervals of Roger writing the so masterly series-impressions, they had but to debate a new name for it.

Above the door was its name carved—Maison Saniosu.

'Let's call is Sans-Sous and be done,' said Roger. And this, because they were very young and very poor and very happy, was a great jest, and almost on that name they decided.

But one morning—a morning early in October—happened that which solved the so urgent matter. In their room Dawn was the first to awake. Upon the window was the urgent tapping of a twig and she looked out on the wonder of a Nile daybreak. Presently she awakened Roger and they sat side by side watching in the sky the silver that changed to amber and so to copper and then into the blind flush of azure.

They had been awakened by the first of the seasonal morning winds which bring the end of the khamsin time, but that they did not know until later. Only that unexpected wind had brought to Dawn an inspiration.

'I know—name for our house! Was there ever such suitable name!'

Roger stared at her. 'What?'

'Why, Daybreak.'

He teased her. 'But that is your own name. It is Dawn.' Then he laughed, and there were words in your English Bible that he remembered, very wonderful and beautiful words ' "*Until the day break and the shadows flee away*——" '.

VII

I met them first in mid-November, in front of the Sphinx,

when Dawn was posing it and her Roger and an Egyptian dragoman for the photograph. I also had come to photograph it for a client I had.

Roger apologised for his Philistine wife who insisted that he and the dragoman should stand beside the Riddle of the Sands. I made her the bow.

'I think she is wise,' I said, 'for this is no Riddle; only a foolish vanity in stone. If I might I would have madame in my photograph with the Sphinx.'

I have that photograph still, with the little madame, slight and sweet and brave, standing beside that owlish carving of the foolish dead. Then I helped them catch the donkeys which had strayed and we went to Mena House and drank the much-needed tea, for the donkey-catching had been a task of the mirth and great speed.

From the first I think their liking was for me as mine for them. Presently, when we had ceased to laugh at memory of a donkey which had raced Roger for almost a mile, they were telling me of the house called Daybreak and that sudden wind from the Nile that now tapped their window each morning.

'It is a *green* wind,' said the little madame, and paused in the doubt of my understanding.

'I know,' I said. 'It is of the Delta crops and harvesting. Yet few know it for a green wind.'

'I am a peasant myself,' she said. 'Is that why?'

I looked at her and wove the fantasy. 'You are of the most ancient race, I think. Of the brunet race that held the Mediterranean lands long before there was Celt or Saxon or Slav. They are not of the history-books: they passed north and south into bleaker lands before history opened. But perhaps there was one of them, some far-father of yours, who once tilled the Delta lands and woke to that green wind. Perhaps it is a memory that has come to you across ten thousand years.'

'That is a wonderful thought,' said Dawn, and looked at her Roger.

'I will steal it for an article,' said Roger, and there was the laughter amongst us.

VIII

In the little I was a frequent visitor at the house called Daybreak. I talked of the Nile and Cairo and gave to Roger good copy for his London gazette. Soon to both of them I was the close friend, and knew this tale of theirs I have told you, even as they knew mine. When I told Roger of those Four Years which ended for me in the storming of Perekop by the Sovyet heroes—heroes they were, though my enemies—I remember the long silence that fell.

'That is life,' he said. 'And it seems blind chance and aimlessness. . . . But there's something behind it greater than a dark malignancy. Though that malignancy is real enough. Perhaps in ancient Egypt they saw it, the Dark Shadow, and built the Sphinx and Pyramids to ward it off.'

'And this other thing,' I said. 'What it is?'

'Oh, something equally nameless and untheological. It has led us up through the dark Defile of history, has turned in many guises to help again and again the stragglers and the lost in their hour of utmost despair. It will lead us to the sunrise yet.'

'That Daybreak the poor Spenglers have never visioned,' I jested at him, though I loved his faith. We heard the singing of Dawn inside the house. 'And the little madame is its prophet.'

He laughed and was a poet. 'She was made in secret when the Dark Gods slept!'

Never since Kazan had I known such friendship as those nights when the little madame and I would sit and talk under our Cairene moon, with the bulking of Bulaq beyond the garden wall and the far wail of native song in our ears. Sometimes was Roger with us, but often indoors, working on the so-great book that was not in the contract with his London gazette—the book that was to bring him reputation and money. I brought my violin to that garden, and Dawn would sing for me peasants' songs that left me homesick for my Volga lands—though they were songs of that Scotland I have never seen. Once she sang that verse which had halted Roger in the hills, and I have forgotten it never:

'Oh, the memory and the ache
They have stown the heart fra me,
And there's heather on the hills
In my ain countree.'

But of course I love her. From the first moment I think I loved her. And with Roger also I was in love. They were to me the surety of my dreams. I loved them as one loves those dream-children, keen and beautiful, who will people our happy world a thousand years after we are dead.

IX

And then, in February, there came the horror into their lives.

At the first I did not understand their silences and strangeness. I said to myself that I was the too-frequent visitor—what need had these lovers of such alien as myself? For a little there was bitterness with me, and I stayed away from the house called Daybreak, going there not at all until the passing of two weeks. When next I went it was to endure their reproach and in the eyes of the little madame a hurt puzzlement.

'You have tired of us? Why have you stayed away?'

I kissed her hand. 'But I had thought you tired of me,' I said, and blundered over words which I desired not to say. 'There seemed a difference the last time I came. . . .'

Then was the silence, though Roger broke it with a sudden laugh and talk of indifferent matter. His eyes were the eyes of a sick animal. And when presently we were alone he went to the window, and looked blindly out on the sunlight and the Nile, then turned and told me.

And then, God mine! I also knew the sudden sickness of mind, and had no word to say because of the horror of the thing.

For another child was coming, and, as they had been told, Dawn could never live through such a thing again.

X

I proposed the committee of doctors which may deal with such cases, but Dawn, modern of moderns though she was, would have none of it. For she could talk of these things being my friend and of her miracle-generation.

'I think—oh, I don't know, but it would be cheating.'

'But this is the absurd fatalism,' I pleaded, as Roger also had pleaded. The little twinkle set its lights in her grave eyes.

'Anton, my dear, was it absurd fatalism that led you to fight a hopeless fight in your White army? . . . And have you lost—even yet?'

That was in the garden of Daybreak, in the late March, and we were silent as she leant on the wall and looked down on the hastening waters. She had a sudden idle thought.

'Oh, that morning wind from the Delta—it does not blow now.'

'Eh?' I said. 'The wind? It will not come again for many months.'

XI

I procured for them Dr. Adrian, the English gynaecologist, who is my friend. Dawn liked him, for he is the droll, but to Roger he talked with a grave face, for he had from London the particulars of the case when the other child had died. The little madame must know no unhappiness or worry. Also, she must leave Cairo.

For the summer months drew on. They blazed their strong heat that summer as never before, I think. Yet Dawn, even when Roger at this would have written to his London gazette and made resignation, refused. They would stay on at Daybreak. On the little madame was the Cairene spell—that spell which makes of a chance house and garden in this strange city more homely than home.

But never so long a summer. . . . A tent was set in the garden, and through those long days of white warmth we watched Dawn with the stealthiness of criminals who fear their gaze may be detected. So she told us, laughing, but with wistfulness, I doubt if Roger comforted her; it was she who gave the comfort. For him it was to start out of even the happiest moment into the blank silence when terror walked his brain and looked from his eyes. And from that would he be awakened with her arms about him, and her teasing tenderness. . . . Then I would stride away, with the sick fear upon me also.

God mine, it was pitiful, heart-breaking.

But I set out to be the droll, even as did Adrian—he who has said that no gynaecologist can be anything but gynaecolatrist—in his visits to the house called Daybreak. We sought to weave the conspiracy, we three—the conspiracy to keep afar the malignant shadow of which Roger had talked. Presently the Egyptian servants also understood and were in that conspiracy. With the ending of the khamsin-time I organised many of the late afternoon excursions—to the Barrage, to Heliopolis, to the desert, borrowing a car from Adrian to take them to those places.

One afternoon in late September I took them to Abu Zabal. For mile on mile we went into that brown country, where stand in sleep the whitewashed villages under their smoke pencillings, and there is no other colour at all, but only the white and black. We had tea as a picnic, making it under the lee of a ruined dyke in the sunset. It was such sunset as seemed to fire the world.

'It is the Ragnarok,' I said, and Dawn poured sand on Roger, who was lazy and lay flatwise, to make him sit up and look at it.

'I've seen a Grampians sunset like that,' he said.

The little madame caught her breath. She began to speak in a whisper.

'It's autumn there now. Oh, my hills, my dear hills! Can't you see them and smell them, Roger, climbing purple into the sunset? And hear the curlews crying down the glen?'

We said nothing, and then we saw that she was weeping— desolately, with uncovered face, she who had been so brave. . . .

And the time drew ever nearer like a black wall of sand.

XII

There came a night when Roger Mantell and I tramped that garden through hours that seemed never-ending. The cruel aloofness of the yellow stars and the whispering Nile! And it seemed to me then, as I think to Roger himself, that the dream of his history was false, that alone and unfriended man wandered amidst the cold immensities of space and time. . . . Beside and above us, against the southwards sky, were the lights of the house called Daybreak.

To and fro, hour on hour, I walked Roger, and talked to him of the stars. I remember I stood pointing out to him Alpha in Centaur when Lesdiguières, the French colleague of Adrian, called him from the garden-door.

For Adrian was not there. That night of all nights he was in Alexandria, and, though we had sent the telegram for him, would not be back until morning. Lesdiguières, good and careful, but of the old school and the old fashion—it seemed but a moment when I next heard him calling me. But it must have been longer, for in the east were the ghost-limnings of the day.

'The child—born alive, yes. A boy, and of the complications none. But the girl'—and I knew he meant the little madame—'is exhausted. She will not see the day, I think. She is calling for you.'

I shall not tell you, my friend, of that so-close room—the windows Lesdiguières had closed against the night miasmas —nor the smells of the antiseptics, nor the stout French nurse who was presently gone out of the room with the doctor. I knelt and kissed the hand of the little madame—so tired, a child herself, lying there, Roger's arm under her head. She was sinking very quickly, dying of exhaustion. But as I rose to go she whispered 'Stay.'

I looked at Roger, but for me he had no eyes. I turned to the closed window and saw in the sky a pallor that waned and flushed and spread. And there came in my mind then, into that silence a bitter memory—the words Roger had quoted the day they named their house.

'*Until the day break and the shadows flee away*——-'

Suddenly there was the rustling sound and I looked round. The little madame had sat urgently up in the arms of her lover, her eyes shining.

'Roger, Roger, look—the hills!'

And then upon the window I heard a little tapping. I wheeled to it and saw the urgent twig beating upon the pane. It was the first of the Delta winds. Of sudden impulse I un-did the catch and flung the window open to the Nile day-break. . . .

And then I heard from Roger the little cry of wonder.

For suddenly, borne on that first Nile wind, out of the dawn the room was flooded with a nameless scent, and it seemed to me a moment I stood in a great valley, and up the grey slopes climbed the dawn, and as it climbed those hill-slopes mantled a misting purple. . . .

A moment the thing was, in a strange, sweet silence, and then gone. I turned and looked at Roger's white face.

'My God!' he whispered. 'Did you smell it? *It was heather!*'

We looked at the little madame lying silent in his arms. I

thought her dead, and then, while we stared, we saw she was asleep.

XIII

And she lived, coming out of that health-giving sleep with no memory of the morning happenings. In the spring Roger took her and his son away from Cairo and Egypt, back to her hills, for he was by then the great man because of his book. And me she kissed farewell—me, the dragoman!—and there was a mist in her clear eyes. . . .

But Adrian when he came that morning: 'You saved her life,' he said to me, while we three stood in the garden and the little Dawn slept in the room above the Nile. 'It was the Delta morning wind that did it—the change in the temperature, you know. That fool Lesdiguières must have half-suffocated her.'

Yet until prevail the years that make all things dim will it seem to Roger and me that once, in an hour of desperate need, we were granted glimpse of the kindlier, nameless thing that verily shines and abides behind all the blind ways and destinies of Nature.

COCKCROW

Eh? That? Only the crowing of a Lemnos rooster! From the fowl-run behind this café it comes—the fowl-run of the little Simon.

You had not suspected in him the tastes bucolic? In our Cairene evenings I think he wanders out there and dreams of a farm in Lemnos—he who would die of the broken heart if he forsook the Khalig's colours and call! ...

The challenge absurd in the sunlight—but in the dawn—how of the haunting it is! Haunting, I think, with memories not our own, the stored race-remembrances innumerable since first the jungle-fowl was tamed and that challenge of the morning heard in an Indian hut. What agonies and waitings has it not ended, what vigils and prayers! That drowsy clamour—surely it is in all memories, vivid and unforgettable, for at least the one night that would never pass, for at least the one stretch of dark, still hours!

That morning the many years ago, my friend—think how it must have shrilled above the hills of Jerusalem!

II

If you walk the Shari' Abbassieh to-day you will see the house of Lucius Ravelston stand shuttered and dusty in the sunshine, with its little garden deserted. Last we heard of him, our Ravelston, he was in Hadramaut, on expedition in search of the sand-cities of the Shiah. In days when that garden knew him he would stride to and fro with the hasting guest by his side, discussing the languages international and the inhabitability of the moon and the character of Marco Polo; of these things he would discuss with the naive fervour that another devotes to scandal or politics. . . .

The guest would pant beside him for a little, then give up with a laugh, and sit to watch his host, pipe-smoking, trample the flower-beds in the heat of exposition.

More nearly the seven than the six feet in height, a giant, with the rapt stare of grey eyes under knit brows and the strange brown hair like silk. He had an athlete's body that Phidias would have loved, though of Hellas the good Aristotle would perhaps have baulked at his mind.

Indeed, this would have been but reciprocal, for the good Aristotle he regarded with the utmost detestation. Giant and genius, he was yet something of a child, and men dead and dust three thousand years he could love or detest with as much fervour as though they wrote in the journals contemporary.

'A snippety surburban mind—the mind of a fossil-collecting curate.'

'But I have heard of him as the Father of the Sciences,' I would say, and so bring upon myself recital of Aristotelian fatuities, the while the drowsy cluckings would cease in the native fowl-run beyond the garden, and the good sun, talked from the sky, went down behind the Red Hills. . . .

He was the crusader essential, hating all neat, unoriginative minds which look on life with the cold, conservative calm. Not yet forty years of age, he had been a surgeon in the Great War, the leader of a Polar Expedition, the assistant of Knut Hammssen in that Odyssey through the Gobi Desert. From such exploits heroic he had settled down in Cairo to study the scourge of cancer. In laboratory and study they fight the last crusades.

Research-worker, student, he yet waged the wars unending in journal and congress and popular press. Enemies in

battalions he loved, though there were occasions when he
would forget the date of a battle, going into lengthy abstrac-
tions as a mystic into a trance. These were escapes to the
super-normal when some thought would suddenly fructify in
his mind and he would wipe the dust of tragedy and comedy
and friendship from his hands, and retreat to the barred room
and the microscope and the notes and the lamplit table for
days or weeks on end....

My friend, Dr. Adrian the gynaecologist, also knew him
and loved him.

'An anachronism, fifty years behind the times, Ravelston.
In the Huxley-Haeckel tradition. Last of the warrior-servants.
Science has more triumphs and heroes than ever, but
Ravelston's the last of her champions to go out into the arena
and defy embattled Stupidity. Pity. They lent colour to life,
the giants.'

'They brought fire from heaven, if I remember,' I said.
'But I do not think he is the last. There will always be
giants.'

Coming from the house called Daybreak, we were passing
through Abbassieh late in the night, and now stood looking
up at the flare of light from the room of Ravelston. Adrian
laughed.

'The Titan, eh? There was also a vulture in the story,
wasn't there? We must warn Lucius!'

III

That autumn the giant went to England, to London, to
see to the publication of a book—not the such book as you
might write, my friend, needing no supervision, but the pro-
duction marvellous and intricate, with the diagrams and
changing print and the chemic symbols much strewn to confusion and despair of printer. Adrian and I made the occasional call at the Abbassieh house and saw to its ordering. It
was a pleasant place, and we spent hours of ease in the great

Q

library, or drank the good Ravelston's wine under the lime-trees in the garden.

Behind he had left, in the rough, the great work on which he had been engaged since coming to Cairo. Though only in first draft, Adrian had promised to read this treatise and contribute to it a preface. He would groan aloud over caligraphy and contractions, yet read on in fascination. Once or twice he interviewed clients of the giant, and of one of those interviews told me. The man was a Greek, who had suffered from the internal pain diagnosed by his own doctor as a cancer tumour. Under treatment of Ravelston he had been made well and whole again in a month.

'A month! Unless it was a mere fluke, colonel, Ravelston's in the process of perfecting a treatment for cancer that'll wipe it from the face of the earth. . . . Beyond the dreams of Lister.'

We would smoke and meditate, and discuss the absent Ravelston. Of his private life we knew nothing.

'He has no private life, no private ambition. He's a Republican of your Plato, colonel, a Samurai out of Wells. . . . Marry? He'd forget a woman in a fortnight—unless she developed *sarcomata!*'

Ravelston telegraphed the date of his return, and I found Cairo's leading gynaecologist, with sleeves rolled up, and the scurry of native servants, flapping the negligent duster around the library. '"Prepare the house," eh? Must be bringing a shipload of zoological specimens.'

It was the afternoon when the boat-train was due from Alexandria. 'It is his jest,' I said. 'Or perhaps he brings a tourist friend.'

'God forbid,' said Adrian, and then we heard a taxicab come in the sharia below and the sound of a key in the door. Then Ravelston's voice upraised.

'Adrian! Saloney! . . . Hell, what a dust!'

We went out and waved to him from the landing. He stood in the doorway, in the winter sunshine, and beyond in the street, seemed a fight in progress between the native porters and the mountains of trunks. These things, and then ——.

Simultaneously we saw her. She stood not in the belt of sunshine, but in the mote-sprayed darkness within the door. I made the bow ineffective and Adrian the fumblement for the collar of his shirt.

'Pamela—Dr. Adrian and Colonel Anton Saloney. You people, this is my wife.'

IV

She called him never by his first name, but sometimes 'Ravelston' and sometimes 'Stealthy Terror'—the first because it was fashionable so to address a husband, the second because of some secret jest they shared together. She ransacked the Abbassieh house from top to bottom, and had shaken from it such showers of dust as seemed to warrant the eviction of the Sahara itself. The roof of one wing was cut away and installed with special glass that interrupts not the violet ray, and for this novelty she was the excited child, as indeed was Ravelston himself.

'He has sun-bathing on the brain,' said Adrian. 'God knows why—unless it's to admire the pretty Pamela. . . . Done without it all his life and now he pretends it's essential to health, whereas it's merely a craze and a fashion.'

'You do not like Mrs. Ravelston?'

'I don't,' he said, with curtness. 'He was a Samurai, and now—Good Lord, look what he's becoming!'

And indeed I also, with amazement and pity, watched the transformation of the giant from research worker and world enthusiast into lover and follower. He planned and rode the excursions with her, the while library and laboratory remained locked and neglected, took her to innumerable balls and festas, humoured her in whims and desires most wayward and foolish. She declared a passion for the language

Russian, and determination to learn it, and I was hired to teach such accent as Ravelston himself possessed not.

She was the pupil impossible—would lie deep in her chair and yawn, or look from the window and comment on the passers-by, or remark on my appearance or her own with startling frankness.

'Why don't you trim that nice brown beard of yours, colonel? . . . All right, then, Sorry. Where were we?. . . . "*Smeyat'cia, posmeyat'cia*—to laugh." . . . But how can they? Laughing in Russian must require a surgical operation. Stealthy Terror would laugh well in Russian.' Would drop the book and clasp her hands about her knees. 'Why have you never married, colonel?'

She would smile sleepily because of the sun-bathing, and stretch like a cat, with the winking of golden eyes.

Beautiful? But no. She had the nose too short and the upper lip too long. Yet the charm that is beyond proportions and measurements—the careless, insolent mouth that was somehow like the mouth of Ravelston himself, and eyes very deeply lashed and wonderful, and the sheen of hair, cut like a boy's, and very dark and fine. Beside Ravelston, she looked on occasion like his son.

She tired very quickly of the Russian, and the lessons in it ceased. She tired of the sun-bathing, and I think the first quarrel with Ravelston was over that tiring. Thereafter she carried it out infrequently, as a boring duty. . . . 'She would tire of the glories of heaven and yawn in the faces of the Archangels,' Adrian would growl.

Light, irresponsible, blindly selfish, insolently cold and insolently passionate, she seemed no more fit mate for Ravelston than a woman of the Warrens. She was daughter of his publisher, and early on his visit to London they had made acquaintance. Ravelston I believed she had married as the new 'thrill,' the new and unprecedented experience—because of his stature and his reputation and that otherness of his—the otherness that now, alas, seemed to have vanished. She had an endless craving for change, for thrill and glitter and running laughter, for the dance and the perfumes, the admiration and the adoration. Anything that savoured of study or the weariness of toil was a horrible thing. All that was enemy of the good time and the careless hour was 'horrible.'

And yet—I could not dislike her. Perhaps because of beauty of gesture and attitude, and the ring of her boy-laughter and that bright scorn she had of things; perhaps because once or twice in her I glimpsed a dark fierceness that might have been her soul, imprisoned and lost, beneath the shifting play of moods that was her life.

V

One morning, near five o'clock, coming from an all-night dance at the Mess Artillery, they overtook Adrian and myself and gave us a lift to the house in Abbassieh. We sat the four of us hunched together in the little car, and the dawn was in the sky into which we raced. Pamela looked tired, and as we turned into the gardenway of the house I saw that she was asleep. The garden was dim and scented, and through it the giant carried her indoors.

And then, suddenly, a cockerel in the native fowl-run next door flapped and crowed with piercing loudness. Pamela awoke with a cry of terror, struggled in Ravelston's arms so that he halted, and then stared from the one to the other of us in slow realisation. But in her eyes was still terror.

We laughed at her, and then stood awkward and embarrassed, for she laid her head against Ravelston's shoulder and wept with an intensity in her amazing. Adrian and I would have gone, but that the giant motioned to us to follow. In the downstairs room he switched on the lights, and set Pamela in a chair, and knelt by her. She stared into his face with the colour slowly coming back to her own.

And it was then, in that moment of the overstrung, that she told us.

She had been a child of twelve in the last years of the War, in the London suburb, in some area unfortunate traversed again and again by the German air-raiders. Often was the screaming of sirens and the falling of bombs, and her child-nerves played on by the inexplicable terrors, her sleep shattered in sudden hurryings to and fro. . . .

And then came a morning that she might not forget. There was the usual alarm and she and her brother, a child of three, were hurried out to hide in a garden-shed, the safest refuge. The nurse left them there a moment the while she ran back for clothes, and in that moment, looking out, Pamela saw the night flash and flash again. She cried out to the nurse, and then in terror ran after her in the direction of the house. Half-way across the garden she heard her brother call her name, and turned, confused and remembering. In that moment came catastrophe. She was flung to the ground by the explosion which wiped out the shed, and the darkness rained splinters of stone and wood around her. She picked herself up, bruised and bleeding, and through the squalling scolding from a near-by chicken-run heard a cock which crowed unceasingly, unendingly, above the clamour. . . .

'Ravelston, I heard him scream—I know I did—and I can't ever forget . . . and that crowing. Oh, I was a coward, a coward! I killed him. He had that lost boy-stare you have when you sit and think. . . . Oh, beastly coward!'

He laughed at her, the giant. 'You could have done nothing. You're brave even to remember it. Tired now. Carry you to bed?'

Adrian and I, forgotten, went out into the morning without the promised refreshments. The laboratory and all the other windows but for one, far up, shone dark as dead eyes.

'What do you think of her now—and this story?' I said.

'Hysteria. Explains a little and doesn't help a jot.' We passed out of the range of that lighted window. 'Poor Ravelston! Titan and Pandora—complete with vulture!'

'Eh?' I said, and would have made remarks regarding the mythology confused, but that he went on:

'Um. You didn't know, of course. There's cancer in her family—*carcinomata*. Hereditary. She doesn't know it herself, but Ravelston did when he married her.'

VI

Here, it seemed to me—I who cannot help finding story and plot in every life I look on—were elements enough of drama. Ravelston, with that secret upon him, with his unsurpassed knowledge of the stages of the cancer-march, turning in desperation from the rigour and slowness of patient research to the sun-bathing and each other of the swift, glib cures; Pamela, insolent, selfish, young, looking forward to years of pleasure and amusement—all that she craved—all unconscious that the most frightful and agonising of diseases lay like a beast awaiting her. . . .

But Nature has little stage-sense. She can make of apparent tragedy the thing ludicrous and meaningless, of comedy the thing horrifying. So at the house in Abbassieh. One morning Pamela complained of unwellness, and the symptoms described to Ravelston. With fear upon him, he made the no-examination himself, but sent for Adrian. The X-ray apparatus was brought from the Citadel Hospital, the many photographs taken, and Adrian made a searching examination. Then he went away with the apparatus and in the evening returned to them.

'Mrs. Ravelston has a magnificent constitution. There is nothing more wrong with her than a passing ailment.'

'Eh?' said Ravelston, and leapt from his chair. Then abruptly he was gone from the room. Adrian was left alone with Pamela, cigarette-smoking, undisturbed, but sitting considering him, chin in hand.

'What was Ravelston fussing about, doctor? What did he and you expect?'

He had never liked her, and it seemed to him then that the truth might sober her. In a moment he was telling her of the suspicions and the facts, and in that moment regretting it.

' . . . Expected I'd develop cancer? Nice. Married me knowing it?—Thought I'd be a convenient subject-study, I suppose? I'll remember that.'

Adrian stared at her in amazed anger. She nodded to him the insolent dismissal. 'That's all, doctor. You can send in your bill.'

VII

More and more rapidly with the passing of the weeks, the lives of these two began to split apart. Ravelston, relieved, exultant, rid of that immediate personal fear, turned again to laboratory and desk. He grew again to the habit of shutting himself up for hours and days at a stretch, immersed in the matters that to Pamela were the incomprehensible unpleasantnesses.

Conscious of his defection from the round of inane pleasure and sight-seeing, he would on occasion burst from laboratory or study to the rooms of Pamela, caress her—and then vanish again in a banging of doors, leaving, I think, one who sat breathless and with singing heart. But so only for a moment.

If Adrian might not, I at least would comprehend something of the startled anger and resentment that followed his revelation. A freak. . . . A 'study.' . . . Even with the cooling of first anger—anger that to her generation is the thing crude and clownish—she forgot not at all. Indeed, the changed behaviour of Ravelston was constant reminder. She had expected, I imagine, that Ravelston would always comport himself as in the days of the honeymoon, with his work relegated to the secondary place. She had expected that Prometheus would continue to bring fire from heaven, but only—in the phrase of Adrian, who disliked her so—'to provide her with a damn little foot-warmer.'

Instead, there were now the moments, in the chance meetings and at meal-times, when he stared at her as though she were a stranger. The 'freak' had ceased to be freakish,

the 'subject' had refused to be satisfactorily cancerous, in dis-
obedience to the expectations of heredity. . . . She had ceased
to interest.

So, knowing that she lied, she must have told herself on
occasion, and so, in the mixture of boredom and pique, and
with that urgency to grasp from life all that it might offer in
sensation, she turned to the gaudy glitter of the European
season, to the dancings and the gatherings, the gossipings and
philanderings, the motor-excursions and the flowering
acquaintanceships; finally, to the growing amusement and
interest in Andreeius de Bruyn.

VIII

I encountered them one afternoon outside the Continental
Hotel, where I awaited the client. I had been dragoman to
him a month before and from his car he nodded to me the
mocking salutation.

'Afternoon, St. Peter!'

This was his crude jest because of the incident during that
month that would smell none the sweeter for the telling.
There had been keys in the incident, and I had saved him
from the slit throat, and a Muslim woman from the atten-
tions of one who imagined he was honouring a 'native.' It
was the incident he had done better to forget.

Before I might reply, she who sat by his side turned her
head, and recognised me, and laughed.

'Hello, colonel! *Kak vi pazhivaiete?* Oh, and—*pocmesy-
ietc'ie!*'

To her and the Russian horrible I smiled then, as she com-
manded. Perhaps there had been other than an expression
pleased on my face at sight of her with de Bruyn. She whispered something to him, and they laughed at me, and the car
shot away. . . . De Bruyn!

He was the young American with the much money and
less perception of responsibility to life than possesses a mayfly.

Villains have gone from life as they have from literature, and perhaps de Bruyn was no more evil than was Ravelston, his antitype. Like Pamela, it was merely that the gross selfishness that is in all of us, the thing instinctive, had never known repression or transmutation. Wants and desires were things to be purchased or cajoled, never to be forgone. In Cairo he had already organised the orgies and excursions and fantastic entertainments innumerable. In his handsome face he had eyes which they said could hold and fascinate any woman. . . . To me they were the bright, shifting eyes of one morally unborn.

That excursion of theirs I witnessed had not been the first. Alike her insolence and selfishness, and perhaps also her fearlessness, fascinated de Bruyn. He laid the cold-blooded siege, without concealment of desire or intention, as is the fashion of the philanderer modern. From Pamela Ravelston was at first the amusement, and then the something else that was still a mocking thing, that mocked even when at last she found herself in his arms. . . . Love or hate, Lucius or Andreeius—what did it matter, so long as boredom was cheated?

As casually as that, and yet quite irrevocably, she must have come to her decision and sat down and wrote the letter which she sent to Ravelston from the Ghezireh ball.

IX

Early in that morning of her writing, I was walking home, all of the meditative way from the Kubbah observatory. In Abbassieh I saw a light in the room of Ravelston, and there came on me a sudden resolve. I would acquaint him with the de Bruyn matter, for in those chill hours it loomed to me as serious.

I went round to the back of the house, through the garden, and pressed the bell that sounded in his room alone. Hardly had I ceased but there was the noise of footsteps, and Ravelston, gigantic, towered in the door-way dimness.

'Saloney!' He gave a strange laugh. 'I thought—but never mind what I thought. Come in.' He banged the door behind me and gripped my arm. 'Come up here. I've something to show you.'

He led me up the stairs of the back, and then, on the landing that led to his study, had a new resolve. 'Not here. Further up, first.'

On that other landing he opened a door and switched on lights and stared round the room. Then laughed again.

'Look, Saloney! She was here yesterday. Everything here is hers. There's not a thing but's known her touch. Eh? And she'd slept in that bed; I've heard her singing up here, going to bed at midnight. . . . Remember the way she had of singing—with that little hoarseness? And of sitting with clasped knees? Eh?'

He bent down and very gently and deliberately picked up a chair. And then he went suddenly berserk-mad. He hurled the chair at the great dressing-glass and brought it smashing to the floor, and then set about deliberately wrecking the room. I stood in helplessness and watched, and when he had finished the place looked, strewn with torn and trampled draperies, like a murdered girl. Once I tried to stay him.

'But why—?'

'Come away, colonel. Out of it! Unclean, this place. Come down below and have a drink.'

Below he poured out the whisky and tossed me a letter. While I read it he walked up and down, his hands twitching. In face and voice was that flare of mirth that is the anger of his kind.

'Good letter, eh? "Not being either a dragoman or a doctor, I'm tired of Abbassieh; not being either a cancerous freak or a beastly disease you're evidently tired of me." Who told her about the cancer? Never mind. . . . A little adultery for amusement, eh? Who's this de Bruyn?'

I told him. 'A lover? A dirty little lover and her days and

nights spent planning dirty little caressings and kissings . . .
while I've been working. I've been made fool and cuckold
because I could not play—the lap-dog! She expected me to
give up for her the world, my work, the things that are me. . . .
For a little loving and mating!'

And suddenly he stopped in front of me and laughed—the
laugh of genuine amusement and relief.

'Lord, why didn't I see? I've been blind as a mole! Oh, not
only to this dirty little intrigue. To fact. Loving and mating,
begetting and desiring—those, or the life without flambeaux
or kindliness, of work unending, with nothing but the surety
that some day the swamps will be cleared away. . . .'

He was walking to and fro again, but no longer in anger.
Rather was it the exultation.

'I know. See it only now. My work's been going to pieces.
One can't have both; one must choose. Warmth and light
and caresses and the safe places—or loneliness and that
vision. . . .'

His eyes were shining now. It was the Ravelston of the
garden-talks, lost and forgotten those many months, and I
thrilled to meeting him again. I stood up and seized his hand.

'You are right. You will press on to the greater work
alone.'

He laughed in ringing confidence, and then dropped my
hand and wheeled to the window like lightning. Upon the
garden lay the dawn. Again shrilled out that sound that had
startled us, and at its repetition he swung round upon me
again, gigantic, with horror on his face.

'My God, if she's scared—alone—with that fool! . . .
What rubbish you've been talking, Saloney! Rubbish! There
wasn't a soul to the world till I found Pam! The future's
trust to me. And I neglected and forgot her. . . . Lost her
now, I who could have kept her mine, could have made her
true and clear and fine as a sword, could have tramped with
her desert and starfield . . . Work! She was light to my clumsy
groping and I've lost her——'.

But I had heard another sound through the hushed morning. I caught his sleeve.

'Listen!' I said.

X

De Bruyn and Pamela, you must understand, had planned to arrive at Alexandria, where was de Bruyn's yacht, early in the forenoon. They danced till as late as the three o'clock at the ball on Ghezireh Island. Then Pamela sent off the letter to Ravelston by the native messenger, and they went out to the car which had been awaiting them.

De Bruyn came flushed with wine and dancing, and as he wrapped the rugs about Pamela he was of the over-affectionate. This she told him, with the usual fearless insolence, and he sat beside her sulkily, driving out of Cairo.

But he was the skilled driver, steering with reckless care, and in the little they were clear even of the grey mud suburbs and the stars were a splendour above them. Pamela Ravelston yawned, and sank deep in rugs, and presently was asleep.

For an hour the great racer fled westwards. along the Alexandria road. Then de Bruyn suddenly swore, and the car bumped and shuddered and fell to a crawl. They were in the midst of a village, shuttered and sleeping, and the roadway was pitted with uneven holes.

The searchlight rays of the headlamps shook and made a standstill. For the moment, amongst the narrow lanes branching from the roadway, the noise of the car was deafening.

'Curse it. Puncture,' said de Bruyn. 'Stay there, Pam. No need for you to get down.'

Pamela stirred sleepily and murmured something the while he got down and fumbled with the lamps. Above the silent, mud-walled village the sky glimmered amethyst in the false dawn.

And then from a mud-hut near at hand a child began to cry, and shrill and clear, awakened by the noise of the car, misled by the false light in the sky, a cock crew and others throughout the village took up the call till de Bruyn lifted a dawn-greyed face, and laughed and swore.

'Those infernal birds! They would waken the dead. Eh?'

And as he stared in amazement at one who sat and wept there in the flickering light, and then sprang to vivid life, and swore at him and made the unreasonable demand, he did not know that that clamour about them had indeed awakened the dead.

XI

'What?' said Ravelston.

But I was looking out of the window as the great car of de Bruyn halted in front of the house, its noise deafening. Out of it leapt someone in the whirl of dance-draperies, someone whose key slotted urgently in the street-door, who came up the stairs with flying feet.

'Ravelston. . . . Old Stealthy Terror. . . . I've come back. . . .' White-faced, but the scared and shivering repentant not at all, she stood in front of him. Not the fear or safety brought her back, but remembrance of that lover with the lost-boy stare. 'Oh, I've been such a fool! Dirty and a coward. . . . My dear, I forgot!'

'We both forgot,' he said, and took her in his arms—those arms in which perhaps she is sleeping to-night in some desert of the Hadramaut.

But I turned away and went down to the street. As I opened the door, de Bruyn, starting up his car, glanced at me with a wry, white smile.

'Morning, St. Peter.'

And then I had the sudden sense of a moment dramatic, of the story told and retold the many times, in many ways.

'Poor Judas,' I said.

GIBBON: FRAGMENTS FROM UNFINISHED MANUSCRIPT

Editor's note

During the last year of his life Mitchell was working under considerable pressure. He had committed himself to a writing output of more than a million words which included three novels, two biographies and an autobiography, and two histories. The difficulties of such a schedule were increased by bouts of ill-health, but although inevitably the target could not be reached the actual output was still remarkable.

In several cases the books were published almost as soon as they were completed—the last words of *Grey Granite* were written during a late-summer visit to the North-east of Scotland and the book was published in November. The other books published in 1934 included *Niger*, *The Conquest of the Maya*, *Gay Hunter*, *Scottish Scene*, and *Nine Against the Unknown*.

It will be readily understood, therefore that very little unpublished material remained. The only remaining manuscript of note is a partially corrected typescript of the first part of a new novel of the Mearns. Selections from this now appear in print for the first time.

Obviously such extracts are of great interest to the Grassic Gibbon scholar and enthusiast, but the writing also holds real value in itself. There is certainly enough here to make one ponder on what the future might have held, and what further masterpieces could have come from a writer who already in a very short literary life had added considerably to his country's heritage.

At least it seems a suitable closing item from a writer who has aroused intense admiration, excitement, and speculation.

Stonehaven had grown the county town, a long dreich place built up a hill, below the sea in a frothing bay, creaming; and it had a fair birn of folk in it by then, bigger it had grown than any other Mearns place, even Laurencekirk with its trade and its boasting; and a Stonehaven man would say to a Laurencekirk man; 'Have you got a Provost in Laurencekirk?,' and the Laurencekirk childe would say 'Aye, that we have; and he's got chains.' And the Stonehaven gype would give a bit sniff, 'Faith, has he so? Ours runs around loose.'

Bervie had mills and spinners by then, when the eighteen eighties opened; and it was fell radical and full up of souters ready to brain you with a mallet or devil if you spoke a word against that old tyke Gladstone. It lay back from the sea in a little curve that wasn't a bay and wasn't straight coast and in winter's storms the sea would come up, frothing and gurling through a souter's front door and nearly swamp the man sitting by his fire, with the speeches of Gladstone grabbed in one hand and Ingersoll under his other oxter.

Now these were nearly the only towns that the folk of the Howe held traffic with, they'd drive to them with the carts for the market, cattle for sale, and bonny fat pigs, grain in the Winter, horses ploughing through drifts, and loads of this and that farm produce. And outside it all was an antrin world, full of coarse folk from the north and south.

*　　*　　*

247

R

Now here was the line of the curling coast, a yammer of seagulls night and day, the tide came frothing and swishing green into the caves that curled below; and at night some young-like ploughman childe, out from his bothy seeking for sea-gulls eggs, swinging and showding from a rope far down would hear the dreich moan of the ingoing waters and cry out to whoever was holding the rope; 'Pull me up, Tam! The devil's in there.'

But folk said the devil maybe wasn't so daft as to crawl about in caves of the Howe when he could spend a couthy night in the rooms and byres of Midden Castle, deserted this good ten years or more, green growing on the slates and a scurf from the sea grey on the windows and over the sills. The last Stratoun there had been the laird John who drank like a fish, nothing queer in that, a man with a bit of silver would drink, what else was there for the creature to do if he was a harmless kind of man? But his downcome had been that he swam like some kind of damned fish as well, he was always in and out of the sea, and the combination had been overmuch, one night his son John was going to bed when he heard far low down under the wall, a cry like a lost soul smored in hell. He waited and listened and thought it some bird, and was just about to crawl under the sheets, douce-like, when the cry rose shrill again. It was summer and clear, all the forward lift over the sea; young John Stratoun ran down the stairs and cried to his mother 'There's a queer sound outside. Rouse the old man.' His mother cried back the old devil wasn't in his bed to rouse but out on some ploy, John should leave him a-be, he'd come on all right, never fear, the devil aye heeded his own. And with that the coarse creature, a great fat wretch, she could hardly move for her fat, folk said, a Murray quean, they aye ran to creash, turn-ed over and went off in a canny snooze. The next thing she knew was John shaking her awake. 'Mother, it's father and I'm feared he's dead.'

So she got from her bed with a bit of a grunt and went

down and inspected the corpse of her man, aye, dead enough, blue at the lips, he'd filled himself up with a gill of Glenlivet and gone for a swim, and been taken with cramp. And folk told that the Stratoun woman said 'Feuch! You were never much Sam lad when you were alive, and damn't, you're not even a passable corpse.'

But folk in the Howe would tell any lies, they'd a rare time taking the news through hand, Paton at the Mains of Balhagarty said the thing was surely a judgement, faith, on both the coarse man and his coarse-like wife, the only soul he was sorry for was the boy. And at that the minister to whom he was speaking, nodded his head and said 'Aye. You're right. Then no doubt you'll have no objections, Mr. Paton, to contributing a wee thing for the creature's support? They've been left near without a penny-piece.' So Paton pulled a long sad face and had to dig out, and it served him well.

They didn't bide long in the place after that, the stock and the crops and the gear in the castle, were rouped at the end of the Martinmas, the Stratoun woman would have rouped Midden Castle as well but she couldn't, it descended to John the son. So instead she left the place stand as it was, no tenant would take it, and went off to the south, Montrose, or foreign parts like that, to keep the house for her brother there, him that was a well-doing chandler childe. And sleet and rain and the scutter of rats came down on Midden and there had bidden for a good ten years, till this Spring now came, a racket of silence hardly broken at all but that now and then on a Sunday night when the minister was off to his study for prayer and the elders prowling the other side of the parish and the dogs all locked up and even the rats having a snooze after their Sunday devotions some ploughman lad and his bit of a lass would sneak into the barn and hold their play and give each other a bit cuddle, frightened and glad and daft about it; and if maybe they thought they saw now and then some bogey or fairley peep out at them there was none to say that the thing wasn't likely Pict ghosts or the

ghosts of the men long before peeping from the chill of that
other land where flesh isn't warm nor kisses strong nor hands
so sweet that they make you weep, nor terror nor wonder
their portion again, only a faint dim mist of remembering.

II

Now the nearest farm to Midden Castle was the Mains of
Bahagarty along the coast, you went by a twisty winding
path, leftwards the rocks and the sea and death if you weren't
chancy and minding your feet, right the slope of the long
flat fields that went careering west to the hills to the cup of
the Howe, and, bright in the Spring, the shape of Auchin-
dreach's meikle hill. The Patons had been in Bahagarty a
bare twelve years and had done right well, though they were
half-gentry, old Paton an elder, precentor, he stood up of a
Sabbath in the old Free Kirk and intoned the hymns with a
bit of a cough, like a turkey with a chunk of grain in its throat,
and syne would burst into the Hundredth Psalm, all the
choir following, low and genteel, and his wife, Mistress
Paton, looking at him admiring, she thought there was no
one like Sam in the world.

Folk said that was maybe as well for the world, Paton was
as mean as he well could be, he'd four men fee'd, a cattler
and three ploughmen, and paid them their silver each six
month with a groan as though he were having a tooth dug
out. But he farmed the land well, in a skimpy way, with
little manure and less of new seed, just holding the balance
and skimming the land, ready for the time when he might
leave and set himself up in a bigger place. He'd had two
sons, or rather his wife, you'd have thought by Paton's holy-
like look his mistress had maybe had them on her own, the
elder would never had been so indecent as take any part in
such blushful work. The one of them, William, was a fine
big lad, a seven years old and sturdy and strong, with a fine
clear eye that you liked, he'd laugh, ''Lo, man. Losh you've

got a funny face.' And maybe then you wouldn't like him so much, queer how fond we all are of our faces. But he was a cheery young soul for all that, aye into mischief out in the court, or creeping into the ploughmen's bothies and hearkening to the coarse songs they'd sing, about young ploughmen who slept with their masters' daughters and such like fairlies, all dirt and lies, a farmer's daughter never dreamed of sleeping with a ploughman unless she'd first had a look at his bank-book.

The second son Peter, a six years old, you didn't much like the look of, fair dark and young and calm with an impudent leer, not fine and excited when you patted his head but looking at you calm and cool, and you'd feel a bit of a fool in the act. But you never could abide those black-like folk, maybe they'd the blood of the Romans in them or some such coarse brood from ayont the sea. The wife, Mistress Paton, was an Aberdeen creature, she couldn't help that nor her funny speak, she called *buits beets* and *speens* for spoons, they were awful ignorant folk in Aberdeen.

Well, that was the Mains of Bahagarty, and outbye from it on the landward side lay the little two-horse farm of Moss Bank, farmed by a creature, Cruickshank the name, that was fairly a good farmer and an honest-like neighbour except when his temper got the better of him. He was small and compact and ground out in steel, blue, it showed in his half-shaved face, with a narrow jaw like a lantern, bashed, bits of eyes like chunks of ice, he'd stroke his cheeks when you asked his help, at harvest, maybe, or off to the moors for a load of peats, and come striding along by your side to help, and swink at the work till the sun went down and the moon came up and your own hands were nearly dropping from their dripping wrist-bones. And if your horse might tread on his toes with a weight enough to send an ordinary man crack and make him kick the beast in the belly, he'd just give a cough and push it away, and get on with his chave, right canty and douce. And at last, when the lot of the work was done he'd nod goodbye, and wait for a dram, and as he moved off call back to know if you'd want his help the morn's morning?

You'd think 'Well, of all the fine childes ever littered you'd give it to the Cruikshank billy, then' and maybe plan to take a bit rise out of him and get him, neighbour-like, for more work. But sure as God in a day or so some ill-like thing would have happened between you, a couple of your hens would have ta'en a bit stroll through the dykes and on to his parks, and picked a couple of fugitive grains, and laid an egg as return, genteel, and turned about to come away home. And Cruickshank would have seen them, sure as death, given chase and caught them, and a bird in each hand stood cursing you and the universe blue, might you rot in hell on a hill of dead lice, you foul coarse nasty robber you. And just as the air was turning purple and the sun going down in a thunderstorm and all the folk within two miles coming tearing out of their houses to listen, he'd a voice like a fog-horn, only not so sweet, had Cruickshank, he'd turn and go striding back to his steading, a hen in each hand, with a doleful squawk, and clump through the oozing sharn of the court, heavy-standing, deep-breathing his bull would be there with a shimmer and glimmer of eyes in the dark. So into the house and brush past his wife and cry 'Hey, bring me a pen and some paper.' His wife, a meikle great-jawed besom, nearly as big and ugly as Cruickshank, and of much the same temper, would snap back 'Why?' And he'd say 'My land's being ruined and lost with the dirt that let loose their beasts on me. Me! By the living God I'll learn the dirt— hey, where's that paper?' And that paper in hand he'd sit and write you a letter that would frizzle you up, telling you he held your hens, and you'd get them back when you came for them yourself and paid the damage that the brutes had made. And for near a six months or so after that when he met you at kirk or mart, on the turnpike, he'd pass with a face like an ill-taen coulter. There were no manners or flimflams about Cruickshank at all, and sometimes you'd think there was damn little sense.

They'd had two sons, both grown up, the one Sandy bade at home with his father and ran a kind of smithy at Mossbank, coulters and pointers and the like he could manage, not much more, the creature half-daft, with a long loose mouth aye dribbling wet, and a dull and wavering eye in his head, like a steer that's got water on the brain. He'd work for old Cruickshank with a good enough will a ten or eleven months of the year and then it would come on him all of a sudden, maybe shoeing a horse or eating his porridge or going out to the whins to ease himself, that something was queer and put out in his world, and you'd hear him give a roar like the bull, and off he'd stride, clad or half-clad, and Mossbank mightn't see him for a month or six weeks, the coarse brute would booze his way away south and join up with the drovers off to the marts, and vanish away on the road to Edinburgh, and fight and steal and boast like a tink. And then one night he'd come sneaking back and chap at the door and come drooling in, and the father and mother would look at him grim and syne at each other, and not say a word, real religious the two of them except when cursing the Lord himself for afflicting decent honest folk that had never done him any harm with a fool of a son like this daftie Sandy and a wild and godless brute like Joe.

Now Joe had been settled in Aberdeen in a right fine job with a jeweller there and was getting on fine till the women got him, next thing there came a note to Mossbank that Joe would be put in the hands of the police unless his thefts were paid to the hilt. Old Cruickshank near brought a cloud-burst on the Mearns when he read that news, then yelled to his mistress to bring him his lum-hat and his good black suit. And into the two of them he got like mad, and went striding away down the road to Stonehaven, and boarded a train, into Aberdeen, the jeweller said he was very sorry, what else could he do, Joe was upstairs, and the sum was twenty five pounds if you please. And old Cruickshank paid it down like a lamb, if you can imagine a lamb like a leopard, and went up the stairs, and howked out Joe and hauled him down and kicked his dowp out of the jeweller's shop. 'Let me never look on your face again, you that's disgraced an honest man.' Joe was blubbering and sniftering like a seal by then, 'But where am I going to go now, Father' and old Cruickshank said to him shortly 'To hell,' and turned and made for the Aberdeen station.

Well, he went there, or nearly, it was just as bad, he joined the army, the Gordon Highlanders, full up of thieves and ill-doing men, grocers that had stolen cheese from their masters and childes that had got a lass with a bairn and run off to get out of the paying for't, drunken ministers, schoolmasters that had done the kind of thing to this or that scholar that you didn't mention—and faith, he must have fairly felt at home. So off he went to the foreign parts, India and Africa and God knew where, sometimes he'd write a bit note to his mother, telling her how well he was getting on; and Cruickshank would give the note a glare 'Don't show the foul tink's coarse scrawls to me. Him that can hardly spell his own name, and well brought up in a house like this.'

For Cruickshank was an awful Liberal man, keen to support this creature Gladstone, he'd travelled down to Edinburgh to hear him and come home more glinting and blue than ever, hating Tories worse than dirt, and the Reverend James Dallas worse than manure. Now, the Reverend James Dallas was the Auld Kirk minister, the kirk stood close in by the furthest of the Mossbank fields, huddling there in its bouroch of trees, dark firs, underneath were shady walks with the crunch of pine cones pringling and cool in the long heats of summer and in winter time a shady walk where the sparrows pecked. Within the trees lay kirk and manse, the kirk an old ramshack of a place, high in the roof and narrow in the body. The Reverend James when he spoke from the pulpit looked so high in that narrow place you'd half think

when the spirit was upon him he'd dive head first down on
your lap. And all the ploughmen away at the back would
grunt and shuffle their feet, not decent, and the Reverend
James would look at them, bitter, and halt in the seventeenth point in his sermon till the kirk grew still and quiet as
the grave, you'd hear the drone of a bumble bee and the
splash of a bead of sweat from your nose as it tumbled into a
body's beard. Then he'd start again on Hell and Heaven,
more the former than the latter for sure, and speak of those
who came to the Lord's House without reverence, ah, what
would their last reward be in the hands of GED? For the
Lord our Ged was a jealous Ged and the Kirk of Scotland a
jealous kirk.

You thought that was maybe true enough, but it wasn't
half so jealous as the Reverend himself, he'd a bonny young
wife new come to the Manse, red-haired and young with a
caller laugh, a schoolteacher lass that he'd met in Edinburgh
when he was attending the Annual Assembly; and he'd met
her at the house of her father, a minister, and fairly taken a
fancy to her. So they'd wedded and the Reverend had
brought her home, the congregation raised a subscription
and had a bit concert for the presentation and the first elder,
Paton, unveiled the thing, and there it was, a brave-like
clock, in shape like a kirk with hands over the doors and
scrolls all about and turrets and walls and the Lord knew
what, a bargain piece. And the Reverend James took a look
at it, bitter, and said that he thanked his people, he knew the
value of time himself as the constant reminder of the purpose
of God; and he hoped that those that presented it had
thought of time in eternity. And some folk that had paid
their shillings for the subscription went off from the concert
saying to themselves that they'd thought of that, he needn't
have feared, and they hoped that he would burn in it.

If he did folk said he would manage that all right if only
he'd his wife well under his eye. For he followed her about
like a calf a cow, he could hardly bear to let her out of his

sight, though while she was in it he paid little attention cold and glum as a barn-door. She'd laugh and go whistling down through the pines, him pacing beside her, hands at his back, with a jealous look at the cones, at the hens, at the ploughmen turning their teams outbye, at Ged himself in the sky, you half-thought, that any should look at his mistress but him. Well that was the Reverend James Dallas then, and his jealousy swished across the Howe and fixed on the other kirk of the parish the wee Free Kirk that stood by the turnpike, a new-like place of a daft red stone, without a steeple and it hadn't a choir, more like a byre with its dickie on, than a kirk at all. The most of the folk that squatted in it were the shopkeeper creatures that came from Howe villages and the smithies around and joineries, the kind of dirt that doubt the gentry and think they know better than the Lord himself. The only farmer in its congregation was Cruickshank of Moss-bank, sitting close up under the lithe of the pulpit, his arms crossed and his eye fixed stern on the face of the Reverend Adam Smith shining above him in the Free Kirk pulpit like a sun seen through a Midden fog.

The Reverend Adam was surely the queerest bully that ever had graced a pulpit, faith. He wasn't much of a preacher, dreich, with a long slow voice that sent you to sleep, hardly a mention of heaven or hell or the burning that waited on all your neighbours, and he wasn't strong on infant damnation and hardly ever mentioned Elijah. Free Kirk folk being what they are, a set of ramshackle radical loons that would believe nearly anything they heard if only it hadn't been heard before, could stick such preaching and not be aggrieved especially if the minister was a fine-like creature outside the kirk and its holy mumble, newsy and genial and stopping for a gossip, coming striding in to sit by the fire and drink a bowl of sour milk with the mistress. But the Reverend Adam neither preached nor peregrinated, your old mother would be lying at the edge of death and say 'Will you get the minister for me? There's a wee bit thing that

I'd like explained in the doctrine of everlasting damnation; forbye, he might put up a bit of a prayer,' and off you'd go in search of the creature, and knock at his door and the housekeeper would come, and she'd shake her head, he was awful busy. You'd say 'Oh? Is he? Well, my mother's dying,' and at last be led to the Reverend's study, a hotter and hotch of the queerest dirt, birds in cages and birds on rails, and old eggs and bits of flints and swords and charts and measurements, a telescope, and an awful skeleton inside a glass press that made you fairly grue to look on. And the Reverend would turn his big fat face and peer at you from his wee twink eyes, you'd tell what you needed and he'd grunt 'Very well' and his eyes grow dreamy and far away and start on his scribbling as before. And you'd wait till you couldn't abide it longer: 'Minister, will you come with a prayer for my mother? She's sinking fast; and he'd start around 'Sinking? What? A ship off the Howe'—the fool had forgotten that you were there.

And when at last he'd come with the prayer and you'd take him along to your mother's room and she'd ask him the point about burning forever, instead of soothing her off, just quiet, with some bit lie to soothe the old body and let her go to hell with an easy mind, he'd boom out that there were Three Points at least to look at in this subject, and start on the Early Fathers, what they'd said about it and argued about it, a rare lot of tinks those Fathers had been, what Kant had said, and a creature Spinoza, the views of the Brahmins and the Buddhists and Bulgarians, and what the foul creature Mohammed had thought, him that had a dozen women at his call and expected to have a million in heaven. And while he was arguing and getting interested, your mother would slip from under his hands, and you'd pull at his sleeve. 'Well, sir, that'll do. No doubt the old woman's now arguing the point with Kant and Mohammed in another place.'

Faith, it was maybe more than a chance, folk said, that the big-bellied brute was keen on Mohammed. What about him and that housekeeper of his, a decent-like woman with a face like a scone, but fair a bunk of a figure for all that. Did he and her aye keep a separate room, and if that was so why was there aye a light late in hers at night, never in his? And how was it the creature could wear those brave-like clothes that she did? And how was it, if it wasn't his conscience, fairly, that the Reverend Adam was hardly ever at home? Instead, away over Auchindreich Hill, measuring the Devil's Footstep there, or turning up boulders and old-time graves where the Picts and the like ill folk were, in a way just as coarse as Burke and Hare.

East, landwards of the Free Kirk rose Auchindreich, spreading and winding back in the daylight, north along the road was the town of the Howe, and south-east before you came to it two small crofts and a fair-sized farm. Now the childe in the croft of Lamahip was a meikle great brute of a man called Gunn, long and lank with a great bald head and a long bald coulter of a red-edged nose, he farmed well and kept the place trig and his wife and three daughters in a decent-like way. And, faith, you'd have given him credit for that if it wasn't he was the greatest liar that ever was seen in the Howe or the Gowe. If he drove a steer to the mart in Stonehyve and sold it maybe for a nine or ten pounds, would that be a nine or ten pounds when he met you down in the pub at the end of the day? Not it, it would be a nineteen by then, and before the evening was out and the pub closed it was maybe nearer twenty-nine, and he'd boast and blow all the way to the Howe, staggering from side to side of the road and sitting down every now and then to weep over the lasses he had long syne, the lasses had aye liked him well, you heard, and once he'd slept with a Lady in Tamintoul, she'd wanted him to marry her and work their estate, and he'd given it all up, the daft fool that he'd been, to take over the managership of a forest in Breadalbane—had you heard about that? And you'd say 'God, aye, often,' and haul him to his feet and off along the road again, up over the hill that climbs from Stonehyve in the quietude of a long June night, you looking back on the whisper and gleam of Stonehaven, forward to the ruins of Dunnottar Castle, black and immense against the sky, the air filled with the clamour of seagulls' wings as they pelted inland from a coming storm.

His wife was a thin little red-headed woman, canty and kind and maybe the best cook that ever had been seen in the district, she could bake oatcakes that would melt between your jaws as a thin rime of frost on the edge of a plough, baps that would make a man dream of heaven, not the one of the Reverend Dallas, and could cook that foul South dish the haggis in a way that made the damn thing nearly eatable, not as usual with a smell like a neglected midden; and a taste to match, or so you imagined, not that you'd ever eaten middens. And she'd say as she put a fresh scone on the girdle, 'But they're not like the fine cakes you had from your Lady, are they now, Hugh,' with a smile in her eyes, and he'd answer up solemn, No, God, they weren't, but still and on, she did not so bad. And she'd smile at the fire, kneeling with the turning fork, small and compact, and keeping to herself, you couldn't but like the little creature.

Faith, that was more than the case with the daughters, the oldest, Jean, had a face like a sow, a holy-like sow that had taken to religion instead of to litters as would have been more seemly. But God knows there was no one fool enough in the Howe to offer to bed her and help in that though she'd seen only a twenty-three summers and would maybe have been all right to cuddle if you could have met her alone in the dark, when you couldn't see her face, you don't cuddle faces. But she never went out of a night, not her, instead sat at home and mended and sewed and read Good Works and was fair genteel, and if ever she heard a bit curse now and then from old Hugh Gunn or some lad dropped in to hear the latest or peek at her sister, she'd raise up her eyes as though she suffered from wind and depress her jaws as though it was a colic, fair entertaining a man as he watched.

But her sister Queen was a kittler bitch, dark and narrow

with a fine long leg, black curly hair in ringlets about her and a pale quiet face but a blazing eye. She was a dressmaker and worked the most of the day above the shop down there in the Howe, sewing up the bit wives that wanted a dress on the cheap without the expense of going to Stonehyve, or needed their lasses trigged out for the kirk, or wanted the bands of their frocks let out when another bairn was found on the way. And Queen Gunn would sit and sew there all day and at night would sit and just read and read, books and books, birns of the dirt, not godly-like books nor learned ones, but stories of viscounts and earls and the like and how the young heir was lost in the snow, and how bonny Prince Charlie had been so bonny—as from the name you had half-supposed. And in spite of her glower and that blaze in her eye she'd little or no time at all for the lads; and the Lord alone knew what she wanted, the creature.

BIBLIOGRAPHY

Except where otherwise stated, all these books were first published by Jarrolds Publishers (London) Ltd.

By Lewis Grassic Gibbon
    SUNSET SONG   1932
    CLOUD HOWE   1933
    GREY GRANITE   1934
    (A SCOTS QUAIR, the trilogy comprising the above novels, was first issued in 1946.)
    NIGER: The Life of Mungo Park, Porpoise Press, Edinburgh/Faber & Faber, London, 1934.
    SCOTTISH SCENE (in collaboration with Hugh MacDiarmid) 1934.

By J. Leslie Mitchell
    HANNO, Kegan Paul, Trench, Trubner & Co., London, 1928.
    STAINED RADIANCE   1930
    THE THIRTEENTH DISCIPLE   1931
    THE CALENDS OF CAIRO   1931
    THREE GO BACK   1932
    THE LOST TRUMPET   1932
    PERSIAN DAWNS, EGYPTIAN NIGHTS   1932
    IMAGE AND SUPERSCRIPTION   1933
    SPARTACUS   1933
    THE CONQUEST OF THE MAYA   1934
    GAY HUNTER, William Heinemann Ltd., London, 1934

By J. Leslie Mitchell and Lewis Grassic Gibbon
    NINE AGAINST THE UNKNOWN   1934